The PLAYERS

Ric Sissons grew up in Nottinghamshire and Derbyshire before studying at the Universities of Sussex and London. He now works in Sydney as the Managing Director of Pluto Press (Australia) and as a cricket historian. With Brian Stoddart, he co-authored *Cricket and Empire: The 1932–33 Bodyline Tour of Australia*. Ric Sissons lives with the writer Stephanie Dowrick and their two children, Gabriel and Kezia.

The PLAYERS

A SOCIAL HISTORY OF THE PROFESSIONAL CRICKETER

Ric Sissons

THE KINGSWOOD PRESS

The Kingswood Press
an imprint of William Heinemann Ltd.
10 Upper Grosvenor Street, London W1X 9PA

LONDON MELBOURNE
JOHANNESBURG AUCKLAND

First published 1988 in association with Pluto Press, Sydney

ISBN 0 434 98140 0

Cover design by Patrick Coyle
Author photograph by Dale Keeling

Typeset, printed and bound in Australia
by Southwood Press, Marrickville, New South Wales

For Gabriel and Kezia

Contents

List of Illustrations

Acknowledgements

Researching *The Players* was always a delight and a debt of gratitude is owed to a number of organisations and individuals. The Surrey and Lancashire County Cricket Clubs in making their records available were particularly helpful. At Trent Bridge the Nottinghamshire Librarian Peter Wynne-Thomas was magnanimous with his knowledge, while Hugh Aixill, of the Nottinghamshire County Council Education Resources Service, kindly shared his own research on the early Notts players. For Frank Peach, the Derbyshire archivist, it was never too much trouble to answer any question and Stephen Green at Lord's was most obliging.

Sir Gubby Allen, Les Ames and Jack Bannister gave freely of their time, as did John Arlott, who very generously agreed to read the manuscript and provide a Foreword. Finally in England, thanks are due to my parents, Ralph and Eileen Sissons, for all their practical assistance and support.

In Australia the New South Wales Cricket Association Library, opened every Monday by the cheerful and helpful Cliff Winning, proved an invaluable source of reference material. It was there that Richard Cashman, Stephen Gibbs and Jack Pollard pointed out many articles and books worthy of consideration, as did George Franki and Dale Keeling on other occasions.

Finally, and most significantly, thanks are due to Stephanie Dowrick for her skilful editing, for her tolerance as I 'shuffled papers' endlessly, and for being such a wonderful mother to Gabriel and Kezia.

Foreword
John Arlott

In *The Players,* Ric Sissons has written what will undoubtedly prove, quite apart from its intrinsic merits, a landmark book in cricket literature. Its breeding is peculiarly Australian; its precursors the works of Richard Cashman and *Australian Cricket Journal*.

That is to say, it is concerned with cricket not simply in the round, but linked to the related aspects of the social scene in which it is played. Cricket has always been a game which reflected the society in which it belongs but it has not previously been written about in this specifically linking fashion. Australian writing about cricket began to break clear of the other traditions with the work of A. G. Moyes and Jack Pollard, but it still lay within the traditional framework.

Its British antecedents had been primarily romantic, sometimes almost poetic, in quality; but still confined by the play of cricket and largely by the established fashions. Now, however, we have a complete breakaway to the setting of the game, not only against its broadly social background, but within the facts, figures and values of that society.

The theme, of course, was the perfect vehicle for such treatment, and this book throws into stark relief the inadequacy of all previous studies of the game in its attention to the realities of life. Many good technicians have been able to write about the realities of cricket *qua* cricket. Now, though, this is cricket within the realities of the life of cricketers as men. Here, for the first time, the living of the professional cricketer is accurately compared with that of the skilled craftsman in other fields.

Neither are the 'amateurs' omitted. The Chapter headed 'The Disguised Professional' includes W. G. Grace, W. W. Read, A. C. MacLaren, S. M. J. Woods and J. J. Ferris. These, of course, were known facts but they had not been clearly and frankly stated before. Neither had the question of shabby treatment of professional cricketers by their employers. This, in other words, is the frank truth about aspects of a subject too often romanticised and distorted in the past. Ric Sissons is a good historian, he has written neither a cosy fireside narrative nor a diatribe; but a careful and objective examination. He is, too, a close researcher. He will surprise many with such items as his chart of the history of the professional touring elevens of 1846-1882. The All-England XI, United England XI, United South of England XI, United North of England XI and the English XI are known to most readers of cricket history in the 19th century: how many, however, could name the other ten?

This is a quite uniquely revealing study. Even those fairly well-read in cricket literature will find fresh facts on virtually every page; the comparisons are valid and often striking. Such subjects as 'Lord Harris and the Respectable Professional', talent money, club profits, benefits, the cricketers' strikes of 1881 and 1896, the lack of worker representation, eventually corrected by the creation of the Cricketers' Association and the abolition of the amateur, are all treated with clear-sighted realism.

This is, indeed, the history of cricket played for money – a game played for pleasure yet paid for – or, in the words of the modern all-rounder good enough to play for England, who is quoted at the end 'A precarious, cut-throat means of earning a living'. Ric Sissons has presented the evidence more clearly and fully – and, for that matter, satisfyingly – than anyone has done before. This reader at least, is happy to record his gratitude to the author.

PART ONE

The Years of the All-England Eleven

CHAPTER 1

The Professionals Take the Lead

THE CONTEXT

THE 1840s in Britain were years of tremendous social, economic and political change. Every facet of the landscape was being re-worked and transformed. In *Cities and People* Mark Girouard describes the North of England city, Manchester, in this way:

> People were fascinated, amazed and appalled by it . . . In Manchester factory chimneys far outnumbered church towers, eight-storey mills towered over squalid little houses, opulent warehouses, some of them as large as the mills, were grander and bigger than the town hall . . . viaducts carried steaming and smoking trains above the roofs of the smaller houses and added another large, bizarre and unfamiliar element to the townscape.

The forces which created Manchester – 'the shock city of the age' as Asa Briggs called it in *Victorian Cities* – indirectly had a profound effect on cricket. The appearance in 1846 of the All-England Eleven, a side of itinerant professionals, occurred only as a consequence of these more general changes in society.

The creation of a national railway network was the first pre-requisite. In the All-England Eleven's tentative debut season, when they played only three matches in quick succession, they had no difficulty in travelling from Sheffield to Manchester and on to Leeds. Manchester was well-endowed with railway connections having been serviced by six lines since 1840. Railway investment reached a peak from 1845 to 1847 and consequently by 1850 6621 miles of track had been laid, linking all the major cities and towns and extending into virtually every part of the country.

In 1830 it took 12 hours to travel by coach from London to Birmingham or Bristol and 20 hours to reach Manchester. Twenty- five years later trains had cut those travelling times to three-and-a-half, four-and-a-half and five-and-a-half hours respectively.

The second important influence was the establishment of the penny post in 1840. From that date a relatively cheap form of communication existed which, significantly, was paid for by the sender and not the recipient.

And thirdly, the 1851 census indicated that for the first time more than half the population lived in urban and not rural areas. In the two decades from 1831 the industrial towns and cities had been consolidated as Table 1 shows.

Table 1: Population growth 1821-61 (in thousands)

	1821	1831	1841	1851	1861
Birmingham	102	144	183	233	296
Bradford	26	44	67	104	106
Leeds	84	123	152	172	207
Liverpool	138	202	286	376	444
Manchester	126	182	235	303	339
Nottingham	40	50	52	57	75
Sheffield	65	92	111	135	185

Source: B. R.Mitchell, *Abstract of British Historical Statistics.*

To a large extent it was from the growing urban middle class and skilled workers that the All-England Eleven found its players and its opposition. During the 1840s industrial life began to be regulated. The 10 Hours Act passed in 1847, although only restricting the working day in textile factories for 13-18-year-olds, did start a general move to curb the number of hours per week that a worker could be expected to toil. Besides, many machines and factories could not function without juvenile labour and by limiting their working day to 10 hours the rhythm of the mill was curtailed. The campaign for a shorter working week would prove to be long and hard fought. Eventually workers won a half Saturday, four Bank Holidays and small reductions in their weekly hours, but it was not until 1910, for example, that miners finally had their underground shifts restricted to eight hours.

The repeal of the Corn Laws in 1846, which removed the duty on imported wheat, was a major victory for manufacturing and laissez-faire capitalism over the traditional agricultural economy. Britain was now committed to live by the export of its manufactured goods and to import its food requirements as the market dictated. The anti-Corn Law agitation which had begun in 1838 had been paralleled by the growth of Chartism among the working class and particularly skilled artisans. Among the Charter's six points, first raised in 1837, were the calls for universal male suffrage, a secret ballot and annual parliaments. Although the Chartists failed to achieve their demands they did mobilise hundreds of thousands behind their banners. In 1847, as the movement was in its death throes, Fergus O'Connor was elected as a Chartist Member of Parliament for Nottingham.

Nottingham, the birthplace of the All-England Eleven and for many decades the epicentre of professional cricket, was also a Chartist stronghold. Although there is no direct connection, Chartism did inspire self-confidence amongst skilled workers and artisans and created an innovative political climate. For a group of professional cricketers to take the initiative and launch their own touring eleven, similar self-confidence and innovative thinking was required.

In the early 1840s the opportunities for a cricketer to earn a professional living from the game were limited. The best players might hope to secure a position on the Lord's ground staff which in 1844 comprised 10 bowlers (William Caldecourt, John Bayley, Thomas Sewell, Tom Barker, Bart' Good, Jemmy Dean, William Hillyer, Henry Royston, William Lillywhite and William Dorrinton). Having achieved this distinction players rarely relinquished it. Caldecourt, Good and Lillywhite died when they were still members of the Lord's staff while Barker, Bayley and Sewell remained with the Marylebone Cricket Club until they were retired. However Lord's did not provide full-time employment as practice occurred only on Tuesday, Wednesday, Friday and Saturday during May, June and July.

In 1846, after the establishment of the Surrey County Cricket Club, the Oval employed two professionals (William Martingell and George Brockwell) and four boys on practice days.

Apart from joining the staff at Lord's or the Oval three other possibilities existed for securing work as a professional cricketer. First, there was the traditional route of seeking employment from a wealthy patron. For example, Alfred Smith of Henfield employed Edward Bushby, a fine batsman and arguably the best long-stop of his day, as a gamekeeper, and before William Martingell moved to the Oval he had a two-year engagement with the Earl of Ducie in Gloucestershire.

Work could also be obtained as a practice bowler with the universities or private schools. Charlie Brown, the Nottinghamshire wicket-keeper and all-rounder, was engaged for two seasons in the mid-1840s at Wadham College, Oxford, while in 1840 his county colleague Samuel Redgate became the first professional to be appointed at Eton.

Additionally, by the early 1840s several of the well-established local clubs employed professional bowlers – Sam Dakin was with the Kingscote Club in Gloucestershire; James Grundy with the Sherwood Forest Club (the Gentlemen of Nottingham); Edmund Hinkly at Watford; William Nix in Derby; Fuller Pilch with the Kent Club in Canterbury; Reuben Roby in Birmingham; Frank Tinley at Southwell (his birthplace); Robert Winfield with the South

Derbyshire Club at Chaddesden and Daniel Day in Southampton. Day had been invited by the gentlemen of the South Hampshire Club to be their ground superintendent. He accepted and also became the landlord of the Antelope Tavern. Subsequently he moved to Itchen where he established a ground of his own, but the venture failed.

Daniel Day was not the only professional to maintain his own ground in the 1840s. William Lillywhite, known as the 'Nonpareil', kept a public house and cricket ground in Brighton which unfortunately also foundered. Consequently Lillywhite moved to London to join the Lord's staff. In 1845 Tom Adams, who had lived all his life in Gravesend, opened the 'Bat and Ball' cricket ground. Previously employed as a labourer in the town's ordnance factory, earning 12 shillings a week, professional cricket proved an attractive proposition. For example, for a short period Adams was patronised by a gentleman from Town Malling at the relatively princely sum of £5 per week. No doubt used to physical toil Tom Adams levelled and fenced his own ground and arranged fairs after matches with the support of his wife who ran the refreshment booth.

One of the great achievements of the All-England Eleven was that it not only directly employed a nucleus of professionals but also helped create the conditions for the employment of many other players with cricket-loving patrons, as groundsmen and bowlers with the rapidly growing number of local clubs, as coaches at private schools, and as practice bowlers with the colleges in Oxford and Cambridge.

THE ALL-ENGLAND ELEVEN

Cricket Song for the Eleven of England

When winter is past, and Phoebus at last
Shines out with his golden light,
When the trees are green and all's serene,
Then Cricket is our delight.
  There is not a hand
  Throughout our loved land
That may not partake of its joys,

Both peasant and peer
Find ecstacy here,
Then Cricket for ever my boys,
Then Cricket for ever my boys.

In the month of May we begin to play,
We're welcomed in County and Town,
We struggle for fame and to keep up our name,
And add to our past renown.
For it must be confest
That Cricket's the best
Means of all to add to our joys,
Both peasant and peer
Find ecstacy here,
Then Cricket for ever my boys,
Then Cricket for ever my boys.

And should we but find the ground to our mind,
Only lively, and level, and sound,
Would you know what to do 'gainst a good twenty-two,
Why – back us then just for a pound.
Though we don't like to bet,
For cricket can yet
Without wagers well add to our joys,
Both peasant and peer
Find ecstacy here,
Then Cricket for ever my boys,
Then Cricket for ever my boys.

What words can reveal the raptures we feel
When we happen to get a long score,
And the girl that we love should be there to approve –
Oh, isn't that luck in galore!
Yes, it must be confest
That Cricket's the best
Means of all to add to our joys;
Both peasant and peer
Find ecstacy here,
Then Cricket for ever my boys,
Then Cricket for ever my boys.

Then long may 'Old Clarke' be up to the mark,
And guide us to triumphs again;

We never shall see better leader than he,
We may look for his like in vain.
  Come join in the toast,
  'Tis a glorious boast,
All classes may share in its joys;
  Both peasant and peer
  Find ecstacy here,
Then Cricket for ever my boys,
Then Cricket for ever my boys.

A.M., Godalming, 1852.

'The Cricket Song for the Eleven of England' was published in 1852 and is an appropriate tribute to William Clarke, the founder of the peripatetic, professional All-England Eleven. Lines such as 'Welcomed in County and Town' and 'All classes may share in its joys' are pertinent reminders of how widely the All-England Eleven was acclaimed. The fact that the song's composer was Alexander Marshall substantiates this point. Marshall was a member of the Surrey Committee in the 1850s, a trustee of the Oval and maintained his own ground at Broadwater, near Godalming. The Marshall family retained a strong Surrey cricket connection; both Henry and General Sir Frederic Marshall were Presidents of the Club.

One hundred and forty years later it is easy to underestimate how the All-England Eleven revolutionised the public's awareness and perception of cricket. William Clarke laid the foundations for the transformation of cricket into a national institution because, as W. G. Grace conceded in his autobiography *Cricket*, prior to the All-England Eleven 'cricket in England was confined to certain districts'. In *Sketches of the Players*, published in 1846, William Denison, the first cricket journalist of importance, includes profiles of 36 professionals from the early Victorian period. The geographical spread of these players provides a rough guide to the influence of the game. Of the 36, 8 were to be found in Cambridgeshire, 7 in Surrey, 6 each in Nottinghamshire and Sussex and 4 in Kent.

Eight years later the pattern had not changed markedly except for the rapid growth of professionalism in Yorkshire. In the 1854 edition of *Fred Lillywhite's Guide* 110 professionals are listed as being engaged or available and of those 27 were in Yorkshire, 21 in Notts, 16 in Sussex, 13 in Surrey, 9 in Kent and 7 in Cambridgeshire. Further, more than one professional was also listed as resident in Derbyshire, Durham and Northumberland, Middlesex and Suffolk.

These figures confirm that prior to the formation of the All-England Eleven in 1846, and during its early years, cricket was concentrated in Cambridgeshire, Kent, Nottinghamshire, Surrey, Sussex and Yorkshire. In fact, of the present first-class county clubs only Sussex (1839) and Surrey (1845) pre-date the All-England Eleven, although a number of other self-styled county teams and clubs had taken the field. For example, from 1826 the Wellesbourne Club frequently played as 'Warwickshire'.

The severe geographical limitations of county cricket in the 1840s is apparent from glancing down the Notts fixture list from 1840 until 1851. In those 12 seasons, home and away, Notts met Sheffield 7 times, Sussex 5, Kent 4, England 3, Hampshire, Leicestershire and MCC twice and Surrey once (and then only in 1851). In 1846, 1849 and 1850 the Notts side played no matches of any significance.

In the late Victorian years the pre-eminent role of Clarke's All-England Eleven was recognised by the more astute writers. In 1883 in the *National Review* Lord Harris commented that it was from Clarke's 'time that the firm hold which cricket has taken on the hearts of the people of England' can be dated. Nine years later in *Cricket*, the Rev. Holmes justifiably commended Clarke as a 'missionary of cricket'.

Thirty-first August 1846 is one of the most notable dates in the history of cricket. On that day the All-England Eleven played their first match against 20 of Sheffield on the Hyde Park Ground, Sheffield. Although the local side won by five wickets, James Pycroft, who generally disparaged the Eleven, subsequently stated in *The Cricket Field* that 'we doubt if any eleven alive could have beaten that eleven'. The first All-England Eleven included nine professionals – William Clarke, Jemmy Dean, William Dorrinton, Fuller Pilch, Joseph Guy, William Martingell, Thomas Sewell, George Butler and William Hillyer – plus two amateurs, Alfred Mynn and the Rev. Villiers Shallet Charnock Smith.

Four days before the Sheffield match William Clarke had organised a benefit match for himself at Southwell in Nottinghamshire. The village of Southwell, a well-known centre of the game in the county, was the birthplace of the three Tinley brothers and provided John Jackson with his first professional engagement in 1850. Clarke arranged for All-England (including Dean, Hillyer, Pilch, Martingell and Sewell) to play Five Gentlemen of the Southwell club and Five Players of Nottinghamshire with Mr A. Mynn. Clarke, Guy and Butler represented the local side. Although All-England won comfortably by an innings, the young George Parr, playing for the home team, top-scored with 51. Unfortunately Parr and Clarke quarrelled during the match after George chose to row to Southwell from his home at Radcliffe-on-Trent. Parr arrived late, as did his passenger Alfred Mynn. As a consequence George Parr was not asked to play for All-England in Sheffield.

After their opening loss in Sheffield the Eleven defeated 18 of Manchester on 3-5 September and 18 of Yorkshire in Leeds on 7-9 September. The following season the fixture list expanded to include visits to Manchester (a match on which, according to *Fred Lillywhite's Guide*, £30-40,000 was wagered in side bets!), Liverpool, Leeds, York, Stockton, Sheffield, Birmingham, Newcastle and Stourbridge. In 1848 the Eleven secured 17 matches and made their debut in Derby, Bradford, Walsall, Coventry, Sunderland, Darlington, Chelmsford and Southampton. By 1851 the All-England Eleven had doubled their programme to include 34 games and for the next 28 years they rarely played less than 20 matches per season.

George Parr, who succeeded Clarke as the Eleven's captain and secretary in 1856, always maintained that the All-

England Eleven would have had to play three times the number of fixtures to meet the demand. This estimate is supported by William Caffyn who made his debut for the Eleven in 1850. In his autobiography *Seventy-One Not Out* Caffyn comments that William Clarke was 'overwhelmed with letters requesting him to take this team to almost every corner of the United Kingdom'.

In the final years of the Eleven's existence it could be argued that the local opposition was often mediocre, but such a proposition is not valid during the 1840s and 1850s. In its first seven seasons, up to and including 1852, the All-England Eleven regularly played against some of the oldest and best sides in the country such as Surrey, Manchester, Manchester Broughton, Liverpool, Sleaford, Newark, Hereford, Leeds, Stockton, Derbyshire and Burton, Bradford, Sheffield, Birmingham, South Hampshire and Edinburgh. The majority of these clubs had been formed prior to 1840 (Manchester in 1816, Birmingham in 1825, Leeds in 1833 and Bradford in 1836) and had well-established playing strengths. Further, the Eleven usually met the opposition on unequal terms playing against 18s, 20s or 22s and invariably with the local side including two or more professional bowlers as 'given men'.

The early visits of the All-England Eleven to Derbyshire show not only the strength of the opposition they faced but also how well they were received. Cricket is known to have been played in Derbyshire since the early 19th century in towns and villages such as Derby, Chesterfield, Ilkeston, Bakewell and Chatsworth. In 1835 the gentlemen-only South Derbyshire Club was created and it quickly attracted 70 members, including the Duke of Devonshire and the Earl of Chesterfield. Thirteen years later the South Derbyshire Club moved their headquarters to the Holmes ground in Derby and the first big match on the ground occurred when the All-England Eleven were the visitors on 21 and 22 August 1848. The local opposition was 20 of Derbyshire and Burton-on-Trent. The Burton Club, patronised by Abraham

Bass the famous brewer, boasted a proud past including an easy victory over the Nottingham Carlton Club in 1814.

According to the *Derby Mercury* the impending visit of the Eleven warranted a rehearsal match in July with players being drawn from Chesterfield, Derby, Burton and Ilkeston in order to select the best local 20. Fourteen amateurs and six professionals were chosen with the latter including Sam Dakin for whose benefit the match was organised. Dakin, although born in Leicestershire, worked in Derby as a lace warp maker when he was not engaged at Lord's. The local 20 also included two excellent professionals in Tom Hunt, 'The Star of the North' from Chesterfield, and Cris Tinley, a fast round-arm bowler engaged in Burton who subsequently transformed himself into one of the best lob bowlers in the history of cricket. The *Derby Mercury* reported that the match created 'considerable excitement' and 'a number of people had come great distances to witness the great players of the land'. Alas the game was spoiled by rain.

A year later the All-England Eleven returned to Derby and were beaten by an innings and seven runs, primarily due to Tom Hunt's 61 which was described by the *Derby Mercury* as made 'in a style that has scarcely been witnessed on the ground', and John Paxton, a fast round-arm bowler from Ilkeston who took 11 wickets in the match. Despite poor weather the local paper reported that 'a large concourse of spectators' attended.

In August 1850 the Eleven drew with 22 of Derbyshire, although it was generally recognised that the home side were in a strong position. Again Tom Hunt, scoring 52 and 39, and John Paxton, claiming seven of the 14 All-England wickets to fall, dominated for the local team.

After the 1849 defeat, with a view to the reputation and drawing power of the Eleven, William Clarke refused to allow any players from Burton to participate. On another occasion, in 1854 in Macclesfield, Clarke threatened to lead his side off if Tom Sherman, the Surrey professional, bowled as a given man for the local 22. Clarke was concerned that his batsmen would be physically 'smashed up' by Sherman on the poorly-prepared wicket. Clearly William Clarke recognised that the popularity of the Eleven was, in part, due to their ability to win.

In 1851, at the fourth attempt, the Eleven finally inflicted a defeat on Derbyshire. Three months later they returned to the county to defeat 22 of Ilkeston by six wickets. Ilkeston, a small lace, hosiery and market town of 7000 people situated mid-way between Nottingham and Derby, was rightly proud of its cricket club, founded in 1829 and a match for any club side in the North of England. The *Derby Mercury* provides an enlightening account of how significant the Eleven's visits were in a town's social calendar:

> Special trains will run from Nottingham and Mansfield. On Thursday and Friday evenings grand galas and *fêtes champetres* will take place at the Vauxhall Gardens, when concerts on a grand scale will be given and there will be fireworks, illuminations, balloons, etc., which will form attractive features of the galas and these, with the interest of the match, will cause, we doubt not, a congregation at Ilkeston such as it has seldom, if ever, witnessed.

Such festivities were typical of the treatment afforded to the All-England Eleven, particularly in country towns. In 1893 and 1894 *Cricket* ran a series of articles by Richard Daft which included his reminiscences about the early years of the Eleven. Daft acted as Parr's assistant when the latter was secretary of the Eleven, although Daft claims he did all the work! Richard Daft did not make his debut with the All-England Eleven until 1857, but the memoirs he wrote for *Cricket* were based on a scrapbook left to him by Dr Yates, a Notts gentleman.

Richard Daft recalled that when the Eleven visited small country towns there was 'such holiday-making and high jinks'. The match was:

> the topic of conversation months before the event took place. Special Committees were formed to get up entertainments in the evening, and when the great day arrived the excitement was often intense.

People would walk from miles around or arrive in whatever carts were available. Daft recounts that when the All-England Eleven met 19 of Devonshire at Teignbridge in 1851 there were great celebrations. Venison, game, the season's delicacies, excellent wines and punch were provided for 50 people in one of the town's hotels, while the following evening another ball took place at the Globe Hotel. Also in 1851 the Eleven made their debut at Trentham Park, the home of the Duke of Sutherland. This match was 'got up' by private subscription and 3-4000 spectators saw the game free of charge – with many hundreds arriving on a special train. Later that season the Eleven visited Hereford and Dr Yates' scrapbook tells the story:

> The ground, under the able management of the veteran Bentley, was in excellent order, and the spirited supporters of cricket in Herefordshire are much to be commended, the expenses of the match being entirely defrayed by subscription. They were honoured by having among them Lord Bateman, who took an active part in the field . . . Amongst the spectators we observed the Hon. Frederick Cavendish . . . A ball was got up by the Mayor for the amusement of the visitors, which went off with great *éclat*.

'THE DOINGS OF THE ELEVEN'

The most valuable account of the All-England Eleven's activities is a two-volume manuscript by Felix entitled 'The Doings of the Eleven, Being a true, full and particular account of the Campaigns of 1851 and 1852'. This remarkable document comprises Felix's reports for *Bell's Life*, additional handwritten commentary and anecdotes by Felix, and a series of delightful colour drawings of matches and incidents.

'The Doings of the Eleven' opens with a map of 'The campaign of the Eleven' in 1851 and Felix maintains that military theme throughout both volumes. The players are refered to as 'warriors', William Clarke as the 'General', bats

Alfred Mynn at Blissworth station by Felix (*Illustration: MCC*)

as 'implements of war' and the Eleven, its baggage and Lillywhite's printing tent, as 'this redoubtable army'.

The Eleven must have given the impression of being a well-drilled military unit as they progressed across the country. Felix describes the journey from Manchester to Wisbech in 1851 by:

> diligence with four horses, coachman and postilion . . . and as the huge thing upon four wheels dragged steadily along . . . throngs of open-mouthed villagers came round, wondering at the strange caravanserai.

Later that season, after the post-match dinner had been concluded in Hereford:

> crowds . . . stood in an admiring gaze around the coach as it heaped upon its roof the trunks, the portmanteaus and implements of war; then came the stirrup cup – then the fond farewell – then the loud huzza, with waving of hats – Then 'on towards Gloucester', the General he cried. Then the lingering look when the fare-well was sighed.

These last two lines are one example from many in the manuscript of Felix's use of verse and rhyme to describe the Eleven's exploits. This departure from Hereford preceded a particularly arduous coach trip. After finding a 'welcome bed' in Gloucester, the Eleven travelled all of the following day via Bristol to Exeter where, after a night's rest, they made an early start for Teignmouth to play Devonshire.

Such coach journeys, occasionally made overnight, could prove hazardous. Felix recalls in 1852 that while travelling by night from Lynn to Sleaford the 'commodious omnibus and four good horses' became lost in Holbeach Marsh and had to wait for day-break to find the correct road.

For the most part the Eleven took trains but that means of transport was sometimes fraught with problems as Alfred Mynn discovered at Blissworth. Felix writes:

> Alfred the Great (so called from his gigantic stature) alighted at the station, and desired the Porter to get his luggage from the van. The Porter surveyed this man of weight and concluding from the size of the British Lion

> that his luggage would be large in proportion hurried to the van – and with the aid of three other sub-porters jolted out the ponderous printing press . . . (the train departed) . . . No hurried expression of rage escaped the lips of the disappointed luggagee. A smile of utmost good nature played upon his manly features . . . With the aid of Telegraph and luggage van – in a few hours all troubles were adjusted.

On the field of play, Felix recognised that in general the standard of the opposition had improved. The local sides, usually 22s (who from Felix's drawings fielded in two concentric circles), were strengthened by such 'given men' as John Berry, Billy Buttress, Andrew Crossland, Alfred Diver and Frank Tinley.

Against strong 22s the Eleven occasionally suffered humiliation. The most notable example being in July 1852 at Captain Willes' ground in Hungerford Park when the local side bowled out the Eleven for 12 in their first innings. The havoc was wreaked by Mr Yonge, who played for the Gentlemen of England, and a professional named Burrin. The match was eventually drawn with the Eleven needing 11 to win with three wickets in hand and George Parr and George Anderson batting well. Felix commented in *Bell's Life* that 'We are sorry it is drawn, as it would have been an extraordinary match for England to have won.'

Through the pen of Felix, the Eleven occasionally complained of partisan local umpires and poorly-prepared wickets. In Wisbech in 1851, despite 'everything else' being 'done with great spirit', the ground was 'full of hard knots and holes with sharp edges'. William Caffyn 'that rising little player, was knocked senseless with a blow in the eye', while Felix put into verse the fate of Alfred Mynn:

> And Alfred the Great, the lion so bold
> Gigantic in stature as Goliath of old
> 'Boshumi procumbit', he laid like a log
> Earth shook as he fell, being fell'd by a Hogge.

During an earlier match in 1851 against 22 of Gainsborough the Eleven encountered a local batsman who refused to move his bat from the blockhole. Felix remarks that he was 'a specimen of blunt good nature . . . his drollery being natural and free from affectation.'

Virtually every one of Felix's match reports contains references to 'numerous and fashionable attendance upon the ground, including most of the principal gentry of the town and neighbourhood and many elegantly attired ladies' (Preston 1852); or 'the splendid entertainment and great evening at the Barracks' (Ipswich 1852); and 'The long room was literally crammed . . . toast upon toast and song upon song' (Sleaford 1852). Substantial sums of money were wagered and attendances were consistently large. When the Eleven visited Newark in 1852 the Mayor closed the town's shops to allow more people to watch the cricket.

Toasts and bumpers of champagne were frequently drunk in honour of the Eleven while the players' social status can be seen in Felix's reference to the menu for 'a compound meal known by the title of "a dinner tea" ' set before the Eleven in Newark. The various courses included 'fried soles, salmon cutlets, chicken, eggs and delicacies of the season' plus 'a glass or so, of Bass and co.' At the time a basic weekly minimum diet for an adult working-class man would have been bread, cheese, oatmeal, potatoes, skimmed milk and bacon, plus very small quantities of tea, coffee, cocoa, sugar, treacle and butter. The very poor would not have been able to afford cheese, while the more prosperous working-class family might have consumed more meat instead of cheese. That is all rather frugal in comparison to the Eleven's 'dinner tea' at Newark.

In 1851 and 1852 the Eleven played 59 matches, winning 26 and losing only 12, but the social significance was much more important than the actual results. Felix's final entry in 'The Doings of the Eleven' is his farewell address for the 1852 season in which he states that the Eleven has:

> brought about a great revolution in the opportunity of witnessing the beauties of this noble pastime . . . But the cricketing county towns yearning for rivalry – at once saw the expediency of such a force as that to which you

> have the honour to belong, and which has been so ably conducted by your indefatigable secretary . . . Year after year the invitations to visit the great cities and towns have increased to an extent unparalleled in sporting history.

So who were these wandering stars local populations clamoured to see?

William Clarke: The 1851 edition of *Fred Lillywhite's Guide* stated that 'it is generally known throughout the country, that owing to the exertions of Clarke, the celebrated slow bowler, cricket has become a very popular game in the North, even as far as Scotland.' William Clarke was a remarkable cricketer and a man of vision and business acumen. He was the first to recognise that in the changed economic and social circumstances of the late 1840s, cricket's local and fragmented popularity could be focused nationally through a professional touring eleven.

Felix described William Clarke as 'painstaking' and 'waggish' and went on to write that:

> There are those who would traduce him, but you have reason to be thankful that you have a man so well skilled in the ways of the world as to have brought about in cricket what he has almost single-handed accomplished.

William Clarke was born in Nottingham in 1798 and by trade was a bricklayer. In the 1830s he was landlord of the Bell Inn, near the Nottingham Market Place, but in December 1837, three months after the death of his first wife, Jane, he married Mrs Chapman who ran the Trent Bridge Inn. The following year Clarke opened the Trent Bridge cricket ground. He took considerable care to ensure that there would be good wickets at Trent Bridge and in 1840 the ground hosted its first county match when Notts met Sussex. Prior to 1838 major cricket matches in Nottingham had taken place on the Forest with the public being able to watch free of charge. Initially Clarke's decision to enclose Trent Bridge and charge a sixpenny entrance caused some public disquiet.

In order to attract the best opposition William Clarke announced various challenges backed by handsome financial stakes. In 1845 he wagered £200 to encourage Fuller Pilch to bring an 'England' side to play 14 of Notts. The home side won by six wickets before a crowd which included two local Members of Parliament, several magistrates and other highly respected Nottingham residents.

Oddly, in 1846 Clarke joined the Lord's staff and held his previously-mentioned benefit at Southwell rather than Trent Bridge. In fact Clarke did not play for Notts at Trent Bridge in 1847 or 1848 which coincided with John Chapman, his wife's son, taking over the management of the ground.

As a batsman William Clarke was by no means inferior, but he was never in the front rank despite occasionally opening the innings. The handicap of having only one eye proved an obvious restriction. Nevertheless, as an underarm lob bowler he excelled. William Caffyn, interviewed in 1892, recalled that Clarke's 'fast under-hand ball' was 'a wonder . . . the spin and the rise would beat any batsman that ever lived'. In an article entitled 'Cricket in 1850', published in *Cricket* in 1889, the comment was made that 'the secret was that his bowling was not so slow as it looked, and it got up very quick off the ground, and the change of pace was considerable.'

The combination of Clarke's ability to spin the ball from leg to off and the veteran's experience helped him claim hundreds of wickets for the All-England Eleven. According to F. S. Ashley-Cooper in *Nottinghamshire Cricket and Cricketers,* in six seasons from 1849 Clarke captured 2385 wickets for the Eleven! With the last ball William Clarke bowled for the Eleven, he took a wicket. Playing for 22 of Whitehaven J. Towerson was stumped by Morton off Clarke for a duck. William Clarke was 57 years old and had been playing the game for 41 seasons. A few weeks later, in July 1856, Clarke made his last appearance on a cricket field as an umpire in the Eleven's fixture against Melton Mowbray. After six weeks in bed, William Clarke died on 25 August of paraplegia at his home, Priory Lodge, in the Wandsworth Road, London.

William Clarke's success might have been due to his lunch of a cigar and a bottle of soda water, or to his ability to eat an entire goose for dinner. But Clarke, or 'Our General' as the players called him, has over time gained a reputation for being an autocrat. In his defence it should be noted that the Eleven did, at least nominally, have a Committee to run its affairs – in 1851 it included Box, Hillyer and Pilch – and that while William Caffyn agreed that Clarke was 'a bit of a despot' he added that he always remained 'a great sportsman'.

Tom Box: 'The best professional wicket-keeper of his day', according to Fred Lillywhite, or, to quote Felix, as 'sharp as a ferret'. William Denison, writing of Box's batting, said, 'few are there who can cut a ball into the slips with more elegance of style, more severity, or with more telling effect.'

Tom Box was born at Ardingley in Sussex in 1808 and by trade was a cabinet maker. After an accident in 1840 or 1841 on the notoriously uneven Lord's wicket, Box's physical appearance was marred by a smashed nose. Nevertheless, he had a reputation for being a dapper dresser. From 1844 until 1863 he kept the Egremont Hotel and the Royal Brunswick cricket ground in Brighton, before becoming a publican in Leicester Square, London.

William Hillyer: 'This lucifer of bowlers', according to Felix, although Denison prefered the more mundane 'now unquestionably one, if not the best, of our bowlers'. Bowling within himself at 'mid-pace', William Hillyer maintained perfect control. In 27 matches in 1845 he delivered only nine wides – in the same season Alfred Mynn bowled 42.

William Hillyer was born at Leybourne in Kent in 1813. He worked as a gamekeeper, possessing a fine shot. From 1839 until 1851 Hillyer retained a place on the Lord's staff before ill-health forced him to conclude his playing career. He then became the coach at Rugby school.

Joseph Guy: By the time William Clarke launched the All-England Eleven, Joseph Guy, who had been born in Nottingham in 1814, was already in his thirties. In 1838 he had made his debut at Lord's in the North versus South and Players versus Gentlemen encounters. Guy played in the latter fixture for 15 consecutive seasons. It was of Joseph Guy that William Clarke made the famous remark that his batting was 'all ease and elegance, fit to play before Her Majesty in a drawing room'. In *Nottinghamshire Cricket Scores and Biographies* C. H. Richards provides a less florid description: 'very forward and his defence perfect; quite a "stonewaller" in his day'. On the field he won renown at long-stop and point. By trade Guy was a baker, but like many of his comrades he became a publican during and after his cricket career.

William Martingell: Although born in Nutfield, Surrey, in 1818, William Martingell played for Kent from 1841 until 1852. Fuller Pilch persuaded Martingell to take an engagement with the Kent Club in Canterbury, however after he joined the Oval staff in 1846 he also played for Surrey. In between these two positions Martingell served under the patronage of the Earl of Ducie in Gloucestershire. This former shoemaker and gamekeeper, with a notably florid complexion, was a right-round-arm, medium pace bowler who was for a time coach at Eton, but ended his life in poor circumstances.

George Parr: 'The Lion of the North' as George Parr was called, played county cricket for Notts from 1844 until 1871. At the age of 45, in his last match for the county, he hit 32 not out and 53. In 1865 *Wisden* wrote about George Parr that:

> His scores have been enormous, and his style of play has long ranked him the best batsman in England; his leg hitting is always a treat to witness, no man approaching him in this department of the game; his position in the field at the commencement of his career was generally long-leg and middle-wicket, he being able to throw a ball a great

The young Richard Daft with George Parr
(*Photo: Nottinghamshire CCC*)

distance, having in a match with a soldier at Lord's, June 16, 1846, thrown it about 109 yards, but of late years he has either taken slip or point.

Parr's hit to square-leg was legendary; Richard Daft described it as a 'country mow brought to perfection' with the ball hit quick, low and hard. It should be added that Parr combined this leg hitting with a splendid defence and a fine range of strokes all round the wicket.

During his 27 years in cricket's front-rank George Parr recorded five centuries – three for All-England and two for Notts. In contemporary terms that list may appear insignificant but in the 1840s and 1850s, with poor wickets and erratic round-arm and lob bowling, an individual hundred was a remarkable achievement. His best innings was generally considered to have been the 130 chanceless runs he compiled in five-and-a-half hours against Surrey in 1859.

George Parr was born in Radcliffe-on-Trent in 1826, one of nine children. His father was a gentleman-farmer who worked land that the family had rented from the Earl of Manvers for over 200 years. In the opinion of Edwin Browne, the assistant secretary of Notts, George had inherited a 'strongly built frame and steady gait' which made him look the part of a 'yeoman farmer'.

In 1856, after the death of William Clarke, Parr took over as captain and secretary of the All-England Eleven – a position he retained until 1870. During that period he also captained Notts. Among George Parr's other notable achievements was his leadership of the first overseas tour in 1859 when he captained the side which visited Canada and the United States. Four years later he took the second party of cricketers to Australia.

As a player, manager and pioneer, George Parr's contribution to cricket was enormous. Off the field the Rev. Holmes described him as 'a man of considerable force of character, shrewd, business-like and enterprising'. However Richard Daft, who undoubtedly was better acquainted with Parr, remarked that he was 'prone to fits of absence of mind and forgetfulness'. In his various memoirs Daft also portrays

Parr as being slightly idiosyncratic, for example, he always carried an old leather hat box to away matches but steadfastly refused to reveal its contents. In *Talks with Old English Cricketers,* Richard Daft doubts Parr's intellect: 'He was a man that wanted knowing. I used to arrange the All-England matches for him, and did nearly the whole of his correspondence.' William Caffyn, in *Seventy-One Not Out,* recalled that George 'prefered one day's shooting to a season's cricket'.

Throughout his life George Parr suffered from gout which made him lame. On 23 June 1891 he died of rheumatic gout. The previous year he had married Jane Smalley, his housekeeper for many years.

Fuller Pilch: No greater compliment can be paid to George Parr than to say that he was the successor to Pilch as the best batsman in England. For a few seasons the pair played together for the All-England Eleven. Fuller Pilch's pre-eminence was established in 1833 when he twice comprehensively beat Tom Marsden, the Sheffield champion, at single wicket. The *Sporting Magazine* concluded:

> Pilch's batting was of the finest description, and a better display of the art of cricket was never witnessed in any former match . . . As a double wicket player he is allowed to be unrivalled, and as a single wicket player his second conquest over the man who was said to be the first, has at once given him the championship which we suppose no one will challenge.

From 1835 Pilch was induced, for an annual sum of £100, to leave his native Norfolk to reside in Kent. In Town Malling, near Maidstone, he managed a tavern and the attached cricket ground. He later moved to Canterbury to work for the Kent Club and remained as groundsman at the St Lawrence ground until 1868. Fuller Pilch died two years later. By profession Pilch was a tailor, a trade to which he returned in collaboration with one of his nephews. From around 1851 he was also in partnership with Edward Martin making cricket bats in Oxford.

By 1851, when the All-England Eleven was firmly established as the greatest cricketing combination in the country, Clarke, Box, Hillyer, Guy, Martingell, Parr and Pilch had been joined by John Wisden and William Caffyn, plus the game's two leading amateurs, Alfred Mynn and Nicholas Felix (né Wanostrocht). Felix was the first President of the Eleven, a position he relinquished when he retired in 1853. It was not common for these 11 players to be available simultaneously but in 1851, of the 34 matches the Eleven played, these eleven each appeared in more than half the fixtures. Caffyn, Guy and Parr played in 33 of the matches, Box in 32, Wisden in 31, Martingell in 28, Clarke in 27 and Felix in 26.

While allowing for the difficulty of making comparisons across generations, this All-England Eleven must rank as one of the strongest sides in the game's history. When this eleven played together, as they did against 14 of Marylebone at Lord's on 9 June 1851, the batting order was Caffyn, Felix, Parr, Pilch, Martingell, Box, Wisden, Guy, Mynn, Hillyer and Clarke. This fixture was one of the season's highlights and ended in controversy. The Eleven needed one run to win with five wickets standing when time was called. This decision, although within the laws, was widely held to have been unsportsmanlike. In MCC's first innings the All-England bowlers were Clarke, Wisden, Hillyer, Mynn and Martingell, while in the second Clarke, Hillyer and Wisden dismissed the 14 for 98.

During William Clarke's 11 seasons as the All-England Eleven's promoter he was well-rewarded financially. When the Eleven appeared Clarke was guaranteed £65 and, in turn, he paid the players. Each individual received an amount that Clarke deemed appropriate according to the player's status and match performance. This match fee varied between £3 and £5, with the established members of the Eleven always receiving the higher figure. William Clarke was left with a good profit.

THE 1852 SPLIT

It has always been assumed that match fees were the cause of the split in 1852 which led to the creation of a second professional touring eleven – the United England Eleven. In his autobiography William Caffyn, who joined the United in 1854, commented that, 'It was thought that Clarke was coining money, and that they (the players) ought to be better paid.'

However, to call the creation of the United England Eleven a split from the All-England Eleven is a misnomer because none of the regular All-England players left to join the United. The United's first fixture occurred on 26 August 1852 when they met 20 Gentlemen of Hampshire at Daniel Day's ground in Southampton. Twelve days later, on 7 September at the Adelphi Hotel in Sheffield, the following resolution was passed:

> That neither the members of the above Eleven shall at any time play in any match of cricket, for or against, wherein William Clarke may have the management or control (county matches excepted) in consequence of the treatment they have received from him at Newmarket and elsewhere.

This statement was signed by John Wisden, Jemmy Dean, Tom Adams, Thomas Hunt, John Lillywhite, George Brown, Thomas Nixon, George Picknell, Sam Dakin, George Chatterton, Tom Lockyer, James Grundy, Thomas Sherman and Henry Wright.

Wisden and Dean were credited as being the main instigators of the United and they became the joint secretaries. Although Jemmy Dean played in the first All-England match in 1846 he did not appear regularly for the Eleven, prefering to remain on the Lord's staff, a position he retained from 1837 until 1861. John Wisden, at the time one of the best cricketers in England, had been an All-England stalwart in 1851 but made only infrequent appearances in 1852. Wisden was a very effective slow round-arm bowler, a good bat and a fine short slip and had opened 'Messrs Parr and Wisden's Cricket Club' in Leamington Spa in 1849, but in 1852 began a four-year term as coach at Harrow school.

Of the other 12 founders of the United, many occasionally played for or against the Eleven but none could be considered regulars. It has to be assumed that the established players in the All-England Eleven were content with the remuneration from Clarke.

In *Seventy-One Not Out* Caffyn writes that Wisden spoke to Clarke about the finances of the Eleven. He 'put the matter straight to Clarke, who answered him somewhat roughly, and caused a breach between them. So the United was formed.' Taking this statement in conjunction with the Sheffield resolution, it seems that some disagreement occurred at Newmarket between Clarke, Wisden and perhaps others. But Newmarket is an enigma given that the Eleven did not play in the town in 1851 or 1852.

On 12-14 August, however, Wisden and Dean played against the Eleven for 22 of Northamptonshire. Although some professionals made their living by travelling the country to play as given men against All-England, Wisden and Dean were never among them. The appearance of the pair in the Northampton 22 remains a peculiar anomaly. Perhaps the altercation between Clarke, Wisden and Dean took place in Northampton and not Newmarket?

Felix's manuscript 'The Doings of the Eleven' covers the 1852 season but makes no detailed reference to the dispute with Wisden and Dean. Felix's only comment came in his farewell address when he remarked that, 'The public mind is not to be occupied with any trifling matters of internal disaffection.' Yet the previous season he had made the general statement that:

> The success of this Corporate Body created the envy of many who by the rule of human nature became jealous of its well doing, and angry because of its purity of principle.

A realistic assessment of the creation of the United is that the professionals who were not regulars in the All-England Eleven, knowing that there was an unfulfilled demand for such fixtures, decided to put a second itinerant eleven into the field. And there proved to be plenty of takers, as well as room for both sides.

The ill-feeling between Clarke and Wisden and Dean did not abate. Two years later when Clarke 'got up' the North versus South fixture in Tunbridge Wells the United pair were either not asked or refused to play. After William Clarke's death relations between All-England and the United improved considerably.

Also in 1854 William Clarke found himself in dispute with Lord's and according to *Fred Lillywhite's Guide* had his name scratched from the MCC's books. The disagreement arose because of the refusal of Clarke, George Parr, Julius Caesar and William Caffyn to play in the Gentlemen versus Players game because of a prior All-England commitment in Maidstone. William Clarke had no intention of releasing those star players who were his main attraction.

On 26 September 1856 at a general meeting the All-England players had decided that despite 'Old' Clarke dying they would continue as before. A new management Committee was elected comprising George Parr, Julius Caesar, George Anderson, Alfred Clarke, H. H. Stephenson and Edgar Willsher. Only George Parr remained from the first generation of All-England pioneers, but who were his fellow Committee members?

George Anderson: W. G. Grace described Anderson as 'superior to the average professional player in manner and education . . a great favourite'. George Anderson, who was born in Bedale, Yorkshire in 1826, first encountered William Clarke in his native village during one of Clarke's regular coaching expeditions. In 1851 Anderson was asked to join the Eleven and for the next 21 years his powerful hitting terrified hundreds of county and club bowlers. Like so many other notable players of the period George Anderson ended his life in difficult circumstances.

Julius Caesar: Owing to his diminutive stature (5 feet 7 inches), 'Julie' as he was universally known, was described by his fellow Surrey professional William Caffyn as 'a big man in a little room'. Caesar's batting strength lay in his fine, free leg hitting and a powerful on-drive. 'Julie', who had been born in Godalming in 1830, was part of a large cricketing family and at various times his elder brother Fred was also a professional. By trade Julius Caesar was a carpenter and joiner, while also being a first-rate boxer and capital shot. He died in Godalming in 1878 in great poverty.

Alfred Clarke: The youngest of William Clarke's six children, Alfred joined the Eleven as scorer. Having graduated to the status of player he gained a reputation for being a hard and vigorous hitter and a useful long-stop. Like his father, Alfred was a licenced victualler by trade and inherited administrative talent – Alfred was responsible for arranging the railway timetable for the busy Eleven. After suffering failing health for some time, Alfred Clarke died in Ruddington, Nottinghamshire in 1878, aged 47.

Heathfield Harman Stephenson: For obvious reasons Stephenson was usually known as 'H.H.'. This Surrey professional was born in Esher in 1833. He was a true all-rounder being a first-rate bat, a good wicket-keeper and a successful fast round-arm bowler. 'H.H.' excelled in all those roles for the Eleven.

Stephenson has many claims to fame, such as captaining the first tour to Australia in 1861-62. Another of his notable feats occurred in September 1858 in Sheffield during the match between All-England and 22 of Hallam and Staveley. Stephenson took three wickets with consecutive deliveries and the Eleven rewarded him with a new hat. This is the earliest recorded instance of a 'hat trick'. By 1860 it had become commonplace to award a white hat for such a feat.

In 1854 Stephenson had given up his position at the Oval to travel full-time with the All-England Eleven. In later years 'H.H.' found employment as a whipper-in with the

Duc D'Aumale before being promoted to the position of huntsman in 1864. At the same time he acted as coach at Rossall and later Uppingham school. In comparison to many of his contemporaries, 'H.H.' prospered socially, purchased a house and achieved respectability as a churchwarden and member of the Board of Guardians in Uppingham. He died there in 1896.

Edgar Willsher: 'The Lion of Kent' was the youngest of 14 children born in Rolvenden into a farming family. Handicapped from boyhood because he had only one lung, Willsher was described in later life by Lord Harris in *A Few Short Runs* as 'an attenuated, consumptive-looking man'. As to Edgar's cricketing prowess Harris commented, 'I do not think he had much idea of the science of the game . . . he had a curious far-away look in his eyes.'

W. G. Grace considered Edgar Willsher to be 'one of the greatest bowlers', while Richard Daft 'unhesitatingly' felt he was the finest left-hand bowler. Writing in 1893 in *Cricket* Daft remembers Willsher as:

> a tall, lanky, cadaverous-looking man, with a very long thin left arm. His delivery was a rather peculiar one . . . He came up to the wicket with a quick-march kind of step; raised his hand high above his head, bringing it down, however, with a very quick jerky movement just as he delivered.
>
> That last movement of his seemed to put a spin and impetus on the ball that caused it to rise like lightning from the pitch.

Edgar Willsher made his Kent debut at the age of 19 in 1847 and for two seasons (1852-53) was engaged by the Kent Club in Canterbury. The following season he played full-time with the All-England Eleven. Willsher was the Eleven's most destructive quick bowler until John Jackson's devastating debut in 1856. During the 1855 season, primarily bowling in combination with William Clarke, Willsher captured more than 270 wickets for All-England. Six years later against 18 of Manchester Broughton, 'The Lion of Kent' produced a remarkable spell of bowling by conceding only one run from 100 consecutive balls.

In 1862 Willsher was at the centre of the bowling controversy which eventually led to over-arm bowling being legalised two years later. In his post-All-England years Willsher led the 1868 tour to the United States. Four years later he became head ground bowler and manager of Prince's cricket ground in Islington. In that same year he organised a successful benefit which netted £794, and in 1875 he opened a cricket outfitters in the Lewisham Road, London.

Throughout the 1850s the popularity of the All-England Eleven showed no signs of waning. *Fred Lillywhite's Guide* is littered with passing comments on All-England matches such as 'a great occasion', 'very large attendance', 'the town was never so much enlivened', 'promenading by the ladies' and 'neither expense nor trouble spared'. Such brief descriptions recorded by Lillywhite make it clear that a visit by the Eleven was an important social occasion demanding attendance by the local aristocracy, their ladies and aspiring tradespeople.

The visits of the Eleven to Derbyshire towards the end of the decade are indicative of the following the Eleven had amongst all social classes. In 1857 the *Derby Mercury* reported that the impending visit by the Eleven had been 'subscribed', that is, sponsored, by a list of notable town and country gentlemen plus three local Members of Parliament. The following season a strong Derbyshire 22 beat the Eleven by 13 wickets in Chesterfield. The local side included the county's best professionals such as Tom Hunt (who tragically died 12 weeks later after being run over by a train in Rochdale), Dove Gregory (the South Derbyshire Club's professional), Thomas and William Attenborough and John Paxton (all from Ilkeston) plus two given men – Rogers and Frank Tinley. The *Derby Mercury* recorded:

> The match was played on the drill ground of the Chatsworth Rifles . . . The trial of skill was got up by a spirited Committee who risked an outlay of upwards of 200 but

> who it is said, have profited by the speculation. On Monday about 1600 persons were present, on Tuesday something like double the number congregated on the ground, and on Wednesday the attendance exhibited a falling off. A number of tents and refreshment stalls were upon the ground and the Chesterfield and Brampton band played selections of popular music during the three days and dancing was indulged in by a great number of young people in the evenings. On the first and second nights there was a display of fireworks by Mr. Copley, pyrotechnist, of Sheffield.

Finally in 1859, back at the Holmes ground in Derby, in a match under the management of the Town and South Derbyshire Clubs, there was, according to the *Mercury*, a 'considerable attendance of spectators, among whom were most of the neighbouring gentry and their families, and gay throngs of ladies.' The home side which held the Eleven to a draw included Lord Stanhope, Lord Paget, the Boden brothers, who ran a very profitable lace business, Unwin Sowter, a local miller, and the professional Dove Gregory.

OPPOSING ALL-ENGLAND

Who were the sides that opposed the All-England Eleven? Were the matches played in the cities or the country? Was the opposition weak or strong? In the first 15 years after the Eleven's debut the teams they played against can be divided into five broad groups.

Established clubs from the cities, such as Manchester Broughton, Liverpool or Nottingham Commercial. These clubs included many excellent gentlemen cricketers who by profession were merchants, clergymen, solicitors and businessmen but who rarely played at Lord's or the Oval. For example, William Lockart of the Liverpool Club and a Birkenhead merchant, was generally considered to be the best amateur wicket-keeper in the country, but during his career he never appeared at Lord's.

Newly-formed clubs in the emerging industrial towns, which in many cases were established after the All-England Eleven began its missionary work. Clubs such as Hull, Huddersfield, Macclesfield, Preston, Stoke and Wakefield fall into this category.

Clubs in market towns, such as Boston, Grantham, Melton Mowbray, Newark, Sleaford and Spalding. In *Kings of Cricket* Richard Daft commented that he always considered that Grantham and Sleaford were the two most pleasant fixtures on the Eleven's itinerary. There, he remarked, the grounds would be 'crowded with the carriages of the neighbouring landowners and farmers'.

Sides under aristocratic patronage, for example, those organised by the Earl of Stamford, Lord Romney, the Duke of Sutherland, the Earl of Lichfield, the Duke of Northumberland and Lord Monson.

The most generous patron was the Earl of Stamford who hosted the All-England Eleven at Enville Hall near Stourbridge each season between 1853 and 1856. Although George Harry Grey, the seventh Earl of Stamford and Warrington, was President of the MCC in 1851 he rarely played at Lord's. According to *Scores and Biographies* the Earl was a hitter and underarm bowler, although Richard Daft remembers him as a mediocre player, but a great patron. Enville Hall, one of the Earl's four seats, boasted a cricket ground in perfect condition. A visit by either All-England or the United was always a grand occasion at Enville Hall, thousands of local people moved through the grounds, a Hungarian band played and a fireworks display brought the proceedings to a conclusion.

Because of his passion for cricket the Earl retained several of the best professionals on his staff. Reuben Roby, by trade a lacemaker, had been the professional at nearby Stourbridge from 1845 until 1851, before he moved to Enville Hall where he remained in service for seven years. Cris Tinley was with the Earl from 1854 to 1858; Samuel Clarke was there in 1856; John Bickley and Charles Brampton from 1855 to 1858; Edgar Willsher in 1857-58; Charlie Brown in 1860 and finally Hiram Slack from 1862 until 1864. The Earl of Stamford's side, with professionals of the calibre of Bickley, Brampton, Tinley and Willsher, was a match for any eleven in the country. But when All-England visited Enville Hall they faced the challenge of a 22. The Earl augmented his professional talent by inviting some of England's best gentlemen cricketers. In 1855 his side included Lord Lyttelton, the Earl of Strathmore, Lord Guernsey, the Hon. Frederick Ponsonby and Colonel Mundy. As *Scores and Biographies* noted, 'no eleven could match such a twenty-two' although All-England had won the two previous encounters.

In 1861 the Eleven made its debut at Beau Desert, the Staffordshire home of Lord Henry Paget, half brother of Alexander Paget, the Marquis of Anglesea. *Bailys Magazine* described the family as having 'interwoven themselves by alliances with the chief noble families of England', as being 'next to the Earl of Stamford and Warrington the most munificent patrons' of the game and Beau Desert as having 'one of the best cricket grounds in England'.

Lord Henry Paget was President of the All-England Eleven in 1860 and it was the Pagets who gave the Eleven their red and white colours. This was exhibited in the form of a white shirt with either small red spots or a fine red stripe.

The involvement of such aristocrats either directly with the All-England Eleven (the Pagets occasionally played) or in sponsoring matches against them is another indication of the high regard in which the Eleven was held. In the 1850s and 1860s the cricket establishment did not perceive the All-England Eleven or the idea of itinerant, professional sides as a threat to the future of cricket.

Matches against the United England Eleven were one of the high points of the season from 1857 to 1869. The two professional Elevens met on 19 occasions with, appropriately, each side being victorious eight times with three draws. The majority of the contests took place at Lord's although the match was staged twice at the Oval (1860 and 1861), twice at Old Trafford (1861 and 1867) and in its final two years at the Savile Town Ground, Dewsbury.

The first encounter in 1857 drew a huge crowd of 20,000 over three days. *Fred Lillywhite's Guide* reported that there were 'never so many lookers on' who came from all over the country and included a large number of the nobility. The All-England Eleven successfully objected to the inclusion of two gentlemen, Messrs Miller and Burbidge, in the United Eleven, establishing the precedent that this was a professionals-only match. All-England won both fixtures in the inaugural season by five wickets and 133 runs.

The 19-match series witnessed some tremendous overall performances. For All-England, George Parr asserted his batting prowess with an aggregate of 622 runs including three half centuries. Parr was the only player on either side who appeared in the first (1857) and the last (1869) games. He commenced with 56 not out and concluded with a duck. He was unavailable in 1862, and in 1864 was on board ship after the tour of Australia and New Zealand.

Richard Daft began disasterously in June 1859 with a 'pair' at Lord's. However he soon made amends and finished with a total of 529 runs from 14 matches, including the only century in the series when he hit 111 not out at Old Trafford in May 1867. The other notable batsman for All-England was Tom Hayward with 469 runs.

The bowling of John Jackson proved decisive for All-England on a number of occasions. Jackson's record of 107 wickets in 16 matches puts him far ahead of any rival. On 11 occasions he took five wickets in an innings and three times 10 wickets in the match (12 for 68, July 1858; 14 for 61, June 1859; 10 for 98, July 1860).

For the United Jemmy Grundy appeared in 17 of the 19 matches but his batting aggregate of 375 runs was overshadowed by the Cambridge crack Robert Carpenter who scored 611 runs in 16 games. Known as 'the old gardener', Carpenter had abandoned his trade as a bootcloser to play

The All-England Eleven versus the United England Eleven at Lord's 1863

professional cricket and, according to *Scores and Biographies*, through his back play and powerful hitting brought a 'scientific manner' to batting. In July 1859 at Lord's he made 97 for the United in a match they won by nine wickets.

Prior to his departure for Australia William Caffyn produced some sterling all-round performances for the United. Appearing in all of the first 13 games he scored 293 runs and claimed 65 wickets. Undoubtedly his most remarkable bowling occurred in June 1859 at Lord's when he and George Atkinson bowled unchanged through both All-England innings to steer the United to a 37-run victory in a low-scoring encounter. Caffyn finished with a match analysis of 11 for 63. This was the second of three occasions that the former hairdresser from Reigate took 10 wickets in a match for the United against All-England.

In 1892 the Rev. Holmes wrote in *Cricket* that the All-England versus United games were 'perhaps the most keenly fought matches in the entire history of the game' and in 1866, as the series was beginning to draw to a close, this clash of professional talent was still attracting a crowd of more than 10,000. But this proved to be the last time the fixture was played at Lord's. The cricket world had split between North and South, exemplified by the fact that all the professionals on both sides were from the North.

THE CRICKETERS' FUND FRIENDLY SOCIETY

Apart from charity appeals or a benefit match the only protection a professional had against an accident or illness restricting his earnings was through the Cricketers' Fund Friendly Society (CFFS) which was established in 1857. In general, friendly or benefit societies were widespread by the end of the 18th century. In *The Making of the English Working Class* E.P. Thompson estimates that in 1793 the membership of friendly societies totalled 648,000 and that by 1815 it exceeded 900,000. The tardiness of professional cricketers in forming such a friendly society is easily explained by the fact that it was only in the mid-1850s that more than 100 cricketers were endeavouring to make a living, at least in summer, from the game. For the first time a coherent group with a community of interests existed and the creation of the CFFS was a logical step.

The Cricketers' Fund had three objectives. First, to provide members with relief if due to 'old age, illness, accident or other infirmity (they were) incapable of following their profession'. Second, to make temporary assistance available to a member's widow and children if they were left destitute. And third, to ensure that the member had a decent burial. This was most important for any self-respecting working-class person – a pauper's funeral was the ultimate social disgrace. Sadly, this was a fate that befell several players.

The successful establishment of the CFFS in 1857 was achieved by a combination of amateur patronage and professional organisation. The Fund's first President was the well-known patron Edmond Wilder; the trustees were the Hon. Frederick Ponsonby and John Walker, one of the famous Walkers of Southgate; Mr James Henry Dark, the proprietor of Lord's, occupied the position of treasurer, while Mr Frederick Lillywhite became the first honorary secretary. However the Fund's Committee was entirely composed of professionals, drawn predominantly from the All-England Eleven, and included Tom Box (chair), George Parr, George Anderson, Julius Caesar, Edgar Willsher, John Lillywhite and Alfred Diver.

To join the Fund a player contributed an annual subscription of one guinea which was due on 1 June each year. Honorary membership was encouraged for an annual sum of two guineas and this represented a donation to the CFFS. If an aspiring member was between 38 and 40 years old they had to pay an entrance fee of 50 shillings; between 40 and 42 £5; and between 42 and 45 £10. No new members over 45 were allowed.

To be eligible to receive benefits a member had to have been fully paid up for five years, or for three years in the case of a claim by his widow. In the event of temporary illness or accident, between May and September in the first year the player could receive a maximum of £2 per week; for the rest of the year the rate was £1 per week. If the claim continued into a second year the maximum benefit was £1 per week and beyond two years no claims were accepted. In the event of permanent illness the maximum that could be awarded was 10 shillings per week, while the sum of £20 was granted for funeral expenses.

The major source of revenue for the Fund, apart from members' subscriptions, was the gate receipts from the All-England versus United fixtures. In 1857 the match raised £158 while in 1860 the sum contributed had risen to £214. Assets accrued to such an extent that in August 1863 it was announced that the Fund held £1630.

After the All-England United match in May 1863 a meeting of the professionals was organised at Lord's to discuss the running of the CFFS. According to the report printed in *Scores and Biographies*, 'somehow or other (like other things at Lord's) it had been neglected'. The meeting decided unanimously that John Wisden should take over as secretary at an annual salary of £20. A new Committee, to meet quarterly, was elected; it comprised George Parr, George Anderson, H. H. Stephenson, Edgar Willsher, John Lillywhite and Robert Carpenter. These six players were chosen to represent the professional-producing counties of Notts, Yorkshire, Surrey, Kent, Sussex and Cambridgeshire respectively. Two years later the Committee was re-elected while Richard Daft replaced Box as the Fund's chairman.

The CFFS prospered in the 1860s and 1870s and by 1874 it held investments to a value of almost £2500. After the conclusion of the All-England versus United fixtures the Fund received the receipts from the annual North versus South match played at Prince's. However, according to the 1888 edition of *Wisden*, in 1886 due to 'very heavy demands' the Fund was 'very impoverished'. Two decisions were made – first, the benefit rates were cut. Sick pay was reduced to 30 shillings in summer and 15 shillings in winter; the permanent illness or superannuation payment was lowered to six shillings per week and the funeral allowance fell to £15.

Second, an appeal to MCC members raised £100, although a similar call the following year brought in nothing. In 1888 Lord Harris, always a great promoter of the CFFS, made a further special appeal.

These measures had a positive effect because the 1889 accounts record that £4770 was invested on behalf of 108 members. That year £338 had been paid out in sick allowances to such famous All-England players as George Parr, Ned Stephenson and Cris Tinley, while John Jackson received one year's superannuation.

In 1902 when the CFFS looked back over its 45-year history it had every reason to be content with its work in providing some security to professional cricketers. In total £6200 had been paid out in benefits since the Fund's foundation and it had retained the support of influential establishment figures such as Lord Harris, Lord Hawke, Mr V. E. Walker, Mr C. E. Green (all trustees) and Mr W. E. Denison (President).

The CFFS, which still existed in the 1970s, was a lasting legacy from the All-England and United England Elevens to subsequent generations of professional cricketers.

THE FIRST OVERSEAS TOURS

Cricket and the British Empire were inseparable. Lord Hawke wrote in his introduction to the aptly titled *Imperial Cricket*:

> The greatest game in the world is played wherever the Union Jack is unfurled, and it has no small place in cementing the ties that bond together every part of the Empire.

George Bernard Shaw made a similar point, albeit from a different perspective, when he commented that 'the most blackguardley agents of capitalism were cricketers to a man'. Until the bodyline tour of Australia in 1932-33 the notion went unquestioned that cricket represented all that was best in the English way of life.

Within the Empire innumerable governors fostered cricket as a means of drawing the colonies closer to Britain and as a device to overcome regional, caste and tribal antagonisms. This was particularly the case in India, while in Australia cricket had an equally important role dating back to Sir William Denison, the Governor of New South Wales, who in 1856 allocated part of Sydney's Domain for use as a cricket field. Ignoring a possible conflict with the military Sir William remarked, 'Never mind the military. If that will make the better wicket, then take it by all means.' In November 1860 Denison became the first patron of the NSW Cricket Association and within 15 months the first tour party had arrived from England. In January 1862 an English professional eleven easily beat a NSW 22 in the Domain.

The involvement of English governors in promoting cricket within the Empire has been well-documented, but it is often forgotten that most of the sides in the Victorian years that ventured overseas were predominantly comprised of professionals. It was the players who undertook the long, arduous sea journeys to carry cricket to the imperial outposts.

The first overseas tour left Liverpool on 7 September 1859, for Canada and the United States. The party of 12, equally divided between All-England and United players, included William Caffyn, Tom Lockyer, H. H. Stephenson, Julius Caesar, George Parr, James Grundy, John Jackson, John Wisden, John Lillywhite, Robert Carpenter, Tom Hayward and Alfred Diver. The team was accompanied by Fred Lillywhite and his printing tent. With a side of such strength it was hardly surprising that the tourists comfortably won all five matches.

The names of the 12 tourists were recorded in a poem by T.R. of Cambridge which was reprinted in *Scores and Biographies*. The last four verses read:

Long may ye rule our peaceful land,
With fortune for a guiding star,
Long may be the champion band,
Beneath the lion-hearted Parr.

Up Lilly, eager for the fray,
And Jackson with unerring aim,
And graceful Hayward – and to play,
And Caffyn, 'cut' thy way to fame.

Up watchful Grundy, and begin,
And Carpenter of plucky skill,
And willy Diver, play to win,
And Caesar, be ambitious still.

Up steady Wisden, sure and free,
And Stephenson, fresh honour reap,
And Lockyer, let the foeman see
The way the simple fort to keep.

The fame of the All-England Eleven was such that since 1856 the Montreal Cricket Club had endeavoured to arrange a tour. To secure the players' services in 1859 each of the 12 was guaranteed £50, although according to Caffyn they cleared £90. *The Times* reported that the party had a 'pleasant voyage' which hardly fits with Fred Lillywhite's descriptions in *The English Cricketers' Trip to Canada and the United States in 1859* of players who 'would not venture to leave England again, under any circumstances' due to seasickness, fierce gales, thick fog and icebergs followed by long train, coach and steamer journeys.

Wherever the England side appeared they were watched by big crowds of which the largest, according to Lillywhite, was in New York when 25,000 saw them beat 22 of the United States. As in England when one of the professional elevens visited a town, there were great festivities. On this first overseas tour the game's moral lessons were already being preached. In a speech to loud cheers, the Montreal Chairman said:

> We live in a country, one of the most glorious dependencies of the British Crown, in which are numerous varieties of races, of creeds, of opinions, of matters political, commercial, and otherwise. May not a lesson be learned from the game in which you have this day been

> engaged – a lesson of moderation, a lesson of good sense? May we not be taught that there may be differences without animosty, emulation without enmity – that people may rival each other not only in cricket, but in all other pursuits of life, and be like brothers, and remain so.

On 11 November, almost 10 weeks after their departure, the England players docked in Liverpool. They had travelled almost 7500 miles. At a dinner on 8 December in Godalming for the six professionals from the South, Henry Marshall, the Surrey President, congratulated the tourists who 'have contributed to give the game a world-wide reputation'.

The second overseas tour party, and the first to Australia, left Liverpool on 20 October 1861. Again the 12 cricketers were all professionals, although less representative of professional cricket than the party to Canada and the United States had been.

For the tour's sponsors, Spiers and Pond – the proprietors of the Café de Paris in Melbourne – a team of cricketers had not been their first choice, but one they accepted when Charles Dickens spurned their overtures. As early as January 1860 Spiers and Pond had sent word to George Parr inviting him to bring an eleven, but it was not until the following season that serious negotiations began.

In September 1861, during the North versus South match at Aston Park in Birmingham, Mr W. B. Hallam, on behalf of Spiers and Pond, offered £150 per man, first-class travel and lodging plus expenses. Ten of the best professionals considered this offer inadequate. Caesar, Daft, Parr, Jackson, Willsher, Lockyer, Hayward, Carpenter, Grundy and Anderson all declined. It is often claimed that it was the northern professionals who refused to undertake the tour, but the list includes Willsher from Kent, Lockyer and Caesar from Surrey and Hayward and Carpenter from Cambridge.

The 12 who accepted and undertook this historic trip were H. H. Stephenson (captain), George Bennett, William

Caffyn, George Griffith, Thomas Hearne, Roger Iddison, Charles Lawrence, William Mortlock, William Mudie, Thomas Sewell junior, Ned Stephenson and George Wells. This side was primarily drawn from the South and the United, but given Parr et al's refusal, it was second-rate. Despite that, the tour proved to be a great success. Four thousand well-wishers met the players when they docked on Christmas Eve in Melbourne and 15,000 spectators watched the first game against 18 of Melbourne. William Caffyn recalls the scene in his autobiography:

> People flocked in from the surrounding country in all directions, in coaches, waggons, cars, and conveyances of every description. The trains, too, were filled to overflowing . . . Each of us had a coloured sash and a ribbon round his hat . . . These colours were printed against each of our names on the score-card . . . The National Anthem was played as we entered the field, amidst the silence of the vast concourse of spectators. When the band stopped playing a tremendous burst of cheering rent the air.

Melbourne and district batted first and made 118. In reply the tourists hit 305, including 79 from Caffyn and 61 from Griffith, and eventually won by an innings and 96 runs. Gate receipts totalled £5000 and a further £1000 was taken by the booths erected around the Melbourne Cricket Ground. Of the 12 matches on the tour, all played against odds, the English professionals won 6, lost 4 and drew 2.

For Spiers and Pond the tour proved a great financial success netting them a profit of £11,000. With the proceeds they closed their Melbourne cafe and moved to Ludgate Hill in London. George Parr and his nine comrades had been proven correct – the tourists had sold their services too cheaply.

Two years later, under the auspices of the Melbourne Cricket Club, George Parr led the second party to Australia, and on to New Zealand. Accompanying him were Caesar, Caffyn, Lockyer, Carpenter, Hayward, Tarrant, Clarke, Tinley, Jackson, Anderson and one amateur, Dr E. M.

Grace. William Caffyn had the distinction of being on all of the first three overseas tours. Of the professionals, eight were All-England regulars.

This was a formidable combination which not surprisingly went unbeaten during their 12 matches in Australia and four in New Zealand. As Caffyn recalls, the team received 'a tremendous reception' and played before large crowds – on 1 January 1864, the first day of the match against 22 of Victoria at the MCG, 15,000 spectators were present. In the penultimate match in Ballarat Robert Carpenter hit the first century (121) by an English player in Australia.

George Marshall, who had emigrated to Australia from Nottinghamshire in 1854, played a significant part in organising the tour. Despite being a wicket-keeper, Marshall had become the first professional bowler engaged by the Melbourne Cricket Club at the rate of 15 shillings per day, but by the time his friend George Parr arrived in Australia he was proprietor of the Cricketer's Arms.

Parr's team generated a £7000 profit for the Melbourne Club and each of the players received £250 plus expenses. Apart from Caffyn and Grace the players set sail on 26 April and arrived back in England eight months after their departure.

At a time when skilled workers were lucky to earn £2 per week the 1863-64 tourists were reasonably well paid for their efforts. Ten years later the professionals on W. G. Grace's tour received only £150 plus £20 spending money.

After the 1861-62 tour Charles Lawrence remained in Australia to coach in Sydney and in the wake of the 1863-64 trip William Caffyn accepted an offer of £300 per year to become the coach at the Melbourne Cricket Club. The following season Melbourne reluctantly allowed Caffyn to move to coach the Warwick Club in Sydney. Caffyn and his wife opened a hairdressing salon in George Street, Sydney's main thoroughfare.

Caffyn and Lawrence were the first two professional coaches in Australia and were instrumental in improving

The 1863–64 tour party to Australia (*Photo: Nottinghamshire CCC*)

the standard of play in NSW and Victoria. Charles Bannerman, generally acknowledged as Australia's first champion batsman and who scored 165 not out in the first-ever Test in 1877, was, in part, a product of Caffyn's coaching. Lawrence died in Canterbury, Victoria in December 1916. Caffyn, who had relinquished the position of professional with the Warwick Club in September 1867, returned to his home town of Reigate in November 1871. He played his last first-class match for Surrey in 1873 before taking a series of coaching appointments, culminating in five years with Hertford College. In 1892, at the age of 63, Caffyn was interviewed for *Cricket* and said that in retrospect he 'regretted I went' to Australia because it cost him a benefit match with Surrey. However, it should be added that the £300 per annum salary he received in Melbourne and Sydney was a very reasonable remuneration. The benevolent Surrey Committee agreed to pay Caffyn an annuity of £36 and gave 'the Surrey pet' a free pass for the Oval.

The work of Lawrence and Caffyn, plus the pioneering spirit of the professionals on the first three overseas tours, contributed enormously to the future of cricket in the Empire. They were followed by countless Victorian professionals who went to coach and play in Australia, New Zealand, the United States, South Africa and India, or participated in the tours organised by Alfred Shaw, Arthur Shrewsbury and James Lillywhite in the 1880s. Lord Harris was fond of commenting that 'cricket has done more to consolidate the Empire than any other influence' but it should not be forgotten who the foot-soldiers were in Harris's imperial cricket army.

NEVER MUCH TO GET FAT ON

With only Lord's and the Oval maintaining a ground staff the professional cricketer in the mid-Victorian years generated his income from match fees. For the best players £5 was the norm, but a professional was liable for all his travel, lodging and other expenses, a situation which would continue into late-Victorian and Edwardian times. George

Pinder of Yorkshire and, among others, All-England, commented to A. W. Pullin in *Talks with Old Yorkshire Cricketers*:

> At the time I was playing we had not so many matches, and we only got £5 wherever we went. The largest number I played in one season was 24. That would be £120. Out of that I had to pay my hotel bills, my railway travelling, and maintain my home, wife and children.

In the same book George Atkinson, a leading member of the United, substantiates Pinder's view. He estimated that he often returned home from an away match with only seven or eight shillings in his pocket. George Anderson, a Yorkshire and All-England player, interviewed for Pullin's companion volume *Talks with Old English Cricketers* recalled that there was 'never much to get fat on'. Before the mid-1890s players lacked the security of winter pay and once the five-month season was concluded they had to live on their savings or find casual seasonal work. Many other groups of workers were in a similar position during the winter and in the years of cyclical depression, when unemployment exceeded 12 per cent, work was very hard to obtain.

A small number of 'star' players did spend an occasional winter on an overseas tour and although Parr's 1863-64 party cleared £250, the team led by Edgar Willsher to the United States in 1868 received only £100. In any case, prior to the 1880s such tours were few.

Each season some additional work was always available for 10 or more professional bowlers at Oxford and Cambridge Universities. For between four and eight weeks bowlers were engaged to provide the students with net practice. In the 1850s the remuneration was £1 per week plus one shilling and sixpence per hour from the batsman. However, Caffyn recalled that he could make as much as 18 shillings per hour if the student was prepared to place a shilling on the wicket – the shilling was also paid if the batsman was adjudged to be out caught. By the 1890s the basic rate had risen to 30 shillings per week and two shillings per hour, but players considered themselves lucky if they earned £3 per week.

Another source of supplementary income for the top professional batsman was talent money and ground collections. For example, during the Surrey-Notts fixture in 1859 Caffyn and Lockyer, who made 76 and 61 respectively for the home side, each received £2 in talent money, while George Parr, who hit 130 in the Notts first innings of 329, benefited from a £20 collection, but given the restricted county programme in the 1850s and 1860s, such bonuses were rare.

In a normal season, when there were no overseas tours, an All-England or United professional, who also found some additional coaching work, would earn approximately £120-150 per annum prior to the deduction of his expenses. In net terms such an income put the professional cricketer on a par with a skilled worker. In 1850 a London shipwright, for example, earned 36 shillings per week, while a Manchester mechanic took home 30 shillings. The average weekly wage was only nine shillings and sixpence. Fifteen years later this national average had risen to 14 shillings and five pence. Dudley Baxter's survey of the distribution of national income, published in 1867, allocated a lower middle-class family an income of between £100 and £300. Very few professional cricketers had an income to warrant their inclusion in that social class.

In the early 1860s life for club professionals or members of the Lord's staff was less rewarding financially. Tom Emmett at Halifax and Allan Hill with Dewsbury remembered being paid two shillings and sixpence per game, although during Dewsbury Feast matches Hill's rate rose to five shillings. When Hill became the professional at Mirfield he received a weekly wage of 15 shillings. A few years later, in 1872, Daniel Campbell, a Nottinghamshire professional but not a county player, was offering his services via an advertisement in *James Lillywhite's Cricketers Annual* for £35 per season, £8 per month or 35 shillings per week. In the same issue W.Fawcett, an ex-Doncaster fast right-arm bowler made known his availability for £2 per week. However, by

1877 R. G. Barlow was earning 50 shillings per week at Saltaire, near Bradford.

In 1866 the MCC decided that the ground staff in the forthcoming season would comprise no fewer than 12 regular bowlers of whom four would receive £2 per week and the others 30 shillings. The Lord's season still lasted only from May until July, although now practice was daily from noon until 8 p.m., except on match days when the bowlers had to be available from 10 a.m. until 8 p.m.

If a ground bowler at Lord's was asked to umpire or score he received £1 for a one-day match and £2 for all others, while if he was selected to play the rate was £1 for a one-day game, 50 shillings for all others and the possibility of a 10 shillings win bonus. Sensibly the MCC deducted at source ground staff members' subscription to the Cricketers' Fund Friendly Society.

A club professional's annual income was only marginally better than that of a well-paid labourer, but playing cricket for a living avoided the harsh, protracted reality of factory life. Raphael Samuel, writing in *History Workshop,* has vividly portrayed mid-Victorian industrial Britain:

> The industrial landscape would be seen to be full of diggings and pits as well as factory chimneys. Smithies would sprout in the shadows of the furnaces, sweatshops in those of the looms . . . On the building sites there would be a bustle of man-powered activity, with housepainters on ladders, and slaters nailing roofs. Carters would be loading and unloading horses, market women carrying baskets of produce on their heads; dockers balancing weights. The factories would be hot and steamy, with men stripped to the singlet, and juvenile runners in bare feet. At the lead works women would be carrying pots of poisonous metal on their heads, in the bleachers' shed they would be stitching yards of chlorinated cloth, at a shoddy mill sorting rags. Instead of calling this picture 'machinery' the artist might prefer to name it 'toil'.

Who could blame a young working-class man for choosing to try to make his career as a professional cricketer?

EARLY EXAMPLES OF BENEFITS

Prior to 1857 when the Cricketers' Fund Friendly Society was established, a professional's future security was in his own hands. Despite CFFS payments a benefit match remained the most important source of investment income for later life.

One of the earliest recorded benefits occurred when Kent met England at Hempsted Park near Cranbrook, the home of T.L.Hodges Esq., on 17 and 18 August 1843. The beneficiary was Edward Wenman, the Kent professional. Born in 1803 Wenman was a renowned wicket-keeper, frequently appearing behind the stumps to the fast bowling of Alfred Mynn. In his benefit match the MCC covered the England side's expenses and Wenman received some hundreds of pounds.

The following month Notts played Sussex at Trent Bridge for the benefit of William Clarke and three years later he had a second benefit at Southwell.

In the absence of the counties taking any responsibility for benefit matches the players made their own arrangements, and what better vehicle than a fixture with All-England? In 1847 Notts met the Eleven for the benefit of the Notts veteran Tom Barker whose career had been severely restricted when he broke his leg jumping out of a carriage after the horse bolted. Barker had two more benefits – Cambridge University versus the players engaged at Cambridge in 1856 and All-England versus the United in 1861. The All-England matches against 22 of Derbyshire and Burton in Derby in 1848 and 1849 were given to Sam Dakin, while the Eleven's visit to Cambridge in May 1849 was for the benefit of Francis Fenner.

Many other examples could be cited but one where the amount raised is known occurred in August 1856 when All-England played 18 of the Nottingham Commercial Club at Trent Bridge for the Notts and All-England stalwart, Joseph

Guy who received £165. More substantial sums were raised when All-England met the Eleven in 1857 for Jemmy Dean (£350) and in 1860 for William Martingell (£260). In 1858 one of the two All-England United encounters was given to George Parr but despite it being known that the French Ambassador donated £1 there appears to be no record of the final total raised. Twenty years later Parr netted £300 from a North versus South fixture.

As cricket became more popular and better organised, benefit returns improved. In 1871 John Lillywhite received £700 when the Gentlemen met the Players at Hove, and the following year Edgar Willsher was the recipient of £794. In 1876, during a grand dinner in Nottingham after a North versus South match at Trent Bridge, Richard Daft was presented with £500 and gifts worth in excess of £250. These included a solid silver tea and coffee service, a silver salver, two clocks, a pair of bronze candelabra, a silver sandwich case and a tankard. This was a tribute worthy of Daft's contribution to the game, but other leading players were not so fortunate. George Anderson had two benefits. The first was the All-England versus United encounter in Dewsbury in 1869 and due to the terrible weather Anderson lost £50! The second, although supported by Lord Hawke, was unofficial as far as Yorkshire were concerned due to an earlier disagreement with Anderson. Many years later Anderson found himself stranded financially.

The precarious financial position of the professional cricketer led to many of the great players from the early and mid-Victorian years ending their lives in poverty or dying in tragic circumstances. Such a fate awaited John Thewlis, Luke Greenwood, Ned Stephenson, George Anderson, John Jackson, William Martingell, Julius Caesar, Cris Tinley, Sam Biddulph, Sam Dakin, Alfred Diver, Tom Hunt, Henry Stubberfield, Tom Box, Tom Plumb, George Griffith, Thomas Humphrey and Edward Pooley.

CHAPTER 2

Following the Professional Precedent

NORTH VERSUS SOUTH

BY 1862 the influence of professional cricket had reached its height. Apart from the match in 1853, the Players had beaten the Gentlemen on every occasion since 1850 and in the early 1860s they inflicted some crushing defeats on their amateur opponents. In 1860 the Players won by eight wickets (Robert Carpenter hit 118) and by an innings and 181 runs (Tom Hayward 132); the following season the victorious margins were an innings and 60 runs (John Jackson 11 wickets) and an innings and 68 runs (Robert Carpenter 106).

With the county programme in its infancy the highpoints of the season were the matches between All-England and the United England Elevens, North versus South (where both sides were dominated by professionals) and the Gentlemen versus the Players. All-England and the United had full fixture lists, while it was all-professional sides that made the first overseas tours.

Cricket, like the rest of the nation's affairs, was highly regionalised with Lord's failing to exert national control. In 1863 the *Sporting Life* launched a campaign, albeit abortive, for a cricket parliament to supercede the MCC as the game's decision-making forum. Within the counties parochialism was rife and very few county clubs existed. The Yorkshire

Club was established in 1863 under the powerful patronage of Mr M. J. Ellison, the agent for Sheffield's principal landlord, the Duke of Norfolk, but it commanded only limited loyalty in the ridings of the county. It was not until 1891 that the Yorkshire County Cricket Club became truly representative. Of the other county clubs as we know them today, only Sussex, Surrey and Notts pre-date 1862.

The dominant position of the professionals waned from the mid-1860s in part because of a disastrous split between the players in the North and the South. This schism was precipitated by a series of quarrels which led to major divisions in the All-England and United England Elevens, the creation of the United South of England Eleven as a third touring eleven, and the suspension of fixtures between Notts and Surrey.

The first incident occurred on 26 August 1862 during the second day of the Surrey versus England match at the Oval. After England had amassed 503 (Hayward 117, Grundy 95 and Carpenter 94) Surrey faced the bowling of Edgar Willsher. In his third over Willsher was no-balled six times in succession by John Lillywhite. The umpire claimed that the bowler's arm was above the shoulder. The professionals on the England side walked off in protest, leaving their amateur captain, Mr V. E. Walker, in the middle with the umpires and the Surrey batsmen. Play did not resume and started on the third day only because Lillywhite was replaced as umpire by George Street.

A strong rumour persisted that the Surrey authorities told Lillywhite to no-ball Willsher. The following May when All-England met the United at Lord's, *Fred Lillywhite's Guide* records that Willsher's first over was bowled 'amidst breathless silence'. In his first six overs, all maidens, Willsher took two wickets, but more significantly was not no-balled. In 1864 the laws of the game were amended to allow above-the-shoulder bowling actions.

In 1863 Willsher returned to play at the Oval without incident, but anti-Surrey feeling remained strong amongst the Notts professionals. George Parr and his comrades refused to play in the Gentlemen versus Players, Surrey versus North and Surrey versus England fixtures at the Oval or in the North versus Surrey game on the Manchester Broughton ground.

Parr maintained his stance, refusing to play at the Oval until after 1866, however relations between Notts and Surrey worsened markedly after Surrey's one-wicket victory at the Oval in July 1865. In *Surrey Cricket*, Alverstone and Alcock provide this summary:

> A decision of the umpire in favour of the batsman gave so much offence (he was out by a yard and a half, Oscroft declared), that the match between the counties ceased until 1868, both sides sensibly agreeing that it would be better not to play at all if the games could not be played pleasantly.

Also in 1865 five Yorkshire professionals – George Anderson, George Atkinson, Roger Iddison, Joe Rowbotham and Ned Stephenson – refused to play for their county against Surrey in Sheffield. The Yorkshire Committee punished the five by leaving them out of the side to meet All-England, a match the visitors won by an innings and 255 runs. The quintet were promptly re-instated for the game against Notts at Trent Bridge before absenting themselves for the encounter with Surrey at the Oval. *Scores and Biographies* accused the five of being 'secessionists', while George Anderson's explanation, quoted in Peter Thomas's *Yorkshire Cricketers*, is that he felt unable to play 'with those who have combined to sweep us from the cricket field, if they could'.

Anderson's remarks refer not just to the Surrey Club but also to the players who had split from the All-England and United England Elevens in 1864 to form the United South of England Eleven. These scissions arose from some acrimonious exchanges over that season's three North versus South fixtures. The first match occurred at Sleaford, but clashed with the Gentlemen versus Players game at Lord's and was obviously unrepresentative. The second, at Old Trafford, featured a South side picked by Willsher and a North side selected by Parr. The third match, according to *Fred*

Edgar Willsher

Cris Tinley

Lillywhite's Guide, was 'a disgraceful affair' played at the Cattle Market ground in Islington, Middlesex. Roger Iddison chose the North eleven and John Wisden the South, but on the day neither Iddison nor Wisden appeared. Twelve southern players – Tom Lockyer, William Mortlock, Edward Pooley, James Lillywhite junior, George Griffith, Harry Jupp, Charles Ellis, Thomas Humphrey, Thomas Sewell junior, George Bennett, John Lillywhite and Julius Caesar – decided unanimously that they would refuse to participate in the fourth North versus South fixture scheduled for Newmarket. As no Surrey or Sussex players would play, the match was re-titled Cambridgeshire and Yorkshire versus Notts and the South.

Of much greater consequence, however, was the meeting that took place in November 1864 at the Bridge House Hotel, London Bridge, when the United South of England Eleven was formed. Julius Caesar, H. H. Stephenson and Edgar Willsher, three All-England stalwarts, resigned to join the new itinerant eleven. The United England Eleven suffered more seriously with the loss of John Lillywhite, Thomas Hearne, William Mortlock, Tom Lockyer, Thomas Sewell junior, George Griffith and Harry Jupp. The meeting unanimously elected Edgar Willsher as secretary, John Lillywhite as treasurer and a Committee of Willsher, Lillywhite, Hearne, Bennett, Ellis, Lockyer and Caesar. The United South of England Eleven, predominantly made up of Surrey professionals, played its first game in 1865 in Dublin against 22 of Ireland.

The founding of the United South of England Eleven divided the professional cricket world into two geographical camps with the southern players grouped around the United South, while their northern counterparts backed the All-England Eleven. Situated rather uneasily in the middle, but leaning north, was the United. After losing so many players in November 1864 the very existence of the United was called into question, but under the joint leadership of John Wisden and Robert Carpenter they perservered and managed to play nine times in 1865.

The north-south schism continued until 1869. Of the professionals who played in the 1866 All-England United fixture, 13 – all from northern counties – refused to appear in the Gentlemen versus Players or North versus South matches. Similar problems affected the Gentlemen versus Players fixtures at the Oval in 1867 and 1868, and the North versus South match on the same ground in 1869. In that game a slight thaw in relations was apparent, marked by the presence of the Yorkshire professionals. On 21 May 1866 the MCC Committee discussed the refusal of the northern professionals to appear in the North versus South match. The Committee concluded that they:

> must decline to enter into the disputes among the professionals, or to take the part either of Northern or Southern players . . . the players in all matches will be selected from those who are willing to play together in a friendly manner in the matches on that ground.

The following season the MCC did intervene implicitly by creating a new benefit fund called the Marylebone Professional Cricketers' Fund which was only for those players who 'have conducted themselves to the entire satisfaction of the Committee'. Various fixtures were played for the Fund, such as MCC versus the South in 1869, and by 1872 it had accumulated £560. The important point is that for the first time the cricket establishment had used their economic influence over the players as a means to exert their authority and impose discipline. Over subsequent decades this precedent was to be repeated many times.

OTHER TOURING ELEVENS

The cricketing success of the All-England and United England Elevens in the 1850s and 1860s brought financial rewards that inevitably led to the appearance of several imitators and rivals. In the era of Victorian free trade or laissez-faire, cricket was being sold in the market place like any other commodity and new 'operations' endeavoured to cash in. Apart from the United South of England Eleven, most of the new itinerant elevens were short-lived. They failed because they were mis-managed or lacked the services of the best professionals whose reputations secured fixtures and drew crowds.

Table 2 provides a genealogical survey of the various elevens. The United All-Ireland Eleven was formed in 1856 and inspired by Charles Lawrence. It played a few fixtures each season, one of the highlights being the visit of I Zingari to Dublin in 1861. That season proved to be the All-Ireland's last. Lawrence toured Australia with H. H. Stephenson's team in 1861-62 and was tempted by the Albert Club in Sydney to remain behind as the coach at their ground in Redfern. In 1868 Charles Lawrence managed the first tour party from Australia to England. This tour has until recently often been ignored, perhaps because the visitors were Aborigines.

The New All-England Eleven was the title claimed by two sides in 1858. The slightly more significant side was founded by Thomas Sherman and Frank Chadband, two Surrey professionals. After making only one appearance in 1858 against 22 of Tunbridge Wells, this eleven did arrange five fixtures for the following season. Despite the patronage of Mr W.S.Norton as President (Norton was also a member of the Kent Committee), and the services of reasonable players such as James Chatterton, Thomas Sewell junior and Henry Stubberfield, the eleven failed to attract opposition and collapsed.

A second New All-England Eleven was formed simultaneously in 1858 by Fred Caesar, the brother of Julius. By trade Fred was a baker; subsequently he became a prison turn-key and a publican in Southwark. His eleven had a fleeting single season existence, but was resurrected four seasons later as 'Another' New All-England Eleven. In 1862 it played five times against odds and despite the presence of professionals such as Thomas Hearne, Thomas Humphrey and Edward Pooley, never won a match.

In order to resolve the issue of who could rightfully call themselves the New All-England Eleven, Sherman and Caesar's sides played a showdown in September 1862 at the

Table 2: A genealogical history of the professional touring elevens, 1846–82

Key

A-EE	All-England Eleven
An NAEE	Another New All-England Eleven
EE	England Eleven
EN	Eleven of the North
NAEE[1]	Chadband and Sherman's New All-England Eleven
NAEE[2]	Fred Caesar's New All-England Eleven
NAEE[3]	Pooley's New All-England Eleven
NEE	North of England Eleven
New EE	New England Eleven
New UNEE	New United North of England Eleven
New USEE	New United South of England Eleven
UA-IE	United All-Ireland Eleven
UEE	United England Eleven
UL	United London
UM	United Midland
UNEE	United North of England Eleven
UNSEE	United North and South of England Eleven
USEE	United South of England Eleven
YU	Yorkshire United

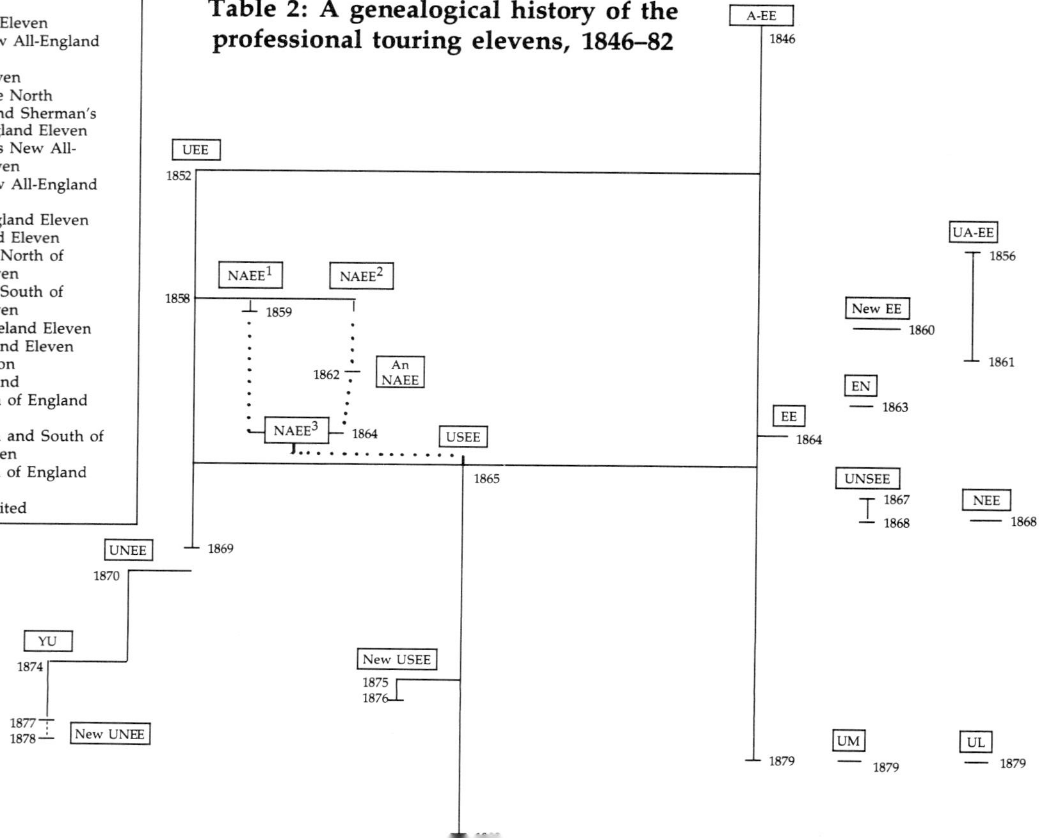

Oval. Although Caesar's eleven won by 10 wickets neither side re-appeared in 1863. Undaunted, Edward Pooley fielded yet another New All-England Eleven in 1864. This side was an amalgam of players from Sherman and Caesar's teams. It played only twice, was ineptly managed and finally its players joined the newly created United South.

Equally transitory were the New England Eleven formed in 1860 by the Notts and All-England professional, Thomas Davis; 'Another' England Eleven which played one match against 22 of Peckham, Dulwich and district in September 1862; and Tom Hornby's An Eleven of the North of England which made its solitary appearance against 22 of Crook in September 1863.

The 'English' Eleven played only three times in 1864, but it gave notice that its organisers, Willsher and Stephenson, were asserting their independence from All-England. Subsequently they joined the United South.

Two other sides made brief appearances in the late 1860s. The United North and South of England Eleven was established in the autumn of 1866 by George Baker, a Kent professional. This eleven managed only two fixtures in 1867 and one in 1868 before it collapsed. Finally in that decade, the North of England Eleven played one match in June 1868 against 20 of Werneth. Among the visitors were Frederick and Cornelius Coward from Lancashire, Joe Thewlis and Joe Rowbotham of Yorkshire, and John Jackson from Notts.

From 1865 there were three main itinerant elevens travelling the country. The All-England Eleven rarely left the North of England due to the hardening of the north-south split and because they found it more lucrative to concentrate their efforts north of the Trent. Under George Parr's leadership the Eleven was never more popular. For example, against 22 of Bolton in July 1867 at least 10,000 spectators attended. Later that month 6000 watched the second day of the encounter with 22 of Sutton-in-Ashfield; remarkably Richard Daft was out first ball in both innings!

Each season, six days per week from May until September, the All-England Eleven fulfilled more than 30 fixtures.

However, the strength of the local 22s was clearly declining. Between 1865 and 1870 the Eleven made six excursions into Derbyshire to play Wirksworth (three times), Staveley, Somercotes and district and Chesterfield. Although the local opposition employed at five guineas each two first-rate bowlers to assist them (in the case of Staveley, George Howitt and Frank Silcock, and at Chesterfield, George Howitt and George Wootton) as well as including some excellent local players such as William Hickton (fast round-arm for Lancashire and Derbyshire) and William Mycroft (an ex-ironstone miner and left-arm bowler), they did not compare favourably with the Derbyshire sides the All-England Eleven faced in the late 1840s and 1850s.

Nevertheless, the All-England visits to villages such as Wirksworth did much to engender local interest in the game. According to the *Wirksworth Cricket Club Centenary Brochure*, the matches 'created the greatest enthusiasm' with bands playing and special booths being erected around the ground. Furthermore, Wirksworth made a small profit on these All-England matches.

After the debilitating split in November 1864 the United England Eleven had rallied to such an extent that they played 22 games in 1867, as compared to the United South's 17. The following season they had just seven local fixtures and in 1869, after the clash with All-England in May, they were seen no more. Sadly it marked the end of the United and the great tussles with the All-England Eleven.

In the wake of the United's demise two of its former players, George Freeman and Roger Iddison, launched the United North of England Eleven. Established in late 1869, this eleven received the distinguished patronage of Lord Londesborough as its President and Mr A. B. Rowley as one of its two Vice-Presidents.

Lord Londesborough, born William Henry Forester Denison, played a significant part in the development of Yorkshire cricket. The Scarborough festival, which he founded, remains a lasting legacy. However Londesborough has to bear some of the responsibility for the lack of a united county club prior to 1891. In 1874 he accepted the Presidency of the Yorkshire United Cricket Club and 14 years later the same position with the North and East Ridings of Yorkshire XI. Over the same period Mr M. J. Ellison, who even Lord Hawke considered to be an 'autocrat', was privately patronising Yorkshire cricket from Sheffield.

Alexander Butler Rowley, one of the United North's Vice-Presidents, retains a distinguished place in the history of Lancashire cricket. Born in 1837 he was educated at Rossall school, but learnt his cricket from Thomas Hunt while the latter was the professional at the Manchester Club. In the 1860s he was considered to be the best all-round cricketer in Manchester and in 1864, with Samuel Swire, was joint secretary of the newly-formed Lancashire Club. As a consequence of marrying Oldham Whittaker's daughter, Rowley became a cotton manufacturer in Ashton-under-Lyne. Like the members of all the other notable aristocratic and capitalist families in Lancashire, Rowley was an Anglican but, unusually, he identified with the Liberals and not the Conservative Party. In line with his Tory-Anglican friends, Rowley was a keen follower of the hunt and in later years a supporter of the Volunteer Movement.

As founders, Freeman and Iddison took on the joint secretaryship of the United North of England Eleven. During Freeman's brief playing career from 1867 to 1871 he assumed the mantle of John Jackson and George Tarrant as the most lethal of fast bowlers. George Freeman retired from cricket to become a successful auctioneer in Thirsk. Roger Iddison, a quick tempered, bluff Yorkshireman, was another talented player born in Bedale. Apart from being a professional with Manchester Broughton, Sefton and Whalley, Iddison worked as a butcher (for which he had a perfect stout build), ran an outfitters shop in Manchester and acted as a commission agent in York. He was a fine batsman, originally a right-hand round-arm bowler but later a convert to the art of lob bowling and an excellent fielder at point.

The United North's notable patronage was matched by some fine players, virtually all from Yorkshire, including George Atkinson, Ephraim Lockwood, Joe Rowbotham and Luke Greenwood. The United North played its first match in June 1870 at Dewsbury against 16 Colts of England, but by 1874 it had been superceded by the Yorkshire United Cricket Club.

Yorkshire United was the outcome of a meeting convened in York on 24 January 1874. Representatives from Bedale, Dewsbury, Hornsea, Hull, Leeds, Malton, Middlesbrough, Scarborough and York decided that a new club was required to advance the interests of cricket in the county. Lord Londesborough accepted the Presidency, with Viscount Downe as one of the Vice-Presidents; appropriately the club's treasurer was Robert Swann, a York banker, while Roger Iddison was assistant secretary to C. D. Barstow, Esq.

In its first season the groundless Yorkshire United played six fixtures against other elevens, such as Derbyshire, but in 1875 they reverted to seeking matches against 22s. In seven such games they managed only one victory and support began to wane. The following season they made just two appearances and in 1877 only one.

In *The History of Yorkshire County Cricket* the Rev. Holmes explains Yorkshire United's dramatic decline by the frequent visits to Yorkshire of the United South, starring W. G. Grace, and the presence of the 1878 Australian tourists who played many of their 41 fixtures in the North of England. Holmes continues that Yorkshire United did 'much good' by providing public pleasure and supplementing the income of the Yorkshire professionals. The United's matches were arranged to avoid clashes with Yorkshire county games and consequently they included the leading county professionals such as the Greenwoods, Thewlis, Lockwood, Ulyett, Emmett, Pinder, Hill and Rowbotham. In 1878 George Pinder endeavoured to organise a New United North of England Eleven but it failed to last more than one season.

In the South the New United South of England Eleven had an equally fleeting existence. Organised by Thomas Sherman and William Caffyn in 1875, this eleven made its only appearance that season against 18 of Edenbridge. The following season, under the Presidency of Mr Arthur Hoare, an occasional Sussex player, and the secretaryship of John Miles of Margate, the New United South fulfilled just two fixtures. Among the side's players were William Caffyn, George G. Hearne and Walter Humphreys.

The All-England Eleven continued to play until 1879 with William Oscroft replacing George Parr as captain and secretary in the last four years. By 1870 its players were mainly drawn from Cambridge and Nottinghamshire and included Thomas Hayward and Robert Carpenter, who vied for the title of the best professional batsman in England; the seemingly tireless, George Parr and Cris Tinley plus new stars from Notts such as Jemmy Shaw, Fred Wild and William Oscroft.

In July 1871 All-England asserted their supremacy over the United North with a victory by an innings and 21 runs. Six years later they defeated the United South, which included W. G. Grace, by an innings. On that occasion the All-England Eleven was strengthened by the inclusion of the Lancashire amateur A .N. 'Monkey' Hornby, although in general by the mid-1870s the Eleven was composed of Notts professionals, including the young Arthur Shrewsbury.

During the 1879 season the London United and the United Midland elevens made their debuts. London United included the best-known professionals from Surrey, Middlesex, Kent and Essex, but the days of the peripatetic professional elevens were numbered. The United South, under the erstwhile amateur W. G. Grace, maintained a presence until 1882.

CLOWN CRICKETERS

The success of the professional touring elevens and the public's interest in the circus led to the creation of various troupes of 'clown cricketers' during the 1870s. For a few seasons, primarily between 1873 and 1877, a small number of players found employment with either Casey's or Treloar's Clown Cricketers.

The original concept had been developed by Harry Croueste, the Queen's jester, although the performances of his 'Original Clown Cricketers' were total buffoonery. However the most successful – and the more serious cricketers – were the Imperial Clown Cricketers otherwise known as Treloar's Clowns. Arthur Treloar, who was born in St Austell, Cornwall in 1848, played one first-class match as a professional for Middlesex against Oxford University in 1872. Treloar scored 10 runs and took one wicket, but he has the distinction of a biographical entry in *Scores and Biographies* as a consequence of his appearance at Lord's in May 1869 when he opened the batting for the Colts of the South against the Colts of the North. He is described as being a 'good average bat' and a bowler of either 'fast round-arm' or 'slow underhand'.

As captain and manager of the Imperial Clown Cricketers Arthur Treloar arranged a full programme of fixtures. In 1874 they played 57 games and in the following 'season' made 63 appearances. In August 1876 Treloar's Clowns undertook a tour of the United States and were not heard of again.

Edmund Peate, a warp-twister from Yeadon and the first in the line of great slow left-arm bowlers produced by Yorkshire, began his professional career with Treloar in 1875 – his Yorkshire debut came four years later. The 'circus' was comprised of eight cricketers, eight acrobats and eight talking clowns, but was not always well-received. Peate recalled being 'mobbed and sodded' in Sheffield and described these exhibitions as 'booby cricket'.

The other major troupe was known variously as King and Casey's, Casey and Exley's, Casey and Robson's and Casey and Mayo's. One of the most notable players with Casey's was Joe Preston who went on to become one of Yorkshire's best all-rounders in the 1880s. Preston played 80 times for

Yorkshire and toured Australia with Shaw, Shrewsbury and Lillywhite in 1887-88. Lord Hawke sacked Preston from the Yorkshire side because of his fondness for drinking. Joe Preston died of a chill at the age of 26.

Among the other players with Casey's clowns were William Slater, the Yeadon professional; Henry Lockwood, the younger brother of Ephraim Lockwood, who played 16 times for Yorkshire between 1877 and 1882; and Samuel Hind junior, who had various professional engagments from 1870 onwards and represented Notts six times in 1877-78.

For a few years the wandering troupes of clown cricketers not only amused the public, but also provided employment for several cricket professionals who were either not in the front-rank or who needed an engagement to start their careers.

CHAPTER 3

The Professionals Lose Control

THE PROFESSIONALS UNDER ATTACK

IN the mid-1860s a concerted campaign was being waged against the influence of the professionals and in particular the All-England Eleven. The main protagonist was James Pycroft, the author of the influential book *The Cricket Field*. This was his most famous work and in it he disparaged the Eleven as 'a travelling circus'; this accusation, and more besides, was reasserted in *Cricketana*.

James Pycroft was a graduate of Trinity College, Oxford who had gone to the bar at Lincoln's Inn in 1836 but abandoned legal practice in 1840 when he took holy orders. In *Cricketana*, which was published in 1865, Pycroft combined the talents of prosecutor and preacher to strong effect. He described the All-England Eleven as 'a very serious nuisance, as superseding those annual contests between rival counties . . . making their livelihood in a silly way', and he urged 'all true lovers of cricket' to have nothing to do with All-England matches. As a means to weaken the Eleven, Pycroft proposed that Lord's and the Oval should refuse to employ any All-England professionals.

What lay behind Pycroft's vitriol was a desire to regain control of cricket from the professionals and, in particular, from leading figures such as George Parr. Having attacked the All-England Eleven, Pycroft questioned the players' cricketing abilities. He wrote that 'a peculiar kind of caution characterises the players' game . . . the player has generally only the common hits . . . a limited game'.

According to Pycroft the dour professionals compared unfavourably with the amateurs who were praised for having 'spirit', 'extra dash', 'sharp running' and being 'innovative'. The reality was very different as the Gentlemen's dismal record against the Players between 1850 and 1865 proves.

James Pycroft was worried about the extent of professional influence. He asserted that it would 'be prejudicial to the game to grow too professional' and 'a mistake to allow professionals so extensively to take the place of amateurs in the great matches'.

The editorials in *Fred Lillywhite's Guide* supported Pycroft, albeit with more circumspection. The 1865 edition argued that matches against local 22s were in danger of ruining cricket, although the editor did recognise that the itinerant elevens had popularised the game, provided local players with practice against the best professional talent and given demonstrations of brilliant play. The last-mentioned point is one which Lord Harris always considered to have been the All-England's major contribution. In 1883 Harris wrote in *Cricket* that 'nothing is so essential for the productionn of a good cricketer as that he should see good cricket'.

Against the itineraries of the peripatetic professional elevens Pycroft and Fred Lillywhite counterposed a programme of county matches, but these would have been insufficient to offer the players a full-time living in summer.

DID THE ALL-ENGLAND ELEVEN STIFLE CRICKET?

The claim that the All-England Eleven and its professional successors blocked the development of county cricket is frequently made and through repetition has tended to become the accepted truth. Occasionally a more accurate voice can be heard. For example, in 1904 in *The History of Yorkshire*

County Cricket, the Wakefield congregationalist minister the Rev. Holmes stated that 'A genuine service was done by the All-England Eleven to Yorkshire, as they kept county cricket going, their matches being the only matches played by Yorkshire in some years.'

In Yorkshire it was regional rivalries which were the main stumbling block to a representative county club. In Kent it was only when a compromise was effected between Canterbury, Gravesend and Maidstone that the Kent County Cricket Club could be formed in 1870. The first Committee comprised of 20 members equally divided between the East and the West of the county. Similarly in Lancashire the rivalry between Liverpool and Manchester hampered county cricket. It was not until 1880 that the Manchester Club finally merged with the Lancashire County Club to form the Lancashire County and Manchester Cricket Club, a title which was simplified to the Lancashire County Cricket Club in 1957. Finally, the present Warwickshire County Cricket Club emerged in 1884 after decades of antagonism between the Wellesbourne Club and cricketers in Birmingham.

In these four important cases the development of county cricket and the establishment of a representative and unified county club was not delayed by the All-England Eleven or the professionals but was a consequence of intra-county rivalries.

Prior to 1850, of the present first-class county clubs only Sussex and Surrey existed. In 1860 this pair were joined by Nottinghamshire and they, in turn, were soon followed by Middlesex, Yorkshire and Hampshire in 1863, Lancashire in 1864 and Worcestershire in 1865. The success of Hampshire was not assured and within a few seasons the Club was virtually moribund. It survived, but from 1889 to 1892 faced local competition from an Isle of Wight County Cricket Club.

The general point that needs to be recognised is that the creation of county cricket clubs and hence a programme of county fixtures could only happen as fast as the counties emerged as unified social, political and economic entities. That entailed overcoming the rivalries between town and country, between different towns and cities within the same county, and between the county aristocracy and the rising urban bourgeoisie. This last point often proved crucial for the birth of a county cricket club. Invariably the local aristocracy gave their patronage and blessing by accepting the positions of President and Vice-President while the urban manufacturers, merchants, solicitors, surgeons and clergymen organised the meetings, undertook the secretarial work and sat on the Committees. County cricket clubs provided another example of the fusion between the aristocracy and the new middle class.

In the case of Lancashire, Samuel Swire and Alexander Rowley – the Club's joint secretaries – were cotton manufacturers, while Edward Rowley, captain until 1879 and an influential Committee member, was a solicitor. A. N. Hornby, who succeeded Rowley as captain, is described in Altham and Swanton's *A History of Cricket* as 'for over thirty years the life and soul of the county's cricket'. In *Work, Society and Politics* Patrick Joyce writes that the Hornby family 'industrialists having adopted the creed of the territorial gentry . . . led local society by divine right of precedence'. A.N.'s brother E.K. was a Conservative Member of Parliament, leaving another brother, Sir 'Harry' to run the family cotton business in Blackburn. The Hornbys were archetypal paternalistic Tory-Anglican employers who had married into Lancashire's landed aristocracy.

The formation of the Derbyshire County Cricket Club in 1870 reinforces the point. Among those at the inaugural meeting were Walter and Henry Boden, partners in the successful Boden and Black lace business; E. M. Wass, a wine and spirit merchant from Wirksworth; John Smith, a solicitor; the Reverends Northey and Anson; Samuel Richardson, a tailor and draper; and Dr Curgenven, a surgeon.

The Earl of Chesterfield, formerly Lord Stanhope (who had played for and against All-England), accepted the Presidency, Mr G. H. Strutt, subsequently Lord Belper, became Vice-President and Walter Boden, who had spent three years campaigning to establish the Club, the secretary. After the Earl of Chesterfield's death from typhoid, the Hon. W. M. Jervis (Eton, Oxford University, resident at Quarndon Hall and Lord Harris's uncle) assumed the Presidency.

A representative Gloucestershire County Cricket Club was not established until after the demise of the Cheltenham and County of Gloucester Cricket Club in 1871. Francis Fenner, the former Cambridge Town all-rounder and tobacconist, formed the Cheltenham Club in 1863 after he took over the Royal Hotel. A significant factor in the decline of Fenner's club was the growing support for the sides organised in the county by Dr Henry Mills Grace. In the new Gloucestershire Club Dr Grace, W.G.'s father, was appointed treasurer, while E.M., W.G.'s brother, became secretary – a position he retained for 39 years – and Henry, the eldest brother, served on the Committee. Grace and all his sons were doctors, but as with virtually every county club the local aristocracy were invited to be President; in this case it was the Duke of Beaufort. The Vice-President was Lord Fitzhardinge.

The incorporation of the county name into the title adopted by the Cheltenham Club was not unique. Other examples were the Devon and Exeter Cricket Club, the Norwich and Norfolk Club, the Yeovil and County of Somerset Cricket Club and the Worcester City and County Cricket Club. None of these sides could lay claim to being representative of the county and it is another indication of the parlous state of county cricket in the 1850s and 1860s.

To secure themselves financially the county cricket clubs had to be based in the urban centres. Their establishment parallels the growth of the industrial towns and cities and, most significantly, the notion of civic pride.

When Queen Victoria acceded to the throne in 1837 there were only six cities and towns in England and Wales with a population in excess of 100,000. In 1891, by which time every contemporary first-class county club existed – Glamorgan being the last in 1888 – 23 conurbations had populations exceeding 100,000. In *Victorian Cities* Asa Briggs traces the expansion of several cities in the Midlands and North of England. He notes that Middlesbrough did not boast a public park until 1868 – the same year that Huddersfield was incorporated; that Manchester's Gothic town hall, which cost one million pounds was not completed until 1877; that Sheffield's sewage system was not functioning before 1884 and the new town hall was opened in 1897.

The gospel of civic pride found its greatest champion in Birmingham's Joseph Chamberlain who, in 1876, was urging that the city should be 'parked, paved, assized, marketed, gas-and-watered and improved'. Two years later work began to redevelop the city centre. Chamberlain and Birmingham provided exemplary national leadership in raising the tone of local government, but Briggs states that the West Midlands city was 'not very different from a large number of other towns and cities'.

The notion that the All-England Eleven and other professional touring sides stifled county cricket must be firmly rejected. Prior to the 1870s the basic economic and political pre-conditions for county cricket clubs did not exist. In fact, one such pre-condition was a greater popularity for the game and in that respect the All-England Eleven made a very significant contribution.

A NEW CLASS OF PROFESSIONAL

Moderate reforming legislation which was passed by parliament in the early 1870s had important repercussions for professional cricket. These laws fall into two categories. The first progressively shortened the working week so that by 1874 a 54-hour week was commonplace. This included a six-and-a-half-hour Saturday which, given an early start, meant that the organised working class had a free Saturday afternoon. The half-Saturday was crucial if workers were to participate in organised recreation. It is not surprising that the expansion of public parks dates from this decade.

Changes in legislation also created Bank Holidays. The 1875 Bank Holiday Act, extending a law passed in 1871, granted the working class four unpaid days off each year. These were Boxing Day, Easter Monday, Whit Monday and the first Monday in August. The two summer Bank Holidays became the occasions for huge crowds to flock to the major metropolitan cricket grounds.

These changes to the pattern of working-class life made organised cricket more accessible and eventually led to a noticeable shift in the social and class background of the professionals. Of 94 professionals who played for Nottinghamshire between 1835 and 1914, and whose previous employment is known, 29 per cent were framework knitters or in the lace trade and 27 per cent were miners. However, their involvement falls into two distinct historical periods. The framework knitters and lace workers (such as Sam Redgate, the Oscrofts, James Grundy, Sam Biddulph, Alfred Shaw, Frank Farrands and Fred Morley) were dominant prior to 1879, while between 1890 and 1914 20 miners played for the county, including such well-known professionals as 'Topsy' Wass, Thomas Oates, Edwin Alletson and Fred Barratt.

Before the 1870s to play or practise as a professional necessitated being able to determine the length of the working day; that is, being self-employed, a skilled artisan or working on piece-rates. R. G. Barlow, Lancashire's stonewalling opening partner for 'Monkey' Hornby, originally worked as a moulder at the Staveley ironworks in Derbyshire. To ensure that he had enough time to practise Barlow began work at 4.30 a.m., finished his piece-work as soon as possible, and 'knocked off' to begin practice for the day.

The framework knitters of Sutton-in-Ashfield and Arnold in Nottinghamshire, and the weavers of Lascelles Hall in Yorkshire, also worked on piece-rates, albeit from home. In Pullin's biography, *Alfred Shaw Cricketer,* Alf, the youngest of 13 children, remembers leaving school at the age of 10 when his mother died to work as a farmer's scarecrow for two shillings and sixpence per week. After his 15th birthday Shaw transferred to hand-frame knitting, the dominant trade in his native village of Burton Joyce and was soon earning 10 shillings a week. Alf told Pullin that he always organised his days so that he could play cricket for at least one hour. Although of a later generation, the Notts-born, Surrey professional William Lockwood shared a similar experience. In 1898, interviewed in *Cricket*, he recalled as a young man hitting 114 in a club match before 'I went back to my lace machine at six o'clock and worked on until midnight'.

In *Talks with Old Yorkshire Cricketers* Pullin interviewed several renowned Yorkshire professionals. The weaving village of Lascelles Hall, described as a gentlemen's residence plus a few cottages, produced a prodigious number of fine professionals including John Thewlis, Luke Greenwood and Ephraim Lockwood. The last-mentioned recounted practising with 'seat-board legs and yarn balls'. Allan Hill, born close to Lascelles Hall in the neighbouring village of Kirkheaton, told Pullin, 'We were all weavers, and spent half our time in playing cricket. The time we spent in practising in the daytime we made up for sticking to the loom at night.'

Framework knitting and handloom weaving were performed as out-work on piece-rates which allowed for a flexible working day, while the nature of the work involving deft movements of the shuttle, pick and treadle encouraged the co-ordination of eyes, hand and feet. The job was dull and repetitive but it did develop mental and physical attributes necessary for good cricketing technique.

The invention of mechanised power looms, plus factory production, meant that the days of framework knitting and handloom weaving were numbered. At the turn of the 18th century handloom weavers were the highest paid and most independent members of the labour force but by the 1840s their social position had declined markedly and many lived on starvation wages. The process of change was geographically uneven and the complete mechanisation of Huddersfield and its Pennine valley hinterland (including Lascelles

Hall and Kirkheaton) did not occur until the late 1860s and 1870s, while in Nottingham the Handframe Workers Society was not finally disbanded until December 1890.

The slower mechanisation in West Yorkshire and Nottinghamshire allowed semi-rural industrial villages to survive and, as a by-product, produce professional cricketers. The significant difference between these two counties and Lancashire was that the cotton trade was rapidly mechanised and organised via factories from the 1840s. The newly-urbanised industrial working class in Lancashire worked long hours and lived in towns and cities which lacked basic recreational activities and space. Consequently Lancashire failed to generate home-grown professional talent and resorted to importing players from Notts and Yorkshire. It should also be added that the best Lancashire club sides, such as Sefton, Huyton, Liverpool, Broughton, Sale, Rusholme and Manchester, restricted their membership to the middle and upper classes via a two guinea subscription which a working man could not afford. In comparison the annual subscription with a good Yorkshire club was half a guinea or less.

Prior to the late Victorian social reforms, factory life and cricket could not survive together. As Pullin commented, 'fast looms have destroyed our fast bowling'. In an interview in the *Cricket Field* in 1893 Ephraim Lockwood noted that once the Lascelles Hall villagers had to travel three miles to work in Huddersfield they were 'almost too tired for cricket'.

Other than being employed as framework knitters or handloom weavers the early Victorian professionals can be divided into three broad work categories. First there were a small number who were self-employed such as Francis Fenner (tobacconist), Roger Iddison (butcher), George Morton (malster), Henry Royston (confectioner) and George Parr, George Picknell and Thomas Butler (farmers).

Second, there were players who had been apprenticed into skilled trades such as George Atkinson (glass blower), Tom Box (cabinet maker), Julius Caesar, James Chester, Henry Stubberfield and Edward Wenman (carpenters),

Charles Pryor (brazier), William Slinn (scissor-smith), Thomas Davis and Thomas Sewell (printers), Edmund Hinkly and Robert Carpenter (shoemakers), Fuller Pilch (tailor) and Bart' Good (blacksmith).

And third, at the bottom end of the social scale, were a number of professionals who were in domestic service, for example, Edward Bushby, William Hillyer and William Martingell (gamekeepers), John Berry, John Boning, George Chatterton and Henry Cornell (servants) and George Brockwell, Daniel Hayward and Thomas Hayward (gardeners).

The 1851 national census indicates that there were more than one million farm labourers, 250,000 building workers, 200,000 navvies constructing the railways and 216,000 coal miners. It appears that no professional cricketer emerged from this substantial section of the population during the 1850s, reinforcing the point that until the 1880s the players were primarily drawn from skilled workers, piece-workers and the self-employed.

Once their playing careers were over Victorian professionals behaved like subsequent generations of players and tended not to return to their original trades or work. Instead they most frequently became publicans, school coaches, sports outfitters and groundsmen.

1873

In 1873 the MCC took two initiatives to exert some authority over the game. First, in collaboration with the counties, it was decided that a cricketer could represent only one county per season either on the basis of birth or residency. Second, Lord's proposed the establishment of a national competition, the Champion County Cup. This was to be played for by a maximum of six counties, but proved to be a dismal failure. In the only match Kent beat Sussex on a typically dreadful Lord's wicket. The idea was then dropped. In February 1873 Surrey had already stated they would not participate on the grounds that such cup contests could threaten 'the honour of victory', endanger county cricket and encourage cup contests elsewhere around the country.

The rejection of the MCC's proposal was an indication of the general ill-feeling that existed between the provinces and the metropolis, which in the cricket world was reflected in Lord's lack of authority. The infant county clubs, whose existence in some cases was still tenuous, were not ready for such a competition. The Champion County Cup was an idea born before its time.

It was not until the 1880s and 1890s that London began to dominate the provinces and national life. Particularly important in this regard was the growth of a national communications network. In *Victorian Cities* Asa Briggs pinpoints 1896 as the watershed. In that year Lord Northcliffe founded the *Daily Mail*, Marconi introduced his wireless invention to the Post Office and the first cinema show was presented in London's West End. Briggs continues:

> The provinces had come to enjoy a vigorous life and a considerable measure of social and political power. Moreover, the provincial cities had developed as cultural centres . . . During the 1890s the pattern was changing again. The decay of the provincial press, which rose to great heights in the mid-Victorian years and down to 1890 was implicit in the rise of the cheap national press, subsidized by advertisement. The power of advertisement threatened the independence of local markets . . . Socially the days of autonomous regional sub-cultures were doomed.

Cricket did not resist such national pressures. On the contrary, it played a part in fostering them. The establishment of *Cricket*, as a weekly record of the game, in May 1882 by Charles Alcock, the Surrey secretary, proved to be a significant development. For the first time a viable national magazine solely devoted to cricket was on the market, retailing for two pence. It reported all English first-class matches and gave extensive details of overseas tours as well as regular items of 'gossip', while the weekly profiles, including many of professionals, began to promote the cricketer as a national hero. *Cricket*, with a slight change in title, existed until 1914.

The general decline of provincialism, the expansion of sports' coverage in the national press, the success of *Cricket*, the establishment of a representative county championship in 1890 and the presence of individual star players combined to cement cricket's place as one of Britain's foremost institutions.

PART TWO

The Not-So-Golden Age

CHAPTER 4

The Respectable Professional

COUNTY QUALIFICATIONS

FOR the professional cricketer 1873 proved to be a decisive year. After considerable discussion the MCC, in conjunction with the counties, agreed on a series of proposals which determined a player's right to represent a particular county.

The crucial clause stipulated that a cricketer could represent only one county per season. Prior to 1873 there were no restrictions so, for example, Roger Iddison played concurrently for Yorkshire and Lancashire in the 1860s. The Yorkshire-born Iddison scored the first century for Lancashire in county cricket. This also explains how William Clarke of Notts represented Surrey, Sussex and Kent, albeit on only one occasion each.

The new laws specified that a player could choose between his county of birth or his county of residence, provided he had lived in the latter for two years. At a meeting of county representatives in the Surrey pavilion in June 1873 Captain Holden of Notts and W. G. Grace had carried a proposal that 'a cricketer may elect to play for the county in which his family home is, so long as it remains open to him as an occasional residence'. This resolution, which the MCC subsequently accepted, obviously discriminated in favour of the amateurs who were geographically more mobile and often from families with several homes, including one in London.

For the professionals these changes had far-reaching consequences. Their mobility of labour was immediately restricted and their earning potential limited. Further, the two-year residential qualification reduced the player's bargaining position. A professional would have to think carefully before he rejected any financial offer from his county, given that he would have to reside for two years in another county before he could recommence playing.

One consequence of these restrictions on players was that counties had to extend their fixture list to provide their professionals with a reasonable source of income. This expansion was quite marked in the mid-1870s. For example, Yorkshire played 13 county matches in 1873 and 20 in 1878, while Lancashire exceeded 10 in 1876 as Notts had done the previous season. By combining county matches with appearances for professional touring elevens, a player could earn a reasonable living.

LORD HARRIS AND THE RESPECTABLE PROFESSIONAL

Lord Harris occupies a mighty place in the history of cricket and his concern for the welfare of the professionals was exemplary in comparison to the shoddy treatment dispensed by many county Committees. Harris maintained a long-standing identification with the professionals. In 1883 in the *National Review* he wrote:

> Professional cricketers are absolutely essential if cricket is to be maintained at its present high standard of excellence . . . Professional cricketers we must have . . . Let us by all means encourage them to persevere in their profession.

Eighteen years later at the Annual General Meeting of the Cricketers' Fund Friendly Society he added that professionals:

> had only tended to raise the game to a higher level . . . The professional had evidently taken care to raise him-

> self. On their part, they (the county Committees) had been glad to provide in many cases better dressing-room accomodation and increased pay.

The Hon. George Robert Canning became the fourth Lord Harris in 1872 after the death of his father, a former Governor of Trinidad and Madras and Deputy Chairman of the London, Chatham and Dover Railway. Lord Harris was part of a traditional landed (3000 acres) Conservative family and his education took the expected course of Eton and Oxford University. However his years at Oxford (1871-75) coincided with the emergence of a new intellectual liberalism more in accordance with late Victorian philanthropy and social reform legislation. The aim of thinkers such as Toynbee was to create a respectable working class distinct from 'the residuum', and within that framework trade unions, friendly societies and the co-operative movement bore the distinctive mark of respectability.

In the cricket world Lord Harris set as one of his goals the fashioning of the respectable professional. This often brought Harris into conflict with other members of the cricket establishment. In 1886 Harris gave notice that he intended to propose at the forthcoming meeting of county secretaries that the residential qualification be reduced to one year. Captain Holden of Notts responded with a call to make the period three years. In arguing his case Lord Harris stated that the two-year residency was a 'double hardship in the case of a professional' and 'arbitrary'. He continued:

> I do not see why professionals should be prevented from reaching the highest ranks by unnecessary restrictions . . . I have been called a cricket socialist. I do not know what a cricket socialist is, but if it means that I have the interest of professional cricketers thoroughly at heart, then I am one.

Despite this astonishing speech (or perhaps because of it) Harris lost his proposal by three votes (Lancashire, Hampshire and Cheshire) to 14. His own county Kent were divided and abstained.

Two years later at the County Cricket Council – a short-lived, national body to control county cricket which Harris had been the prime mover in creating – the vexed issue of players' qualifications was raised again. Derbyshire, bitter over the defection of Crich-born Frank Shacklock to Notts, proposed that, 'So long as any county requires the services of any of its duly qualified players, such players shall not be allowed to play for any other county.' In speaking to the motion Mr J. Smith, a Derby solicitor, said, 'What would they think of any gentlemen who tried to bribe their private servants from their employment.' The resolution was seconded by W. G. Grace and supported by the patriarch of Yorkshire cricket, Mr M. J. Ellison.

Clearly the idea that the players were private servants of the county clubs was widely held. Lord Harris was vehement in his opposition to this attitude. This was 'a most dangerous proposition . . . I view it with the utmost disfavour.' Harris continued that he could not support 'anything that had any suspicion of interfering with a working man from selling that which was his property – his labour.'

The resolution was defeated by seven votes to five. This proved to be the last Cricket Council meeting Lord Harris attended as shortly afterwards he left for India to become the Governor of Bombay. In 1891, with Harris still overseas, the Cricket Council voted itself out of existence on the casting vote of Mr Ellison.

Lord Harris returned home to Kent in 1895 and three years later was advocating 'A Register of County Cricketers' as a means to control the movement of players between counties. Harris's idea was that cricketers would register which county they intended to represent either on the basis of birth or residency. If a professional wanted to move to another county Harris argued that both counties had to agree and the player had to serve either a residency of two years or, if he was returning to his county of birth, one year. In his Lordship's opinion this system allowed for 'greater elasticity in the first instance . . . but would make cricketers very cautious before getting themselves registered . . .

(and) discourage as much as possible changing from one county to another.'

Around this time a number of bitter disputes occurred between several counties over the qualifications of particular professionals. The most notable cases were between Notts and Lancashire over John Crossland, Derbyshire and Notts over Frank Shacklock, and Surrey and Somerset over Len Braund and William Montgomery. It was ironic that Surrey, never shy about luring northern professionals to the Oval, should have taken offence when Len Braund left to join Somerset in 1899. Braund, an ordinary member of the ground staff, had shown little indication of the great 'doubles' he was to perform for his adopted county in 1901-03. Relations were strained between the two counties but when Montgomery left for the west country in 1904 Surrey responded by cancelling their fixtures with Somerset; a state of affairs that lasted until friendly relations were re-established in June 1907!

Lord Harris's thinking may have been affected by cases such as these but his solution was significantly more restrictive than his 1886 and 1888 proposals. Harris's 1898 Register advocated the maintenance of the two-year qualification and would have weakened the professionals' bargaining position.

Within the Conservative Party Lord Harris was aligned with the 'democratic Tories' who sought populist and working-class support for the Party's policies. One of Harris's more public commitments to the Conservative Party was his acceptance of the Chancellorship of the Primrose League in 1887, 1888 and 1896. The Primrose League had been founded in 1883 by a small group of disaffected Tories led by Lord Randolph Churchill. The original aim had been to create an organisation to unite the younger, more democratic and 'militant' Tories, but the League quickly assumed a more general role in mobilising broad popular opinion and support for the Party.

By 1890 the Primrose League had one million members and 20 years later they claimed the figure exceeded two million. The League's *Manual*, published in 1894, states as its objectives the maintenance of 'Religion', 'Estates of the Realm' and the 'Imperial Ascendancy of the British Empire'. The manual continued:

> The social aspect of the Primrose League, which has been the means of bringing high and low, rich and poor, together, breaking down social barriers and uniting all classes in a common crusade against the forces of Atheism and Revolution.

This description bears a great similarity to the ideological role which Lord Harris and Lord Hawke assigned to cricket. It is not surprising that on another occasion Harris deemed cricket a 'great Conservative institution' or that in his memoirs Hawke wrote:

> High and low, rich and poor, greet one another practically on an equality, and sad will be the day for England if socialism ever succeeds in putting class v. class and thus ending sports which have made England.

By the 1890s Lord Harris and the Primrose League were more concerned with imperialism than promoting social reform and had become obsessed with the dangers of socialism and atheism. Neither opposed trade unions but they rejected institutions such as the closed shop, while also cautioning the unions against strike action and the dangers of socialism. Lord Harris was now Chairman of Consolidated Goldfields, whose founder in South Africa had been Cecil Rhodes, and the Naval Construction and Armaments Company in Barrow, as well as being on the Board of the London, Chatham and Dover Railway.

Lord Harris's part in successfully fostering the respectable professional cannot be denied. In 1902 J. T. Hearne was the first player to be accepted on the Middlesex Committee; Maurice Read was described in *Cricket* as 'refined alike in appearance, manner and speech; Louis Hall, the Yorkshire opening batsman and teetotaller, named his children Londesbrough and Edith after Lord and Lady Londesborough, and R. G. Barlow, often cited as the model professional, was complimented in *Scores and Biographies* for being a 'teetotaller and non-smoker'. Yet despite Barlow's long service and widely acclaimed demeanour the Lancashire Committee sacked him in 1892 for 'lack of courtesy' after he complained about being left out of the side 'much too soon'. When the matter was raised at the Club's Annual General Meeting the vote went 200 to 4 against the player. Barlow played league cricket successfully for a further seven seasons.

Wilfred Rhodes was another professional invariably identified with this new respectability, but the great Yorkshire all-rounder was never completely satisfied with the Committee's treatment of their players. In Sidney Rogerson's biography, *Wilfred Rhodes*, Rhodes states that he considered himself 'a VIP who was in a sense a hired servant on a low wage'.

CHAPTER 5

Professional Earnings in the Golden Age

AT the turn of the century the average weekly earnings of a county professional could vary from a minimum of 30 shillings to a maximum of around £8. The annual sum was totalled from several sources of which only the basic ground staff wage and winter pay, for those fortunate enough to receive it, were regular and guaranteed.

Being selected for the county first eleven and subsequent match performance determined whether a player lived well or struggled to survive. Match fees, win bonuses, talent money, end-of-season bonuses and ground collections explain why such wide variations could occur. While the professional county cricketer did receive a basic retainer, to a large extent his income was derived from a payments-by-results system. If a regular first eleven player lost form and his place in the county side, his earnings would drop dramatically.

GROUND STAFF WAGES

Lord's, the Oval and Old Trafford had always maintained a ground staff of bowlers. In 1890 there were 42 professionals on the staff at Lord's; by 1898 the Oval boasted a ground staff of 32 and that year Old Trafford employed more than 20 professionals. Elsewhere the situation varied. Nottinghamshire, for example, despite the county's pre-eminence, did not have a ground staff until 1897 – four years later it had grown to 13 players, while Warwickshire, although not a first-class county until 1894, maintained a small staff at Edgbaston from the early 1890s.

A place on the Lord's staff was a much sought after position providing regular summer employment as a ground bowler, possible selection in MCC and Ground fixtures and a guarantee from the MCC that a player would always be allowed to play for his county in championship matches. For the counties who could not afford a staff, Lord's was an ideal place to try to place their professionals, while for the players it offered a good, secure income. In 1886 John Selby, the Notts professional, in a letter to the county Committee, wrote that, 'almost all of the county eleven have had good engagements at Lord's where their profits are three or four times the amount of what any man's are that plays for Notts county.'

In 1890 the season at Lord's lasted 16 weeks. A ground bowler was paid between 30 and 50 shillings per week plus £3 for a MCC and Ground match at Lord's, £6 for an away game, the possibility of a 10 shillings win bonus and occasional gratuities from MCC members. In a good week a professional at Lord's might earn £10. Eighteen years earlier the staff had been divided into two classes. There were no more than five in the first class and they received 35 shillings, which was five shillings more than those in the second class. The rate for a match at Lord's was £3 for a win and 50 shillings for a loss, while away fixtures or 'out' matches, as they were then called, paid £5.

An established professional at the Oval or Old Trafford in the 1890s would expect to be paid between £2 and £3 in ground staff wages for a 22-week summer season commencing on 1 May. A member of the Oval staff who was not a regular in the first or second elevens received only £1 per week. Their contract stated that they must be available to bowl at the nets and play in matches when required, not enter service elsewhere and were liable to dismissed at a week's notice or with one week's pay in lieu. They received no pay in winter.

At the turn of the century a ground bowler worked long hours during the summer. At Old Trafford they were expected to be available to bowl to members in the nets until 7.00 p.m. and until 4.00 p.m. on Saturdays.

WINTER PAY

The introduction of winter pay by the Surrey Committee in 1894 represented a significant achievement for the players. The professional cricketer had ceased to be a seasonal worker. Surrey's lead was quickly followed by Lancashire in 1895, Yorkshire in 1896 and eventually every other county.

Initially winter pay split the counties into the rich, who could afford such an expenditure, and the poor, who could not, and divided the ground staffs at the Oval and Old Trafford into those players whose services were recognised as worthy of retention and those who were expendable.

The 1897 edition of *Wisden* includes a comment that Yorkshire's decision to spend £600 on winter pay created 'a feeling of anxiety, not to say alarm' among many other counties. The precedent set by Surrey, Lancashire and Yorkshire forced the rest to follow or risk losing their best professionals, despite the two-year qualification period. As late as 1905 Sir Spencer Ponsonby-Fane, speaking at the Somerset Annual General Meeting, attacked winter pay for professionals as 'a most unwise thing and bad in principle. It was paying a man to idle away eight months out of twelve'. But as every other county paid it Somerset had 'to do the same'. Ponsonby-Fane was a very influential member of the MCC being treasurer from 1879 until his death in 1915 and a trustee from 1900.

Specific cases of winter pay are indentifiable as early as 1882. Surrey and Lancashire compensated for their lack of local professional talent by offering players from other counties, notably Notts and Yorkshire, pay throughout the year while they fulfilled the two-year residential qualification.

From October 1882 Lancashire paid John Crossland, the Notts-born bowler, 25 shillings per week in winter. Notts had already complained about Crossland playing for Lancashire and in November 1883 the Notts secretary wrote to the Lancashire Committee stating that they could not agree to the coming season's fixture because of the dubious bowling actions of Crossland and George Nash. The following September Lancashire terminated Crossland's engagement at Old Trafford and finally in June 1885 the MCC ruled that Crossland 'no longer possesses a residential qualification to play for Lancashire'.

Arthur Mold was another Lancashire import whose career was over-shadowed by doubts about his bowling action. In September 1887 the Lancashire Committee offered Mold, who had been born in Northamptonshire, 25 shillings per week in winter and £3 in summer 'in order that he may become qualified'. The arrangement was repeated in 1888. This right-arm fast bowler served his adopted county well, making 260 first-class appearances as well as playing three times for England in 1893.

The two Yorkshire-born brothers, Alfred and Henry Tinsley, were also enticed to qualify for Lancashire and from 1893 received £1 per week in winter. Ten years earlier Surrey had offered Edwin Mills and Tom Bowley, both from Notts, 15 shillings per week in winter in order to qualify.

It was the danger of Surrey's leading players moving elsewhere that prompted the Committee to establish the 'player retention sub-committee'. The sub-committee put forward a proposal for winter pay which included wide differentials. For example, in 1895-96 Abel, Baldwin, Henderson, Lockwood, Marshall, Richardson and Wood received 30 shillings per week in winter, while 10 other Surrey players were recipients of between 10 and 25 shillings. By 1900-01 23 Surrey professionals were being paid a total of £843 in winter or an average of 24 shillings over 30 weeks.

Lancashire introduced a simpler two-tier system of £1 or 10 shillings. In 1901 out of a ground staff of 24, seven (Webb, Huddleston, Hallows, Tyldesley, Sladen, Broughton and

Turner) were offered £1, a further four were given 10 shillings, while the remaining 13 received nothing.

The Yorkshire approach of £2 for their first eleven professionals was straightforward, but it should be added that the players only received £1 per week. Half of the winter pay was retained by the Committee and given to the professional on his retirement. Four per cent per annum interest was added, but it hardly adds up to the 'very liberal winter pay' and 'generous percentage' that Lord Hawke claimed in the introduction to *The History of Yorkshire Cricket*. Undoubtedly this was another of Hawke's attempts to 'encourage thrift' amongst the Yorkshire players.

In October 1903 the Surrey Committee undertook a survey of the winter employment prospects of the Oval ground staff and of the 16 who replied only four felt they had any chance of finding work. Bobby Abel ran his own bat-making business, but added that his earnings were 'uncertain'; Len Gooder, a paperhanger, expected irregular work; Tom Rushby, by trade a carpenter, seemed to have the best prospects and Fred Stedman, a bricklayer, had a chance of some piece-work. The other 12, including the young Jack Hobbs and the renowned William Lockwood, felt they had little likelihood of finding employment.

The covering letter from the Committee makes the point that:

> Bowlers in receipt of winter wages are trying to make this a living wage, when granting winter wages the Committee had no such idea . . . (winter wages were) to help them while unemployed and to supplement such earnings as they could secure.

It is hardly surprising that the Surrey professionals found it impossible to find winter work in London in 1903. A substantial part of the London workforce was in seasonal employment and during the winter the glut of unskilled workers made casual work very hard to obtain.

Clearly the Surrey Committee envisaged winter pay as a retainer and a supplement which would ensure the players' loyalty to the Oval, but the lack of work had a demoralising effect on the professionals. Fred Holland, who joined the ground staff in 1892 when he was 16, wrote to the Committee in these terms:

> When my first season was finished, I had nothing to do and for the first winter or so, until a retainer was granted, I was dependent upon my parents. For the past twelve winters I have done nothing, and the long closed season hangs terribly . . . This mode of living is not conducive to one's success at cricket. It amounts to saving as much money as possible in the summer and worrying whether it will carry you through the winter, and then in the winter worrying again in case success should not attend your efforts the following summer . . . My idleness has been enforced, inasmuch as I have tried hard to secure winter employment . . . To know, whilst cricketing, that some employment was certain in the winter, would be the greatest tonic and boon.

Holland's sentiments were echoed in six other letters to the Committee; all the players had been unable to find work.

The Surrey Committee were not always consistent in the view that winter pay was a retainer. In 1903 they withdrew the payments to Tom Hayward and Herbert Strudwick when they were chosen to tour Australia; five years earlier Lancashire had treated J. T. Tyldesley in the same manner when he visited South Africa with Lord Hawke's party. It was not until 1909 that Surrey agreed to pay their professionals in winter even if they were on tour or coaching overseas.

Winter pay had been achieved as the game prospered during the so-called golden age. However, prior to the First World War attendances declined and even clubs such as Lancashire reported annual losses. Between 1910 and 1913 inclusive the red-rose county lost £3617.

At the Advisory County Cricket Committee in February 1913 Pelham Warner advocated solving the game's financial problems at the expense of the professionals. First, he urged the clubs to select more amateurs and therefore reduce the amount due to the players in match fees and second, he proposed cutting winter pay to a level 'such as would make him keen to find work'. Warner ignored the fact that winter pay was neither a living wage nor sufficiently generous for players to avoid seeking employment. As we have seen, the professionals would have prefered to work in winter.

Three months later, again at the Advisory County Cricket Committee, Warner continued his attack on winter pay stating that 'a great deal of money was wasted especially with regard to the professional's winter pay'. He wanted a system which would 'keep the wolf from the door but not be so much that he need not look for employment . . . it was bad from a national point of view that these people should do practically nothing in the winter.' (A facetious professional, forgetting his 'place', might have been excused for asking what Mr Warner did for the nation in winter!)

By eight votes to five a sub-committee of the county clubs was established to examine the issue of winter pay. In March 1914 the Advisory County Cricket Committee had before it a proposal from Sussex, seconded by Yorkshire, that 'winter pay should not be given to professionals after they had had their benefit'. The advocates of this view added that their proposition would have the additional advantage for the clubs of persuading players to request their benefits later in their careers. The players must have been relieved to hear that the Sussex motion was defeated, albeit by the narrow margin of five votes to four. The debate over winter pay, concluded by the War, was re-opened in 1919.

MATCH FEES

By the onset of the 'golden age' £5 for a home match and £6 for an away or 'out' game was well established as the rate for the job. Although the All-England Eleven players had received £5 per match throughout the 1860s it was not until the MCC Annual General Meeting in 1871 that this amount was agreed for the professionals at Lord's. The resolution also added that an additional £1 would be paid for matches which took place 100 or more miles away. Surrey and Yorkshire did not agree to the extra £1 until 1898. The previous year, Lancashire had simplified their match payments system to £5 at home and £6 away, whereas from 1885 until 1897 they had paid the additional £1 only for games in the South and South-West.

The players paid all their own travel and lodging expenses for 'out' matches and so that extra £1 was very significant. The professionals had to find not only the third-class rail fare and the cost of bed-and-breakfast accommodation, but also the cost of cabs, lunch, evening meals and tips.

FEES FOR REPRESENTATIVE MATCHES

The MCC Annual General Meeting in 1871 agreed that the professionals would receive £10 for their services in the Players versus Gentlemen fixtures at Lord's. The decision was made 'to secure the best available talent' and was endorsed by the authorities at the Oval.

While £10 remained the rate for that particular fixture there was little uniformity in payments for other representative matches. For example, in 1882 when Lancashire arranged a match between the North of England and Australia they offered the players £12 if they lost and £15 if they won. But eight years later when Lancashire met the Australians the local professionals received only £10, which was still the rate in 1902. In July 1886 Walter Wright of Notts had asked for £10 when the county met the Australians; the Committee rejected the request and dropped him for the rest of the season. This harsh judgement led to Wright leaving the county of his birth and qualifying by residence for Kent. The Notts decision seems even more ridiculous given that they had paid, albeit reluctantly, their professionals £20 when the county met the 1880 tourists. On that occasion seven Notts professionals, including Arthur Shrewsbury and Alfred Shaw, had persuaded Captain Holden, the Club secretary, to accede to their request but, exhibiting considerable petulance, 'Hell-Fire' Jack Holden gave £21 to the four players who were not party to the demand for more money. It is worth noting that the 'amateur' Australians cleared an average of £34 for the match.

By 1896 the rate for representative and England matches had been uniformly reduced to £10. The strike by George Lohmann, William Gunn, Tom Richardson, Bobby Abel and Tom Hayward prior to the Oval Test against the Australians in 1896 may have failed to win their request for £20, but two years later, in October 1898, a meeting at Lord's agreed to such an increase. The full story of that strike is told in Chapter 8.

WIN BONUS

The £1 win bonus was universally paid by the counties in the 1890s. It was one of the longest-established features of the professionals' payments system. For example, as early as 1853 the Surrey Annual General Meeting established that players in county matches would be paid £4 for a win and £3 for a loss.

TALENT MONEY

Payments, in kind or money, for outstanding performances were another tradition, the most obvious example being a white hat to a bowler who had taken three wickets with consecutive balls.

The precedent for rewarding performances had been established at Lord's in 1854 when fine batting, by an amateur or a professional, warranted the award of a new ball. At the Oval the gift of a bat to an amateur, although these were usually ornamental, and money to the professionals, was the norm, but in May 1872 the Surrey Committee decided that 'talent money and hats were to be abolished'.

Fifteen years later the Committee agreed to John Shuter's request that as captain he be given a fund of £100 to dispense during the season in talent money. The following season, 1888, the amount was increased to £150.

By the 1890s a consensus had been reached amongst the counties on the scales for talent money. In 1892 Yorkshire paid £1 for 50, 30 shillings for a score of 75 and £2 for a century; Lancashire paid £1 for any score over 50 while, according to Jack Hobbs in *My Cricket Memories*, Surrey granted £1 for 50, £2 for a hundred and £3 for 150. The details of talent money for bowlers are less well-recorded, although the Gloucestershire professional, William Woof, in Pullin's *Talks with Old English Cricketers* credits Dr E.M.Grace as being the pioneer of the award of £1 for six wickets in an innings.

As a payments-for-results system talent money on the basis of £1 for 50, etc, contained the obvious flaw that it took no account of the circumstances in which an innings might be played, its relative worth to the side and the state of the wicket. Thirty runs accumulated on a sticky wicket could be more significant than a century on an easy-paced pitch.

Lord Hawke recognised this problem and instituted the mark system. In *Recollections and Reminiscences* he outlined the procedure:

> I gave marks according to my view of the importance to the side of what was done. Not only did I reward good batting and really excellent bowling, sometimes when not particularly successful though exceptionally good, but I also allocated marks for fine wicket-keeping and smart fielding. The mark was always worth the same sum, namely, five shillings, but I bestowed a half-mark for a smart catch.

During Lord Hawke's years as captain there was no upper limit to the total amount available for disposal. One season it was claimed that more than £800 was distributed, although Hawke states that the highest individual payment he ever awarded was £52 10 shillings to George Hirst; in the post-Hawke period, Wilfred Rhodes received as much as £66.

A. O. Jones, the Notts captain from 1900 to 1914, instituted the mark system from 1905. Again, each mark was worth five shillings, but Jones allocated four marks for 50, eight marks for 100 and 12 for 150, while a bowler received four marks for five wickets and 10 for eight wickets in an innings. In effect this approach was little different from the original talent money system, although Jones did operate it with some discretion and flexibility. In 1907 when Notts won the county championship with 15 victories from 19 matches, the players shared £147 5 shillings in mark awards.

During the 1904 season the Surrey Committee enquired of Lord Hawke how the mark system worked and four years later they implemented a similar procedure. In his letter Hawke remarked that, 'the player is not told the different marks he receives but the total amount is handed to him at the end of the season.' Lord Hawke distributed the sealed envelopes during 'my annual day to my boys at Wighill . . . the red-letter day of my year, and I believe it was to them too'.

Annual open days, when paternalistic northern employers invited their employees to their country properties, was common practice, and Hawke's reference to 'my boys' makes that paternalism all the more apparent. That the professionals were kept in the dark during the season about the allocation of marks reinforced the authority of the amateur captain and the Club over the players.

END-OF-SEASON BONUS

1887 saw the first of six consecutive Surrey championship wins. In October the Committee allocated the first of what became regular end-of-season bonus payments. George Lohmann, with 154 wickets, was the season's leading wicket-taker prompting *Cricket* to comment that 'this was a remarkable performance'; the Surrey Committee rewarded him with £25. The other regular professionals were given £5, while the 'amateurs' were even more generously remunerated. Walter Read received £100, the captain John Shuter 25 guineas and Messrs Key and Roller 10 guineas each.

Two years later Surrey shared the championship with Notts. The Committee at the Oval decided that Walter Read was worthy of a £100 bonus, while the nine leading professionals (Abel, Beaumont, Bowley, Henderson, Lockwood, Lohmann, Maurice Read, Sharpe and Wood) shared £100 between them. George Lohmann's haul of 202 wickets put him well ahead of his nearest rival in the season's averages and yet again asserted his prowess as the leading bowler in England. The aggrieved Lohmann sent a brief letter to the Surrey secretary:

> Your cheque to hand for which I thank you.
> I fail to see why my services should be less worthy of recognition in 1889 than those rendered in previous years. Kindly place this before the Committee.

In March 1890 the Committee rectified the situation, awarding Lohmann £50 and the other leading players £20 each, but added the proviso that they would 'not pledge themselves' to an honorarium at the end of each season. Despite this, throughout the 1890s the Surrey players continued to receive such end-of-season bonuses, but no professional, not even George Lohmann or his equally legendary partner Tom Richardson, was ever given more than £50, although the 'amateur' Walter Read always received £100 at the end of the season.

Only Yorkshire matched the generosity of Surrey. In 1897, subsequent to Yorkshire winning the championship in 1893 and 1896, the Committee established a Bonus Fund into which they paid £2 for each county match played by one of the leading professionals after 1 May 1897. In 1901 and 1903 the Committee contributed additional 'handsome cheques' into the Fund. Once again Hawke used these payments as a potential disciplinary measure by stating that a player's money could be forfeited if the Committee was dissatisfied with his conduct.

Other counties were much less generous. When Notts won the championship in 1883, and Lancashire were successful in 1904, their respective Committees rewarded their professionals with only £10 per player.

GROUND AND PUBLIC COLLECTIONS

Taking the hat around the ground to allow the crowd to show their appreciation of a particular player's performance became a regular occurrence in the 1890s. *Cricket* recorded some of the more notable collections, although the published information tends to be from the Oval due in part to the large crowds and also because Charles Alcock, the Surrey secretary, was also editor of *Cricket*.

The largest collection listed in *Cricket* was accorded to Tom Hayward during the Test match against Australia at the Oval in 1899. The crowd of 25,000 contributed £131 after Hayward hit 137 out of England's first innings total of 576. A few days earlier Hayward and Bobby Abel shared £73, donated by a Bank Holiday crowd in recognition of their 448-run partnership in six hours against Yorkshire. The Oval crowd frequently dug into their pockets for the popular 'Guvnor' Bobby Abel. In 1886 he shared £72 with Maurice Read during the Surrey-Australia game; in 1897 after his 215 against Notts he received £65 and later that season shared £36 with William Brockwell after their first wicket partnership against Hampshire.

No doubt these collections, for the most part made up of silver and copper coins, were very welcome additions to the professional's earnings. To the chagrin of the bowlers these collections were usually taken only after fine exhibitions of batting, although in 1907, after Notts won the county championship, a public shilling fund raised £800 for all the Notts players in the first eleven.

STAR CONTRACTS AT THE OVAL

Virtually every professional in England during the 'golden age' lived a precarious life with an income primarily dependent on their maintaining form and good health. Prior to the First World War George Lohmann, Tom Richardson and Tom Hayward, the three outstanding professionals employed at the Oval, managed to negotiate contracts which guaranteed their income over several seasons. It is not surprising that this development occurred at the Oval, given

George Lohmann

the wealth of the Surrey club and its more liberal wages' policy.

George Lohmann set the precedent in September 1891. At this time he was unquestionably the best all-rounder in the first-class game; he had taken over 800 wickets during the previous four seasons. Lohmann informed the Committee that he had been approached by Middlesex, the county of his birth, with a view to his playing at Lord's. During a meeting between Lohmann and Viscount Oxenbridge, the Surrey President, satisfactory terms were agreed as follows:

a) a retaining fee of £100 for 1892 as well as the usual match payments;

b) the end-of-season bonus of £50 was to be 'made a fixed and absolute payment';

c) total payments in 1892 would be not less than £300 and

d) the agreement applied only to the 1892 season.

During the 1895 season Tom Richardson claimed the unprecedented tally of 290 wickets at an average of 14.37. From a position of such strength Richardson was astute enough to negotiate a special contract with Surrey. Basically the agreement reached gave him the 'usual summer wages, match fees, talent money and bonus' plus 'a lump sum of one hundred pounds to cover and include all winter pay'. This latter sum was to be reduced to £50 if Richardson accepted an engagement between 1 October and 1 May. Finally, and of most importance for the player, the Committee agreed that 'no doubt he would have a benefit match not later than 1900'.

Tom Richardson happily accepted these terms and wrote from Mitcham:

> I feel I can safely leave my interests in your hands . . . I shall therefore for the future consider Surrey to have the first call on my services no matter how flattering any offer is that may be held out to me.

As in the case of George Lohmann, it appeared that Tom Richardson had been approached by another county. It was the danger of losing their star players that prompted the

Tom Richardson

Surrey Committee to give them relatively lucrative contracts. In line with the agreement, Richardson was given a benefit in 1899 which raised approximately £1000; his contract was renewed annually until 1903 when his winter wages were cut from £100 to £50.

Surrey certainly had good value from Tom Richardson. Following his astounding effort in 1895, he took 246 first-class wickets the following season and another 273 in 1897. In those three seasons he had delivered more than 24,000 balls! At the age of 26 he took his 1000th wicket in the shortest-ever period of 134 matches and six years later in his 327th game his 2000th wicket. Both of these feats remain records. To put those achievements in perspective, Malcolm Marshall was 28 and in his 228th match when he captured his 1000th wicket, while Derek Underwood was 36 and needed 518 appearances before claiming his 2000th wicket.

Despite Richardson's renowned strength (which was remarkable given that he had been refused entry to the police force prior to becoming a professional cricketer because of a weak heart) the strain began to tell and after the 1897-98 tour of Australia with Stoddart's party he did not recapture his previous superlative form. Nevertheless, in five of the following six seasons he captured more than 100 wickets. In November 1904 Richardson wrote to the Surrey Committee to 'sever my active connection' with the Club after a failure to agree terms. Tom Richardson moved to Bath where he kept a hotel and qualified by residence for Somerset. His only appearance for his adopted county was against the 1905 Australian tourists, a drawn match in which the visitors compiled a total of 4 for 609 (Warwick Armstrong 303 not out) in their only innings. Richardson bowled 13 overs and conceded 65 runs.

Tom Richardson had begun to put on weight, perhaps as a consequence of his fondness for stout – James Lillywhite claimed Tom drank 'a bottle to each hour of bowling and he had it, too' – and his cricket career came to a close. Subsequently Richardson returned to his native Surrey to keep the Prince's Head at Richmond Green and was interviewed

Tom Hayward

there about Dr Williams' Pink Pills for an advertisement that appeared in the 1910 edition of *Wisden*. Tom listed his health problems, 'nervous system impaired . . . appetite fell off . . . memory often failed me . . . insomnia . . . depressed . . . tired easily . . . rheumatism' but the Pink Pills proved 'a splendid tonic'. Tom Richardson, described by Herbert Strudwick as 'never a more kind-hearted or genuine man' and by Jack Hobbs as a 'delightful fellow', died of congestion of the brain in July 1912 in St Jean d'Arvey, France aged 41. He left an estate worth £629.

Tom Hayward was the pre-eminent professional Surrey batsman prior to the First World War. For 20 successive seasons from 1895 he exceeded 1000 runs, while in 1904 and 1906 Hayward topped 3000. Among his many other notable achievements was to bring his fellow Cambridge-born opening batsman, Jack Hobbs, and the fast bowler, Bill Hitch, to the attention of the Surrey authorities.

From 1898 Hayward was receiving £60 in winter wages, separating him from the rest of the professionals except Tom Richardson. In February 1906 that amount was raised to £80. After scoring 3518 runs that season, which remained an aggregate record until it was broken in 1947 by Denis Compton, he was given a three-year contract to be concluded by a complimentary match in 1909. Tom Hayward, having made his debut in 1893, had received a benefit in 1902, but in October 1908 asked the Committee to allow him a second benefit rather than a testimonial game. The Committee would agree if the benefit took place after Hayward's retirement from first-class cricket. Under those conditions Tom opted for the testimonial, whereupon the Committee added the rider that he must put 'his services at the disposal of the Committee for five years'. Six months later the Committee decided that Hayward's testimonial would take the form of a £200 donation from the Club, a subscription card in the pavilion, but no list to be circulated to the other counties; and a ground collection at one match of Hayward's choice. Not surprisingly the total reached only

£383, which must have left Tom Hayward a disappointed man.

However, when his father, Daniel Hayward junior, died in May 1910, Tom's inheritance made him comfortably off. Four years later he married Matilda Emma Mitchell, who worked variously as a detective for the South-Western Railway Company, the Royal College of Veterinary Surgeons and Selfridge's. The bride's father gave the couple £500 before they left for a honeymoon in Paris. Tom Hayward announced his retirement from the first-class game during the First World War to take up a coaching position at Oxford University where Robertson-Glasgow remembered his 'florid face . . . quasi-military moustachios . . . enormous collar of his sweater'. He later moved to Cambridge to work in the family business.

In negotiating 'star' contracts, George Lohmann, Tom Richardson and Tom Hayward were exceptions among the players, but the deals agreed with 'amateurs' such as Walter Read at Surrey and Archie MacLaren at Lancashire substantially exceeded the remuneration afforded to that trio of professionals. Payments to 'amateurs' were common and often generous; they are examined in Chapter 7.

SUMMARY – ANNUAL EARNINGS

As we have seen the professional's earnings were totalled from various sources and most of these were dependent on the player's on-field performance. Table 3 summarises the position of the Surrey professionals at the turn of the century. Yet it should be remembered that Surrey was a generous and wealthy club and that these are gross earnings prior to the deduction of travel, lodging and expenses for away matches.

These figures highlight the wide differentials between the professionals which was a product of the payments-by-results system. For a ground staff member, not in the county side, the only opportunity to increase his earnings came from second eleven matches. For these Surrey paid 50 shillings at the Oval, an extra £1 for an away game and a 10 shillings win bonus, while at the end of the season second eleven regulars usually received a £5 bonus. Such a professional would do well to make an extra £25 per season from second eleven matches.

In comparison William Lockwood, a first eleven member who played in two-thirds of the first-class games, could earn in excess of £250 per year. In 1901 Lockwood represented Surrey 18 times, of which nine were 'out' matches; in six he received a £1 win bonus (this was a relatively disappointing season for Surrey who finished sixth in the championship); he scored one century, three 50s and took five wickets on three occasions which gained him £7 in talent money; he was selected for the Players twice which was worth £20, and received an end-of-season bonus of £40.

Table 3: Earnings of the Surrey professionals, 1896-1901 (£)

Category of player	Summer	Winter	Total	Weekly ave. (shillings)
Ground staff and second eleven	50-70	30	80-100	30-38
First eleven regular playing in half the first-class games (1)	130-160	30	160-190	62-73
Leading first eleven playing in two-thirds of the first-class games (2)	215-245	45	260-290	100-112
Star contracts (3)	200-350	100	300-450	115-173

(1) Based on Frederick Holland, 1901
(2) Based on William Lockwood, 1901
(3) Based on Tom Richardson, 1896-99

Source: Surrey CCC minutes.

The information for the fourth category of 'star' players is based on Tom Richardson's performances between 1896 and 1899. Tom Richardson was one of the handful of professionals who played in virtually every first-class Surrey fixture and had increased opportunities for win bonuses, ground collections and talent money. For example, in 1896 Richardson took five wickets on 15 occasions to earn an additional £15. He was also selected three times for England, twice for the Players and twice for the South of England during the Hastings festival which contributed a further £70; additionally, he received a £50 end-of-season bonus. Three years later Richardson's decline in form was apparent from the fact that he took five wickets on only three occasions and was not chosen for any representative fixtures. A reasonable estimate of Tom Richardson's earnings in 1896, leaving aside overseas tours and any other coaching work, would be £425, as compared to £350 in 1899.

Table 4 compares the position of the professionals at the Oval and Old Trafford. Despite the fact that the Lancashire Club invariably recorded a reasonable profit every season, their players received between 20 and 30 per cent less than their Oval counterparts, the most significant differences being the lower winter pay, the lack of an end-of-season bonus and the fact that no Old Trafford professional was ever rewarded with a special contract.

Table 4: Comparison of the earnings of Surrey and Lancashire professionals around 1900 (£).

	Annual earnings	
Category of player	Surrey	Lancashire
Ground staff	80-100	70
Regular first eleven	160-190	150
Leading first eleven	260-290	200
'Star' contracts	300-450	not exist

Sources: Surrey and Lancashire CCC minutes.

OVERSEAS TOURS

From 1873, when W. G. Grace led the third English party to Australia, overseas tours became a regular feature in the calendar of the top professionals. In the 30-year period prior to 1903, when the MCC undertook to organise Australian tours, 13 parties had travelled to Australia. With three exceptions they were predominantly made up of professionals and, in fact, four of the six tours during the 1880s were financed and organised by three professionals – Alfred Shaw, Arthur Shrewsbury and James Lillywhite junior.

In his diaries James Southerton recalls that the 1876-77 trip entailed 'very rough travelling by land and sea' and despite the hearty receptions the tourists invariably received, such trips were hard work. The Shaw, Shrewsbury and Lillywhite tours involved the cricketers being away from home for seven or eight months and playing more than 30 matches in Australia, many of which would be 'up country' against 18s and 22s. Inevitably such an itinerary included long, laborious journeys by coastal steamers, the recently extended railways and the traditional horse and carriage. The 1886-87 English party was the first team to be able to travel overland by railway from Adelaide to Melbourne. From 1 January 1887 an 18-hour sleeping car service was inaugurated, but there was still no unbroken link between Adelaide and Brisbane.

After George Ulyett's death in 1898 *Cricket* estimated that during his Yorkshire and England career 'Happy Jack' had travelled 258,000 miles playing cricket, of which 157,000 had been undertaken during his five trips to Australia.

For Shaw, Shrewsbury and Lillywhite the four tours in the 1880s eventually proved to be a financial liability. The profits on the first three were eliminated by the substantial loss of £2400 on the 1887-88 cricket tour and the £800 deficit from the 1888 rugby tour which followed on immediately. For Shaw and Shrewsbury this outcome was worsened by Lillywhite's inability to make any contribution to the losses. Of the 1884-85 tour Shaw and Shrewsbury wrote in their self-published account:

> Financially it had not been all we had hoped for, but we were not dissatisfied, for besides the pleasure of the visit, we had been enabled to extend the large wholesale

The 1887-88 England side to Australia organised by Shaw, Shrewsbury and Lillywhite

> business in requisites for cricket and other games, which we had already opened up with the Colonies.

For the professionals who visited Australia, the first Shaw, Shrewsbury and Lillywhite effort in 1881-82 marked a significant improvement in pay and conditions as compared to 1873-74. On that earlier occasion Grace had offered the players £150 and second-class travel. Alfred Shaw considered such terms unacceptable and refused to go. Eight years later the memorandum of agreement, signed on 29 August 1881 between Shaw, Shrewsbury and Lillywhite – 'the employers' – and George Ulyett, John Selby, William Bates, Edmund Peate, Thomas Emmett, Richard Pilling, William Midwinter and R.G.Barlow – 'Professional cricketers of England' – included seven points of which the most important were:

* a tour fee of £200; £50 on departure, £50 after the first match in Melbourne and £100 after the last match in Australia;
* £20 to cover all personal expenses 'such as refreshments during and after matches';
* a first-class saloon passage and payment of all travelling expenses during the tour; and
* in the event of impropriety or misconduct the player will be fined £20 – such 'fines shall be equally divided between the said team at the close of the tour'.

According to R. G. Barlow in his memoirs *Forty Seasons of First-Class Cricket*, five years later Shaw, Shrewsbury and Lillywhite paid him £320 plus first-class travel to undertake the Australian tour. And that became the going-rate up to and including the MCC tour in 1907-08.

In his reminiscences, recorded by Pullin, Alfred Shaw wrote that:

> with ordinary care he (the professional) could return from the trip with £100 or £150 in his pocket. This was occasionally done, but I am sorry to say that the majority of the players returned with practically nothing.

Shaw continued that this was due to 'expensive habits' and 'feasting and merrymaking'. Yet in a letter quoted in *Give Me*

Arthur, Shrewsbury details that after the 1887-88 tour they still owed Lohmann £80, Read £100, Briggs £60, Pilling £55, Preston £45, Pougher £75 and Ulyett £73. Interestingly, the two amateurs on the trip were owed even more – 'Mr' Newham £147 and 'Mr' Brann £190. Excessive payments to prominent amateurs to encourage them to undertake Australian and South African tours rankled with the professionals. In another letter Shrewsbury commented that 'the expenses of each amateur member of Lord Harris's team was more than double those of any one of the professionals' and later, writing to Shaw about Lord Sheffield's 1891-92 party, he added, 'I told you what wine would be drunk by the amateurs. Grace himself would drink enough to swim a ship.'

The Australian tours highlighted for the English professionals the inequitable way they were treated socially in England as compared to their Australian counterparts. Players such as Shrewsbury, Lohmann and Briggs were fêted in Australia and considered no differently from the Australian cricketers, but when the latter visited England they were deemed amateurs and treated better than their English fellow players. In class terms there was virtually no difference between the players. For example, before Victor Trumper opened a sports shop in Sydney with the Australian wicket-keeper Hanson Carter, he worked as a clerk. Carter subsequently left the partnership to work for his family's undertaking business. Joe Darling, the Australian captain on three tours to England, also ran a sports shop, although later he became a farmer. Monty Noble was a dentist by profession; George Giffen worked as a letter sorter; 'Tibby' Cotter was employed in the accounts department of a meat works; Warren Bardsley was a trainee teacher; C. T. B. Turner serviced coaches; Harry Boyle laboured in a warehouse; Harry Trott was a postman; Clem Hill became stipendary steward and handicapper for the Adelaide Jockey Club, while Warwick Armstrong was the pavilion clerk with the Melbourne Cricket Club on a pre-War salary of £228.

Most Australian Test players had a testimonial match towards the end of their careers. In 1906 Joe Kelly received £1300, while in the same season Syd Gregory benefitted by £630. Three years later Monty Noble made a profit of £2000 from an Australian XI versus the Rest fixture, and in 1913 Victor Trumper was rewarded with £2950.

Australian players did very well financially from their tours to England. In 1903 *Cricket* reported a case from the Sydney law courts where an unnamed test player recounted his earnings from tours to England. This was almost certainly Syd Gregory who was declared a bankrupt in 1903 and under oath he stated that he earned £400 in 1890, nothing in 1893, £4-500 in 1896, £700 in 1899 and £800 in 1902. Seven years later *Cricket* noted that the 1909 tourists each made a profit of £473.

The Australian tours to England were organised very differently from their English counterparts. Until, and including, the 1905 tour the players elected the captain and the manager and divided the tour profits between them. After the Australian Board of Control was finally established as a representative body in 1907 when South Australia and Tasmania were incorporated, the players' position steadily weakened. For the 1909 tour the Board appointed Monty Noble as captain, but he insisted that the players hold an election, which he duly won. On this occasion the Board offered the players a lump sum of £400 or a share of the profits. Three years later four of the Australian tourists to the triangular tournament wisely accepted the £400 fee; the rest of the party shared a loss.

The 1912 triangular tournament was in part a failure because of the wet English summer but also because of the weak Australian side which made the journey. Clem Hill, Warwick Armstrong, Victor Trumper, Vernon Ransford, 'Tibby' Cotter and Hanson Carter – the six leading Australian players – refused to accept a significant change in the status quo whereby the Board intended to appoint the manager and charge his expenses against the tour takings. The 'big six' proposed the same procedure as in 1909 when the Board selected the team and the players chose a player-manager on the same financial terms as the rest of the party. In a letter to the *Sydney Morning Herald* on 29 February 1912 Monty Noble wrote:

> I am a strong supporter of the Board as a Board, and I believe in the principle of Board control, but I am strongly against its present personnel . . . In these six years they have not been credited with one single act of conciliation or forbearance. They have held the pistol of coercion at the heads of the players the whole time, and gradually taken from them all their privileges.

The dispute in 1912 proved a bitter culmination as the Board sought and finally gained control over the Australian game and its players. The English authorities had won that battle many years before and in 1907 the MCC offered the players a basic £300 and a first-class passage for the Australian tour, that is, £100 less than the Australian Board offered their players two years later. Other terms had improved for the English professionals; they were given 30 shillings per week during the sea voyage to cover expenses such as wine, spirits and tobacco; 40 shillings per week while in Australia for expenses; and washing bills and tips to servants would be covered by the MCC. Despite those inducements Tom Hayward, J. T. Tyldesley, George Hirst and A. A. Lilley declined the offer and stayed at home.

COMPARISON WITH THE REST OF THE WORKING CLASS

The average weekly earnings of the professional county cricketer in the 'golden age' exceeded those of a skilled worker. However, it was to this social group that the players belonged. In his book *Useful Toil*, John Burnett describes the skilled worker as being 'possessed of a degree of skill – a combination of manual dexterity and acquired knowledge'.

According to G. D. H. Cole in *The Common People*, skilled workers, such as fitters, turners, ironfounders, compositors or craftsmen in London in 1900 could expect to earn between 38 and 42 shillings per week, that is, approximately

£100 per year. In the provinces similar jobs would pay about two shillings per week less, that is, approximately £95 per year. At the other end of the social scale Cole estimates that an agricultural labourer would be lucky to earn £40 a year.

Even taking into account the professional cricketer's expenses, which were obviously greater than the norm for a skilled worker, he remained one of the more prosperous members of the working class. And like other skilled workers, the professional provided his own tools of the trade and exhibited a growing pride in his personal appearance. John Burnett comments in *Useful Toil* that:

> the over-40 shillings-a-week 'aristocrats' were increasingly concentrated in the metal and engineering trades. It is also significant that with the exception of railway-engine-drivers and one grade of engineer, all these were occupations paid by piece-wage rather than time-wage.

As we have seen payments-by-results or piece-wages were an important part of a player's earnings and, as Burnett explains, it was piece-work which ensured that wage differentials existed between the skilled and the unskilled – or, in the cricket context, between the first eleven professional and the ground staff bowler.

In comparison to soccer players' earnings, the professional cricketer was potentially in a more lucrative position as a consequence of the football clubs' decision prior to the 1901-02 season to enforce a maximum annual wage of £208. Footballers and cricketers' earnings were in turn, dwarfed by the rewards gained from horse-racing by a few top jockeys. Wealthy owners, such as Lord Rosebery, Leopold de Rotchschild and Lord Beresford, were willing to pay up to £5000 as retainers to jockeys such as Tod Sloan and Danny Maher.

In the years from 1873 until 1900 an increase in a worker's standard of living was assured provided they avoided a reduction in wages. During the last quarter of the 19th century the cost of living fell by more than 30 per cent and consequently the consumption of meat, tea, beer, cigarettes and sugar rose.

The small financial advances made by the players, such as an extra £1 for away matches, winter pay and higher remunerations for England games, helped to raise further the standard of living of the professional cricketer. But as Lord Hawke conceded in 1904 the players' wages and conditions were 'even now none too good'. There had been an improvement but clubs such as Lancashire, Surrey and Yorkshire could have been more generous. As spectator sport boomed the attendances at the Oval and Old Trafford, soared and so did the clubs' annual profits.

THE BOOM IN ATTENDANCES AND CLUB PROFITS

In 1849 Surrey had a debt of £70; from 1856 to 1865 they registered a total loss of £1271; but in 1895 the Annual General Meeting was informed that more than £10,000 was invested in stocks. Within three years a new pavilion and tavern had been built at a cost in excess of £38,000. Club membership had increased significantly from 230 in 1855, 1000 in 1861 to 3300 in 1895, but from the 1880s the general public flocked to the Oval in their tens of thousands. It was their sixpences that laid the financial foundations for the great years of the Surrey Club. Table 5 highlights this point.

Table 5: Attendance figures at the Oval, 1881-97, cricket only

	Total 1881-97	Yearly average
Free (anybody in uniform including rail and tram workers)	742,016	43,648
Paid entrance	4,681,341	275,373
Members	719,168	42,304
Total	6,142,525	361,325

Surrey gave free admission to soldiers, sailors, telegraphists, railway workers, police officers and fire fighters, provided they were dressed in their uniforms. On the first day of the 1897 clash with Lancashire more than 1300 took advantage of the offer. *Cricket* regularly reported that new attendance records had been set at the Oval, for example, in 1892 over the August Bank Holiday, 63,775 paid to watch Surrey lose to Notts in a sensational match. The previous record for an inter-county game had been set by the same two sides in 1887 when 51,607 paid to see the home side gain a four-wicket victory.

Attendances and club profits had exhibited a comparable increase at Old Trafford. In 1885 the Lancashire Annual General Meeting was informed that the Club had 1792 members and 336 lady members, whereas 11 years later the figures had risen to 2637 members plus 659 ladies. In 1896, for the first time, total paid attendance exceeded 200,000. A similar peak of 207,000 was attained in 1899; in both seasons the three-day Manchester Test boosted the totals. During the 1890s in non-Australian tour years, the figure fluctuated around 150,000.

In 1899 the Lancashire Committee reported that £3090 had been invested, with a further £1808 remaining in the Club's bank account. Throughout the 1890s, with the exception of 1894, Lancashire made an annual profit in excess of £2000 and in the winter of 1894-95 a new pavilion was constructed at Old Trafford, while in February 1898 the Club purchased the ground for £24,082.

In *Lord's and the MCC* Lord Harris and F. S. Ashley-Cooper recount that in the winter of 1889-90 the MCC spent £21,000 on a new pavilion. Ten years later they state that the Club had liabilities of £26,000 but by 1904 the full amount had been re-paid.

Of course not all the counties could boast such attendance figures, profits and building programmes – many simply did not have a sufficiently large constituency. At various times during the 1880s and 1890s Derbyshire, Essex, Sussex and Warwickshire only survived financial crises thanks to public appeals or generous one-off donations. Other clubs, such as Leicestershire, lived on a knife-edge, reporting small profits or losses, but nevertheless in 1901 the new Aylestone Road ground was opened after the Club spent £7400 on improvements. The position of these counties was improved in 1898 when it was agreed that future net receipts of the home Test matches against Australia (that is, after the deduction of the tourists' share, all other expenses and 20 per cent for the home ground authorities) would be divided amongst the MCC and first-class counties. This proved to be a boon to the non-Test venues and began a process of revenue re-distribution within the game.

It is undeniable that in the last quarter of the 19th century cricket as a spectator sport had grown dramatically in terms of attendance figures and gate receipts. The four leading sides in the period 1864-94, when the first-class game emerged as we know it today, were Lancashire, Notts, Surrey and Yorkshire. They were the only sides to win more matches than they lost (Lancashire 154-93; Notts 162-75; Surrey 199-150 and Yorkshire 175-115) and their elevens were dominated by professionals. The magnificent Notts side of the 1880s was even captained by a professional until J. A. Dixon accepted the position in 1889, and while Lord Hawke flippantly commented that prior to his arrival in 1881 the Yorkshire eleven comprised 'ten drunks and a chapel parson', a strong case can be made that the successful Yorkshire side at the turn of the century was so packed with professional talent that it hardly needed an amateur captain.

In the same period you cannot think of Surrey without immediately picturing great professionals such as George Lohmann, Tom Richardson, Bobby Abel, Tom Hayward and William Lockwood. These were the cricketers who became the heroes of the working-class fans in the sixpenny stands. Ordinary people readily identified with players who shared their class background and who, in theory, offered their own sons the chance of a temporary exit from the routine drudgery of work. In a similar vein, William Howard in *Fifty Years Reminiscences of a Non-Player* reminds the reader that it was Johnny Briggs who 'attracted more people to Old Trafford than any player I could mention'.

In the context of the major contribution the professionals made to popularising cricket as a national institution they were undervalued and underpaid.

CHAPTER 6

Close of Play

A SHORT CAREER

FOR the time that a professional retained his place in the county's first eleven his earnings exceeded the best rates of pay of any skilled worker. But the number of years in which he could earn such money was often all too few and most men had no other trade to fall back on either in winter or after their cricketing career ended.

In an essay in *Sport: Money, Morality and the Media*, Wray Vamplew concludes that:

> the experience of three leading counties (Yorkshire, Lancashire and Surrey) suggests that many players failed to make the grade, with the median career-length being only three years for cricketers who made their debut in the last three decades of the nineteenth century.

Available information on 131 Notts professionals who played for the county between 1870 and 1913 supports Vamplew's findings. Fifty-three players, or 40 per cent of the Notts professionals, played in only one season; more than half had careers which lasted fewer than three years; while 28, or 21 per cent, appeared for more than 10 years.

Many of the players whose services were dispensed with after one season returned to, or found positions with, the emerging leagues in the North of England. Former Nottinghamshire players had a strong influence in the Lancashire

League, which on its formation in 1890 was known as the North East Lancashire Cricket League. Of the 13 clubs in the League in the 1890s at least eight had a Notts professional on their books at some stage during the decade. But with few exceptions these Notts examples point to the hazardous brevity of the cricketers' professional lives.

Accrington: Robert Mee, 1897: Mee represented Notts 37 times over 10 seaons. Prior to joining Accrington he had a three-year spell at Lord's and in later life became a publican in Burslem.

Burnley: Henry Reynolds, 1880-93: Reynolds made his Notts debut in 1872 but his first-class career finished three years later. His long engagement with Burnley was ended by his death from dropsy in April 1894.

Church: Thomas Flowers, 1894-95: Flowers, a cousin of the well-known Notts professional Wilfred Flowers, played only once for Notts.

Colne: Silas Hardy, 1897: Hardy, a miner from Ilkeston, played five times for Notts in 1893 and 1895. Like so many other professional cricketers he died of phthisis (consumption).

Lowerhouse: Silas Hardy, 1894-96, and Ben Gregory, 1898: Gregory, a miner and subsequently a publican, was 30 years old when he began his very short county career. He represented Notts five times between 1895 and 1897.

Nelson: Frank Shacklock, 1894, and Arthur Wilkinson, 1894: Shacklock is the most illustrious name in this list, having played for Derbyshire in 1884-85 before transferring his allegiance to Notts which he represented until 1893. He played 118 times for his adopted county before the Committee suspended him for ill-discipline in August 1893. It was rumoured that he emigrated to New Zealand in 1894 to avoid prosecution or escape debts. Thirty years later he was living in Christchurch and engaged by the Canterbury Cricket Association. Arthur Wilkinson played 19 times for Notts in 1894-95.

Rawtenstall: Richard Hardstaff, 1893-95: Hardstaff, another ex-miner, played regularly for Notts from 1894 to 1896. His

county career ended in 1899 when he was no-balled for throwing.
Todmorden: William Wilkinson, 1894-1900: Wilkinson represented Notts five times in 1892-93 and in the wake of his cricket career became a cinema proprietor.

Of these nine professionals only Frank Shacklock had a first-class career of length or note. For the others Notts offered only sporadic employment as compared to the relative security of league cricket.

If, however, a player did gain a regular place in the county side he might anticipate playing for a decade or more and retiring in his 40s. Playing for 10 consecutive seasons was the first, crucial pre-requisite before the county Committee would consider granting a professional a benefit match.

THE BENEFIT

'His hopes were centred on his benefit' recalls Jack Hobbs of Ernie Hayes. But Hayes must have been a sad man during the Surrey-Lancashire fixture in 1908 when not a ball was bowled due to rain, although at a cost of £150 he had taken the precaution of insuring the gate receipts against inclement weather. The insurance plus the subscription list lifted Hayes' benefit to £1264 which was a reasonable outcome given the Surrey record of £1750 established two years earlier by Walter Lees, but not so generous when it is remembered that Hayes represented Surrey on 500 occasions.

For the Victorian professional a benefit match represented his future security – an opportunity to invest for later life or perhaps start a small business. With capital from this source, and trading on their names, many players opened athletic and sports outfitters. Although the benefit was often spoken of in terms of an old-age pension – at that time the state made no such provisions – it was, in effect, a deferred payment against a minimum of 10 years consecutive service, and usually against the player's entire first-class career.

For the county Committees the benefit was another means to impose discipline over the professionals. In 1881 the seven striking Notts professionals demanded that the Committee guarantee a benefit to any player who completed 10 years with the Club. The Committee rejected that proposition out of hand; nor would they accept the seven's milder proposal that the Committee 'express an opinion that the players are entitled to one'. For the Notts Committee to guarantee or even accept an entitlement to a benefit would have been a concession that removed its disciplinary aspect. It was hardly surprising that the only senior Notts professional who did not join the 1881 strike was William Oscroft who had been promised his benefit in 1882.

Similarly William Woof, the Gloucestershire player, reckoned he never received a benefit, despite 11 years with the county, because W.G.Grace was 'greatly offended' when he accepted a coaching position at Cheltenham College.

The Rev. Holmes, writing in *Cricket* in 1894, argued:

> Respecting benefits, it is open to question whether they are not wrong in principle . . . If professional cricket was remunerated as it should be, there would be no necessity for such matches. I like to pay people adequately as they go along, at the time when they do the work.

Such a proposition was anathema to the county clubs. Not only would it have raised their wages bill but it would also have placed all the responsibility for the players' financial welfare on their shoulders.

Prior to the First World War benefits were inherently uncertain. First the player had to advance a case for a benefit and often the Committee rejected or deferred the request. For example, Fred Wild, who made his county debut for Notts in 1868, applied without success for a benefit in December 1882, January 1886, January 1887, January 1888 and December 1888. Finally on 11 January 1890 it was agreed that Wild could have the coming season's match against Lancashire, from which the player eventually received £270. Fred Wild appeared 110 times for Notts, but by the time of his benefit he had been in retirement for almost 10 years and he died only three years later.

Alfred Shaw, one of the all-time great bowlers, suffered a similar fate. His requests to the Notts Committee in January 1888, January 1890 and December 1890 for a benefit were turned down, but finally prior to the 1892 season the Committee relented. Unfortunately the match was rain-affected and raised only £130. Alfred Shaw had made his debut for Notts in 1864 – 28 seasons before his benefit! In the meantime, however, he had been a leader of the 1881 strike and from 1883 was employed by Lord Sheffield coaching young Sussex cricketers.

Players' uncertainty about being allowed a benefit was always followed by uncertainty surrounding the game itself because of the weather. Rain adversely affected the gate receipts and ground collections. Of the eight benefit matches arranged in 1894 four were partly spoiled by rain, including the Lancashire versus Yorkshire clash for Johnny Briggs. Acting in the best interests of 'Boy' Briggs, Lancashire prepared two pitches for the roses match, including one which was covered. Lord Hawke refused to play on the covered wicket and although fully within the law it was generally perceived as an unchivalrous decision. The game was concluded early on the second day. In their first innings Lancashire struggled to 50 after losing their first four wickets before a run was scored. Inevitably Johnny Briggs was 'awfully cut up'.

Earlier in the season the MCC benefit for Mordecai Sherwin also finished in less than two days. Poor Mordecai – two years later when he took the Notts versus Cambridge University fixture for his benefit from the county the attendance was so poor that he made nothing. The most extreme case of a benefit being over quickly appears to have been the MCC benefit in 1887 for Walter Price when the North met the South. In less than seven hours 34 wickets fell for only 288 runs and the game finished on the first afternoon! This was a poor reward for Price who had joined the Lord's staff in 1868 and remained there until his death 26 years later.

To avoid such calamities players began to insure the gate receipts. Sadly, Somerset and England's Len Braund failed to take this precaution in 1908; the match was washed out and he collected nothing. A desperate Braund even tried to dry the pitch with blankets brought from the hotel he kept near the Taunton ground. The other procedure which was increasingly adopted was to pre-sell tickets, usually offering the incentive of a three-day ticket for the price of two days.

The players were further disadvantaged by sometimes being given one of the less lucrative matches. During the 1890s the choice of game began to be restricted by a number of county Committees. For example, Surrey specified that neither George Lohmann in 1896 nor Tom Richardson in 1899 could have the Bank Holiday fixture; after 1902 Lancashire withdrew the Yorkshire Bank Holiday match; Kent excluded Canterbury week games and from 1892 to 1894 Notts decided that benefit matches would be outside the county programme, consequently Alfred Shaw's 1892 benefit featured Notts and Lord Sheffield's XI.

Nor was the beneficiary always allowed all the gate receipts. In 1895 Surrey gave Bobby Abel the Yorkshire fixture, but specified that the revenue from the stands would not be included. Abel wrote the Committee a plaintive appeal asking them 'to brake (sic) your rule and give me the stand money'. He continued by reminding them of his past services, the needs of his wife and six children and that during the same season there was going to be a testimonial for Walter Read. The Committee remained unmoved: 'the stand money could not be granted'.

Despite all these limitations a good benefit could be a great financial bonus for a player. Table 6 provides the results of many of the benefits from 1881 until 1911. Assuming reasonable weather and three days play, a Lancashire, Surrey or Yorkshire professional would expect to make at least £1000. From 1890 the average amount raised at those counties was £2080, £895 and £1888 respectively.

George Hirst's benefit in 1904 netted £3703 which was the highest sum made prior to the First World War. During the first three days of August 78,792, spectators paid to see the roses match. Total receipts for Hirst's benefit fund exceeded £4887 of which gate receipts made up £2879, subscriptions contributed £1442, ground collections added a further £103 and the county club donated £432 (15 per cent of the gate receipts). The expenditure for which Hirst was responsible totalled £1185, including £270 for the Yorkshire team's expenses at Leeds and Manchester, a 25 per cent ground commission of £720, insurance £116 and the printing, advertising and stationary costs of £79.

In terms of the beneficiary's income the subscription list was often as significant as the match gate receipts. The list was headed by the county and apart from Yorkshire, who donated 15 per cent of the gate receipts, took the form of a specific sum – in the case of Lancashire and Surrey £50. A healthy subscription list might provide some compensation if weather interfered with the game. In 1895 Wilfred Flowers netted only £64 from the Notts versus Lancashire fixture but a further £350 was generated by subscriptions. Similarly in 1910 Warwickshire's Walter Quaife netted a mere £6 from his benefit game but £335 was raised in subscriptions. Nevertheless, it was a poor return for a player capped seven times by England, who represented Warwickshire on 665 occasions and hit 1000 runs in 24 seasons. One of the reasons a beneficiary's expenditure could match or exceed his income from the game was because the county deducted their expenses for the match in question and the return encounter.

A shilling fund became an increasingly popular method of raising money for the beneficiary from the general public and was usually arranged under the auspices of a local newspaper. Of the £1442 subscribed to Hirst's benefit fund £147 came from the *Leeds Daily News* shilling fund. Smaller contributions were also often made. For example in 1897, for the benefit of the Essex fast bowler Henry Pickett, hundreds of local schoolboys dug into their pockets. A penny subscription launched by some Essex schoolboys realised a handsome clock, while the boys of Leyton and East Ham donated half-pennies and presented their hero with a minature set of stumps, bat and ball in gold and silver. Pickett, who took 10 for 32 in Leicestershire's first innings in 1895, was yet another player to die tragically. On 27 September 1907 he disappeared; a week later his body was found on Aberavon beach but it was not identified until the end of December.

The most widely acclaimed Surrey professional prior to 1900 was the incomparable George Lohmann. In seven successive seasons from 1886 Lohmann took more than 150 wickets including 209 in 1888 (average 10.90), 202 in 1889 (average 13.43) and 220 in 1890 (average 13.62). In an article in *Wisden* in 1889 Lohmann explained that the essence of his bowling was 'good length, break, a tendency to rear up quickly from the pitch, and a deceptive delivery'. He continued that the last-mentioned feature was the most important – 'surprise is usually the fatal one'.

George Lohmann could command a place in the Surrey side as a bowler, but as the white marble gravestone paid for by his county colleagues states, he was also 'a splendid fielder and a resolute batsman'. Lohmann's pre-eminent status was put into verse and recorded in the 1894 edition of *Cricket Songs*. The first lines read:

When Surrey ladled out defeat,
Who did it?
When Notts and Yorkshire and Kent were beat
Who did it?
Lohmann did – George Lohmann –
Something like a yeoman,
Neither fast nor slow man,
George!

On 30 July 1896 Surrey met Yorkshire for Lohmann's benefit; *Cricket* set the scene:

> So much importance was attached to this match, and so popular is Lohmann, that a crowd far greater than that which had attended the match between Surrey and the

Australians went to the Oval on Thursday. Fortunately for Lohmann the match lasted well into the third day, and altogether some 33,000 people paid for admission.

As early as November 1894 the Surrey Committee had agreed to Lohmann having a benefit in 1896 and the minutes record that they would be 'glad to give him the match between England and Australia'. The following July, with Lohmann suffering the effects of consumption which eventually took his life, the Committee stated he could have any county match except the Bank Holiday fixture. As usual in 1896 that match was against Notts and 28,000 attended on the Bank Holiday Monday.

Gate receipts from the Yorkshire match, which Surrey won by an innings and 61 runs, totalled almost £812, but after the deduction of expenses at the Oval and the corresponding 'out' fixture in Bradford, George netted £625. The Committee headed the subscription list with £50.

Such was George's popularity that a number of other collections were organised on his behalf. James Logan, the well-known South African cricket patron from Matjiesfontein in Cape Province, gathered £25 from the passengers on the *Norman* en route to London, while Charles Pond, George's step-brother, handed over £100 after his performance of Othello at Covent Garden. At this time George's elder brother Stewart, a former solicitor's clerk, was a professional in the United States with Staten Island. Previously he had been professional with the South Shields Club in County Durham. In 1898 Stewart Lohmann abandoned professional cricket to seek his fortune in the Klondike gold fields.

George Lohmann's benefit totalled about £1000 which must have been disappointing for a player of his stature. Five years later, on 1 December 1901, George Lohmann died of consumption aged 36. Since October 1892 he had been spending as much time as possible in South Africa's dry climate in an effort to throw off the disease and it was there, near Matjiesfontein, that he died and is buried.

Table 6: Selected benefit returns, 1881-1911 (amateur testimonials in italics)

	Lancashire		Notts		Surrey		Yorkshire		Leicestershire (L) Warwickshire (W)	
1881	McIntyre	1000			Jupp	450				
1882			Oscroft	622			Lockwood	591		
1883					Pooley	500				
1884			Shaw J	460			Hill	376		
1885	Watson	1102			Humphrey R	81				
1886	Barlow	1000								
1887			Selby	184			Ulyett	1000		
1888							Emmett	620		
1889	Pilling	1600					Bates	1000	Rylott (L)	125
1890			Wild	270			Hall	570		
1891										
1892			Shaw A	130						
1893			Shrewsbury	600	Read M	1200				
1894	Briggs	n/a	Barnes	350	Wood	450	Peel	2000		
1895			Flowers	457	Abel	621			Shilton (W)	415
					Read W	829				
1896			Sherwin	0	Lohmann	1000+				
1897	Sugg	n/a	Gunn	730	Henderson	798	Hunter	1975		
1898	Baker	1900	Attewell	1000			Wainwright	1800		
1899					Richardson	1000			Law (W)	380
1900	Mold	2100	Shrewsbury	300	Brockwell	490	Moorhouse	500+	Pougher (L)	228
1901					Lockwood	1000+	Brown	2282	Lilley (W)	850
1902	Ward	1718			Hayward	700+			Whiteside (L)	430
1903			Gunn	300	Abel	464	Tunnicliffe	1750	Woodcock (L)	0
1904							Hirst	3703		
1905	*MacLaren*	1000+								
1906	Tyldesley	3000+			Lees	1750			Knight (L)	471
1907			*Jones*	1578	Holland	1202	Denton	1916	Devey (W)	406
1908					Hayes	1264	*Hawke*	1843		
1909					Hayward	383	Haigh	2071	Santall (W)	400
1910	Sharpe	1680							Quaife W G (W)	341
1911					Strudwick	1216	Rhodes	2200		

The figures in Table 6 indicate the stark contrast between the fortunes of leading professionals with counties like Yorkshire and their less fortunate brothers employed by the newer and poorer first-class counties such as Leicestershire and Warwickshire. Among the Leicestershire beneficiaries are Dick Pougher who made his county debut in 1885 and carried the burden of the county's bowling until 1901, but who will always be remembered for the sensational spell of bowling for the MCC against the Australians in 1896 when in three overs he captured five wickets without conceding a run as the tourists were dismissed for 18!; or Arthur Woodcock who for many years was considered one of the fastest bowlers in England, but who poisoned himself in 1910; or A. E. Knight, a Methodist lay preacher, who held the batting together prior to the First World War. In *A History of Leicestershire Cricket* E. E. Snow comments that Knight was 'widely read and a keen student of the classics'.

None of this trio could have been satisfied with the outcome of their benefits, but their plight was typical of leading professionals – even England players – employed by the lesser first-class counties. The two-year residential qualification was a strong disincentive against such players moving elsewhere to maximise their earnings, but that commitment to their county could never be adequately rewarded.

Table 7: Nottinghamshire professionals' benefits, 1885-99

Player	Amt (£)	No. of seasons prior to benefit	Deferred payment per season (£)
Selby	184	17	10.82
Wild	270	22	12.27
Shaw (Alfred)	130	28	4.64
Shrewsbury	600	18	33.33
Barnes	350	19	18.42
Flowers	457	18	25.38
Sherwin	0	20	0
Gunn	730	17	42.94
Attewell	1000	17	58.82
Average	413	19	21.14

Nottinghamshire, despite their on-field successes, was a less affluent club than Lancashire, Surrey and Yorkshire and this is reflected in the benefit figures given in Table 7. Two general points are worth noting. First, these nine well-known players had to wait on average 19 years for a benefit, not the usual 10 years. And second, the information shows that a benefit as a form of deferred payment represented a very poor return for the professionals. An average of £21 per season for such an illustrious list does not do them justice. John Selby's situation was exacerbated when he was declared a bankrupt in 1887 and the official receiver claimed all his benefit money. Ten years later *Cricket* wrote that William Gunn's benefit was 'a very inadequate return for the great services "the Agamemnon of the North" has rendered his county'. The Notts Committee recognised this failing and in the cases of Gunn and Shrewsbury allocated them second benefit matches.

The most notable absentee from the Notts list is William Scotton, who made his county debut in 1875, but had not received a benefit by the time he committed suicide in 1893, three years after his last game for the county.

BENEFIT PATERNALISM

In his biography of Wilfred Rhodes, Sidney Rogerson comments:

> To the end of his days he never stopped 'chuntering' about the unfairness of talent money as it was awarded, or the closeness of the Yorkshire County Club in the matter of the proceeds from benefit matches or testimonials. He would never subscribe to the Yorkshire Club's claim to treat their professionals generously.

Wilfred Rhodes considered it a 'scandal' that the proceeds from a player's benefit were 'never the property of the player again . . . At his death it will be paid to his nearest relation or to whomever he may will it'. Rhodes quoted the case of Schofield Haigh's widow who wanted to use some of her husband's benefit money to buy a cottage. The Yorkshire Committee refused and instead lent her £250 and charged her interest; Rhodes concluded 'I can't think this was right . . . I expect it was one of Lord Hawke's ideas.'

In 1899, at a meeting of county representatives at Lord's, Lord Hawke successfully proposed that 'counties should reserve direct control over the investment and disposal of all benefit monies'. Three years later, in line with this decision, the Yorkshire Committee decided that only one-third of the benefit proceeds would be given to the player and that the remaining two-thirds would be held for the player's wife and children in a 'trust to terminate with the death of his widow'. At the same meeting the Committee also agreed that they would guarantee that the net sum from a Yorkshire benefit would never be less than £1000.

From 1902 Surrey also began to invest the players' benefit monies on their behalf. That year they purchased £1000 of debenture stock in the Mexican Railways for William Lockwood. Nine years later the Committee addressed the issue of making an Oval benefit a more financially secure event. The Committee proposed that in future the Club would keep all of the gate receipts from the player's benefit match, but in return guarantee a payment of £500 plus the usual £50 donation at the head of the subscription list. The Club had calculated that between 1901 and 1910 the average return to the beneficiaries in gate receipts had been £530. Under this new system the Club would lose financially because they would be responsible for additional match expenses, but they recognised that the inclement climate added an 'unfair' dimension to the 'deserving' professional's benefit and that this new system might save the player from 'much anxiety and so temporary loss of form in a benefit year'.

As with most questions of money involving the players, the issue of authority and control emerged in the Committee's discussions. The minutes record that if the Club could guarantee a player £500 it 'would place the Committee in an even stronger position as regards dealing with the professionals'.

This paternalistic attitude, promoted by Lord Hawke, stemmed from a fear that a professional cricketer was unable to organise his own financial affairs and might waste, gamble or drink away his benefit. From the players' point of view it seemed unacceptable that money given to them should not be theirs to dispose of as they pleased. Further, it seems inconceivable that the beneficiary could not have been given the money as well as some sound advice about managing and investing it.

THE NOTTS BENEFIT FUND

The only significant benefit innovation prior to the First World War occurred in 1908 when the Notts Committee established a Benefit Fund. Rather than organising an annual benefit for one particular player it was decided to open a six-year fund and in 1913 to divide the proceeds between six players (George Gunn, John Gunn, Albert Hallam, James Iremonger, Thomas Oates and 'Topsy' Wass). The Committee agreed that each year they would contribute £300, or half the gate receipts of the Whitsun fixture against Surrey, whichever proved to be the greater sum.

When the Fund was distributed each of the six received £506 which although not significantly higher than the average Notts benefit in the 1890s, proved a more equitable arrangement in that no player was discriminated against due to the uncertainties of the weather or a match that was concluded in less than three days. However, a 'star' professional might have felt he was subsidising his less-talented team-mates. The Benefit Fund was not resuscitated by Nottinghamshire after the War; in 1920 they awarded Joe Hardstaff a traditional benefit game.

AFTER THE GAME

Many Victorian professionals had previously been skilled workers, or at least served some years of an apprenticeship, but very few returned to their original trade. In that respect Sydney Barnes was only partly correct when he commented in his biography written by Leslie Duckworth that players:

> . . . after fleeting years as famous cricketers, fêted and fussed, dropped out, returned to the mine or factory, or, at best, took a fourth-rate beerhouse, trading as best they could upon their faded glories.

Taking a public house was the most popular course after a professional's career ended. While many of these establishments were 'fourth-rate', nevertheless, as Patrick Joyce noted in *Work, Society and Politics*, 'the drinkseller had his own local fame and standing' and was 'a leader of street and neighbourhood opinion' in Victorian northern England.

Information on players after they left the game is not easy to obtain, however data is available on many of the Notts professionals who represented the county between 1835 and 1914. Only seven occupations were listed – 35 players became publicans, 24 umpires, 19 coaches, 10 ran sports goods' manufacturers or retailers, nine were groundsmen, two opened off-licences and one became a cinema proprietor.

A similar pattern emerges from details gathered on players throughout England who were born prior to 1837 (the accession of Queen Victoria) and who played between 1850 and 1870. Of those 60 professionals 25 became publicans, nine coaches, six groundsmen, four umpires, four sports outfitters, three opened shops and two worked as batmakers. There were also individual cases of a bank actuary, a laceworker, a lodging-house keeper, a coffee-shop owner, a labourer, a tobacconist and a stationary-engine driver.

From these two surveys a number of conclusions can be drawn. First, players used their cricketing success as a means to avoid returning to the discipline and anonymity of factory life. Second, they retained a connection with cricket and presumably used contacts made while playing to secure employment in jobs such as school coaches. And third, their principal asset was their name and sporting reputation.

As the 19th century progressed and cricket became even more popular, players increasingly began to open athletic and cricket outfitters or traded as bat and ball manufacturers. Richard Daft pioneered that course when he opened his sports emporium in 1873 in Lister Gate, Nottingham. Nine years later, when Shaw and Shrewsbury had opened their doors, followed in 1885 by William Gunn and T. J. Moore, a former Daft employee, Nottingham boasted three sports outfitters and manufacturers – all owned by renowned cricketers.

During the 1880s and 1890s several Lancashire professionals established retail outlets in various cities and towns in the county. Johnny Briggs, in partnership with Richard Pilling and then Pilling's widow, and Alec Watson, both opened shops in Manchester, Albert Ward in Bolton, George Baker in Bury, R. G. Barlow in Blackpool and Frank Sugg in Liverpool. In 1922 Sugg's advert in the *Cricketer* listed eight shops, including two in the Netherlands.

Many of the Yorkshire players from this era found positions as school coaches. John Tunnicliffe went to Clifton, Tom Emmett to Rugby, Louis Hall to Uppingham, Robert Moorhouse to Sedbergh, Joseph Mounsey to Charterhouse and Schofield Haigh to Winchester. This situation continued well into the twentieth century. From 1921 George Hirst was employed at Eton, that year too David Denton was forced by spinal trouble to turn down a seven-year contract at Haileybury; while in the 1930s Wilfred Rhodes coached at Harrow.

From the great Surrey side of the 1890s George Lohmann, living in South Africa, worked for the Johanessburg Waterworks as well as coaching variously with the Cape Town Club, Western Province and the Wanderers. Bobby Abel ran a bat and ball manufacturing business and a sports outfitters. William Lockwood coached at Westminster and for two years from 1925 at Denstone before his health broke down. Ernie Hayes eventually found similar work at Winchester and after the First World War with Leicestershire. Tom Bowley coached at Sherborne and Fred Holland with

Oundle. Tom Richardson became a publican in Bath and subsequently in Richmond. Maurice Read announced his premature retirement to go into service with Sir Henry Tichborne – *Cricket* commented that he was 'wisely making provision for regular employment'. *Cricket* also reported that all cricket-lovers at the Oval were delighted to learn that after his benefit in 1897 Robert Henderson had been employed by Lord Harris in the Consolidated Gold Fields office in the City.

HOW THE MIGHTY ARE FALLEN

Lord Hawke was always keen to claim that 'his' Yorkshire professionals were well cared for by the county Club. While that may be true of the professionals who appeared in the great Yorkshire elevens from the 1890s onwards, the same cannot be said of those players who represented the county in the previous three decades.

A. W. Pullin (Old Ebor) completed his *Talks with Old Yorkshire Cricketers* in 1898. Having tracked down and interviewed more than a dozen notable veterans he was forced to conclude that:

> The position in which a few of Yorkshire's old cricketers were found in the search for these interviews was not an agreeable testimony to the influence of cricket itself upon the fortunes of those who adopted it as a profession.

Pullin continued that some players had been 'cast aside like an old shoe' and 'sunk into oblivion, and even poverty'.

John Thewlis was the most tragic case. Eventually Pullin found him living in Failsworth, near Manchester, aged 70, going blind and toothless, but still having to work carrying 'a heavy basket of laundry clothes' many miles every day. After Pullin's article appeared in the *Yorkshire Post* Thewlis was offered the job of groundsman with the Greenfield Club and Lord Hawke arranged for him to receive a winter allowance from the county. Thewlis, formerly a handloom weaver from Lascelles Hall and part of a prodigious, extended cricketing family, had appeared 46 times for Yorkshire between 1862 and 1875 and is credited with hitting the

George Anderson

John Jackson

first 'official' century for the county when he made 104 against Surrey in 1868.

Luke Greenwood, another handloom weaver from Lascelles Hall, was discovered by Pullin 'sadly down on his luck'. An appeal in the *Yorkshire Post* in 1896 raised £50. A similar appeal had been launched in November 1894 via the pages of *Cricket* for George Anderson who 'after 21 years of service as Actuary of the Bedale Savings' Bank at the modest salary of £90, finds himself stranded at the age of 69, through the closing of the bank.' Anderson had represented Yorkshire from 1851-71, played for the All-England Eleven for 21 seasons and toured Australia in 1863-64. Ned Stephenson had been one of the pioneers on the first Australian tour in 1861-62. Ned was a colleague of George Anderson's in the All-England and Yorkshire elevens, but after his death in 1898 *Wisden* recorded that he passed away in 'very poor circumstances'.

Obviously not every Yorkshire professional from the period prior to the so-called golden age lived out his life in poverty. George Freeman, described in *Cricket* as the 'finest fast bowler of his generation', established a thriving auctioneers in Thirsk in 1869, in partnership with a Mr Boulton. Two years later he became secretary of the Thirsk Agricultural Society and when he was interviewed by the Rev. Holmes for *Cricket* in 1895, he was living in a house with five acres of grounds, but, as he commented, his 'fortunes were not reaped' at cricket. Ephraim Lockwood, the premier Yorkshire batsman of the period was interviewed by the *Clarion* in 1892 in his 'handsome cricket material warehouse', while 'Happy Jack' Ulyett, an ex-pitman who played 350 times for Yorkshire, became a successful publican and left £1064 in his will.

Pullin's research exposed the reality that before the turn of the century the Yorkshire Committee paid scant attention to the fate of their former employees. They were not alone. After the death of John Jackson, Frank Sugg, the former England, Yorkshire, Derbyshire and Lancashire professional commented bitterly that the 'Notts County Com-

William Martingell

mittee chose to entirely forget one who has rendered yeoman service'. At the time Sugg was appealing for donations so that Jackson's grave would not 'remain unmarked'.

John Jackson's sad demise is well documented in Pullin's companion volume *Talks with Old English Cricketers*. The fast bowling of 'The Demon' Jackson was legendary from 1855 to 1870. One unknown aspiring poet wrote of a Jackson over:

The first ball hit me on the hand,
The next I played in doubt;
The third ball smashed my finger,
And the fourth ball bowled me out!

The illegitimate John Jackson was born in Bungay, Suffolk but raised in Nottinghamshire. According to Richard Daft he learnt how to bowl by practising with stones using a milestone for a wicket. Jackson's professional career blossomed from 1850 with engagements at Southwell, Newark, Ipswich and the Grange Club in Edinburgh. It is apparent from Daft's various memoirs that John Jackson was something of a character who 'often got into scrapes' and insisted on being paid in 'hard cash' rather than notes. After being injured while playing for Notts, Jackson retired from county cricket in 1866, although he continued to represent All-England until 1870. This was followed by a series of professional engagements, the last of which was for three years with Birkenhead Grammar School. Subsequently Jackson could only find work as a labourer; a cricket professional all his life, he had no other trade.

When Pullin found Jackson he was 67 and living in Liverpool on five shillings and sixpence per week from the Cricketers' Fund Friendly Society. He had no permanent address and was close to the workhouse. In fact the latter proved to be his final abode. He died in the Liverpool workhouse infirmary as a pauper in 1901; his estate was valued at £15. Ten years earlier W. G. Grace in his autobiography had described John Jackson as 'one of our great bowlers'.

The Surrey Committee, which generally exhibited a most benevolent attitude towards its professionals, was also capable of lapses. William Martingell, who had been the first ground bowler at the Oval in April 1846, represented Surrey between 1839 and 1859 and acted as a professional at Eton for many years, found himself 'in a state of great destitution' in 1883. An appeal was launched via *Cricket*; Surrey contributed £10. On his death 14 years later Lord Harris, who knew 'Granny' Martingell from his Eton days, made a further appeal on behalf of Mrs Martingell who had been left in 'very straitened circumstances'.

William Martingell played in the first All-England Eleven match in 1846. A few seasons later Julius Caesar, another Surrey player, had established a regular position in the itinerant eleven. 'Julie's' batting style was described in *Surrey Cricket*:

> He was a man of smaller proportions, but a steady, sturdy cricketer of the best type. A most difficult man to get out, he showed to the front when runs were wanted, and had a knack of frequently bringing off a good leg hit, which was more in vogue then when the 'glance' had not been invented.

Apart from All-England, Julius Caesar also played with the United England Eleven and the United South of England Eleven, he toured North America in 1859 and Australia in 1863-64 and represented Surrey until 1867. 'Julie' took great pride in his personal appearance and Richard Daft recalled that he always travelled with a huge portmanteau and a hat box.

Eleven years after his retirement Julius Caesar was found dead at the Railway Tavern in Godalming. His final years had been spent in the depths of poverty. The only representatives of the cricket world at his funeral were three former Surrey professionals. This was a sad finale for a man who was always considered the life and soul of the county eleven.

1878 also marked the death of Thomas Humphrey, another notable Surrey professional. Known as the 'Pocket Hercules' Humphrey's name was often associated with Harry Jupp. In *Surrey Cricket* Charles Alcock writes that they created 'a sensation' with 'their bright and attractive cricket, their long partnerships, by their speed between the wickets'. Despite a benefit in 1876 which netted Thomas Humphrey £300, he died two years later, aged 39, in the Brookwood Asylum of congestion of the lungs.

Thomas Humphrey was one of three brothers who represented Surrey during the 1860s and 1870s. Richard Humphrey, a former plumber, made 145 appearances for the county between 1870 and 1881. His benefit match in 1885 was a financial failure. The Surrey Committee donated 20 guineas; three months later they gave the 'amateur' W. W. Read a wedding present of £250 plus a clock worth £16. From 1883 to 1889 Richard Humphrey was employed as the coach at Clifton College, but in November 1890 the Surrey Committee voted him £10 in relief and the following August began paying him a weekly six shillings. In October 1894 the Committee decided that this grant would cease at the end of the year, despite the fact that the Annual Report stated that 'the finances of the Club are in a very satisfactory state' with more than £10,000 invested in stocks. On 28 February 1906, aged 57, Richard Humphrey drowned in the River Thames after living in very poor circumstances for several years. The *Wisden* obituary concluded that 'no doubt his mind became unhinged', a euphemism for suicide.

Edward Pooley was a contemporary of Thomas and Richard Humphrey and his story is no less tragic. Playing for Surrey from 1861 to 1883 Pooley was generally considered the best wicket-keeper in England. In four consecutive matches for Surrey in 1868 he held 16 catches and completed 16 stumpings. This sequence included the Sussex fixture at the Oval when he established the record of 12 dismissals in a match. From such heights Edward Pooley's life fell apart and Sir Home Gordon wrote in the *Badminton Magazine*, 'to see him in shabby clothes, with grizzly-white hair, and a strained, sordid appearance, gazing at the Oval on the scene of his former triumphs, was pitiable.'

Pooley's relationship with the Surrey Committee had never been incident-free. In 1873 he was suspended due to 'disgraceful conduct' in the Yorkshire match in Sheffield. According to the Club minutes Pooley was charged with not trying to win the game, betting against his side and using abusive language to his captain. In his defence he pleaded that he was 'unwell' and 'out of sorts', 'sincerely' apologised for 'using coarse language' and did admit to taking 'one bet of five shillings to half a crown that five Yorkshire players would not get seventy runs', but he rejected the implication that he had sold the match.

The United South of England Eleven also suspended Pooley and his livelihood as a professional cricketer was in jeopardy. To no avail he wrote to the Surrey Committee urging them to 'reconsider a judgement that takes the bread out of my mouth and family' and added that 'it is impossible for me to enter any new business with confidence or credit with a cloud hanging over me'. Six other professionals, including the Humphreys and Jupp, pleaded that they were 'happy to play with him again', but the Committee remained unmoved. Finally, in February 1874, Pooley was 'summoned before the Committee' and reinstated.

In 1881, 20 years after his debut, the Surrey Committee agreed to Pooley's request for a benefit match. It occurred two years later and netted around £500, including £25 from the Club. Prior to it *Wisden* recorded, 'no professional is more popular . . . no man better deserves three days of splendid weather'. However, by March 1885 the Surrey minutes note that Pooley was soliciting for work and five years later the Club was paying him a weekly allowance of 15 shillings, although that was discontinued at the end of 1894.

In 1880 Edward Pooley found work in a billiard saloon in Clapham, eight years later he was a groundsman, by 1890 a timekeeper on a building site and finally in 1898 sought relief in the workhouse. That year the press mistakenly printed his obituary; he lived for a further nine years before dying in the Lambeth workhouse infirmary. In an interview with Pullin, Pooley remarked 'it was the workhouse, sir, or the river'.

Wisden claimed Pooley's difficulties arose from 'faults of private character', while *Cricket* stated that he 'had only himself to blame for his misfortunes'. But in the years prior to the First World War, with its dominant laissez-faire attitudes, and in the absence of the welfare provisions which can now be taken for granted, formerly great professionals, such as Pooley, could end their lives in desperate circumstances. Clubs such as Surrey, which made their wealth through the drawing-power of players such as Pooley, have to accept some of the responsibility.

The sad demise of William Brockwell, a member of the great Surrey eleven of the 1890s, has been well documented in James Coldham's pamphlet *William Brockwell – His Triumph and Tragedy*. William Brockwell was the nephew of the old Surrey professional George Brockwell and was born in Kingston-on-Thames where his father was a blacksmith and his mother a woman of some substance. Coldham writes that 'Brockie' was 'known for his immaculate attire, hat box and dandyism, and as a frequenter of London's theatres'. Undoubtedly 1894, when he topped the first-class batting averages, was his best season, while between 1893 and 1899 he represented England on seven occasions.

At the turn of the century William Brockwell was a leading professional and the owner of four cottages, although he lacked a trade. By 1915 the properties had been sold and five years later *Sporting Life* ran an appeal on his behalf. He then had a number of jobs including that of groundsman at the Sundridge Park Golf Club. In *Background of Cricket* Sir Home Gordon recounts being shown a 'partially roofless hovel' in which Brockwell lived. J. T. Hearne was the only first-class cricketer to attend his funeral in 1935.

William Brockwell's case epitomises the plight of the professional with neither trade nor provision for later life. Once his playing days were finished he quickly faded from view and was forgotten.

The 10 cases quoted in the preceding pages were not exceptional and there are numerous other examples. In 1890 an appeal was launched for Cris Tinley, the great All-

England lob bowler, who had become an invalid, while such renowned players as Sam Biddulph, Sam Dakin, Alfred Diver (all three died in 1876), Tom Hunt and George Davidson (the mainstay of the Derbyshire side in the 1890s) died leaving their wives and families impoverished. In 1906 *Cricket* reported the situation of Henry Stubberfield who at 71 was 'in serious trouble' being unable to find work despite being strong and well. 'Stubber's' wife had been sent to the asylum. Henry Stubberfield, having declined to join All-England, played for Sussex and took a wicket with his first ball in county cricket. He earned a fine reputation as a schools' coach, but in later life returned to his trade as a carpenter.

Tom Box was the best professional wicket-keeper of his day but died in 1876 a fallen man while working the score board at Prince's cricket ground. Tom Plumb, a wicket-keeper who was invariably compared in the 1860s and 1870s with George Pinder of Yorkshire and Edward Pooley of Surrey, after years of poverty died in 1905 in the Northampton workhouse.

William McIntyre, the Lancashire bowler who headed the first-class averages in 1872, 1873 and 1876, died in the Prestwich Asylum. Four years earlier, in 1888, his brother Michael, who played for Notts, died in the Nottingham workhouse. John Crossland was another Notts-born bowler who proved a great asset for Lancashire. According to the Committee minutes in 1894 he was 'in very poor circumstances' and was given two £5 donations. When Crossland died of pneumonia in 1903 Lancashire paid for the funeral as Surrey had for Harry Jupp 14 years earlier. The Warwickshire professional John Shilton died, according to his biographer, 'virtually a pauper, despised by his wife and daughter, friendless and almost unmourned', in 1899.

Richard Humphrey was not the only player whose eventual desperate circumstances led to suicide. George Griffith, known at the Oval as 'Big Ben', took this course in 1879, as did William Scotton, the famous Notts stonewaller, 14 years later. Scotton became depressed after losing his

Arthur Shrewsbury

place in the county side. Arthur Shrewsbury, who went to school with Scotton, shot himself in 1903 under the mistaken belief that he was suffering from an incurable disease. Seven years later Arthur Woodwock, the Leicestershire fast bowler, died of self-administered poison, while in 1914 the legendary big-hitter Albert Trott, in failing health and poverty, shot himself. 'Alberto' left his few remaining possessions to his Willesden landlady.

'When the popular applause dies away, how often indeed the old cricketer is forgotten', commented the *Evening Standard* in 1907. The London paper advocated establishing a 'Home for Aged Cricketers' that is 'a national asylum for the decayed professional'. And where better to locate this 'memorial' than Hambledon. Nothing came of this proposal.

CHAPTER 7

The Disguised Professional

'NICE customs curtsey to great kings' was how *Wisden* in 1897 explained away the substantial and widely-known payments to W. G. Grace. They were considered 'anomalous'.

Ten years later Sir Home Gordon, writing in the *National Review,* took up 'the amateur question' in more forceful terms:

> The case of Dr W. G. Grace became an accepted anachronism and that of the late Mr W. W. Read was also treated as a thing apart. For those two then there are probably a score today, and the matter is euphemistically cloaked under the guise of 'expenses', the item for washing alone being on occasion preposterous.

These were not new revelations. In the 1878 edition of *John Lillywhite's Cricket Companion* Frederick Gale had criticised the 'gentlemen professionals' who posed as amateurs. During the 1890s the Rev. Holmes, through the pages of *Cricket,* had occasionally drawn attention to the matter. In 1893 he criticised the 'idiotic class barriers' which ensure there are 'amateur-professionals' or 'highly paid pros who pose as amateurs'. Two years later he attacked 'the snobbishness of the disguised professional'.

Joe Darling captained Australia on 18 occasions, toured England four times between 1896 and 1905 and was subsequently elected as an Independent in the Tasmanian Legislative Council. In 1926 he stated that 'very few of the amateurs in England in my time – or today – were amateurs. They were highly paid professionals.' Darling cites Grace, Stoddart, MacLaren, Jones and Jessop as the prime offenders.

It is clear in retrospect that for many years the MCC and the county Committees either turned a blind eye to the amateurs' remunerations or were directly party to contravening the ethics of the game as they claimed it should be played.

W. G. GRACE

Examples of Grace's earnings from cricket are well-documented. In Eric Midwinter's biography of the 'Old Man' it is estimated that he grossed £120,000 from cricket.

For the 1873-74 tour to Australia Grace was paid £1500 or 10 times the amount each professional received, yet the party included such talented professionals as Harry Jupp, Richard Humphrey and William Oscroft. Eighteen years later Lord Sheffield obliged with a fee of £3000, generous expenses and a locum for Grace's medical practice for the tour of Australia. Lord Sheffield lost £2000 on the 1891-92 tour, in part, according to Alfred Shaw, because of the captain's 'princely fee'. Arthur Shrewsbury, through the intermediary of his business partner Shaw, had given pre-tour financial advice to Lord Sheffield, but on being told he had substantially underestimated the tour costs he wrote:

> I didn't know that Lord Sheffield had to pay for Grace's wife and family expenses in Australia. I thought he had repudiated that before leaving England. If he hadn't taken Grace out, Lord Sheffield would have been £3000 better off at the end of the tour, and also had a better team.

As secretary-captain of London county from 1900-04, Grace received an annual payment of £600 which was virtually double the earnings of the best paid professionals, despite his being well past his best by this time. The most blatant examples of payments to Grace were his two testimonials. The first, in 1879, raised £1458. The MCC hoped that the money would be used by Grace to buy a medical practice. The second, in 1895, was much more substantial. It totalled almost £9000. The *Daily Telegraph*'s 'National Shilling Fund' accounted for more than £4000, the *Sportsman* and the MCC contributed £3000 and Gloucestershire a further £1500. In *Background to Cricket* Sir Home Gordon claims that 'a substantial portion went to pay his betting debts'. Before the turn of the century the highest sum ever achieved in a player's benefit was £2000 for Bobby Peel in 1894.

W. W. READ

Although always regarded as an amateur, Walter Read was the best paid pre-War Surrey cricketer. Until 1897 he held the nominal position of assistant secretary at the Oval with a salary package as follows:

* £150 per annum,
* a railway season ticket to and from the Oval,
* four guineas per match,
* an annual bonus of £100, albeit proportional to the number of matches he played.

In September 1896 the Committee proposed to end the arrangement. Read replied that he was 'at a loss to understand why' and countered by suggesting that his engagement continue until 31 December 1897. The Committee agreed and paid him off with £400 with the provisos, which he accepted, that he had no claim whatsoever on the job of assistant secretary and that he undertook to play in the Surrey first eleven fixtures in 1897.

It is obvious from the Surrey minutes and correspondence that there was never any question of Read working as assitant secretary. The payments to Read clearly contravened the MCC definition of an amateur, that 'no gentlemen ought to make a profit from his services on the cricket field'.

Walter Read was born in Reigate in November 1855. His father kept a school and the youthful Read worked as an assistant master. He made his debut for Surrey in 1873 but it was not until he became assistant secretary in 1881 that he appeared regularly for the county. And as Altham and Swanton state in *A History of Cricket*, Walter Read was 'the greatest run-getter in the county's history up till that date, and probably the finest batsman that had appeared in its ranks since William Beldham.' Undoubtedly the revival of Surrey's fortunes in the 1880s were due to the batting of Read and the brilliant all-round skills of George Lohmann.

The Oval Committee was keen to retain Read's services and gifts were lavished on him. In 1883 after his successful tour of Australia, for which the press claimed he had been paid £1000, Surrey members presented him with 250 guineas and an address on vellum; two years later he received £250 and a clock as wedding presents; while from 1884 the annual £100 end-of-season bonus commenced. George Lohmann never received more than £50 as his end-of-season bonus.

In 1895 Read was given the Surrey versus England match as a testimonial. It netted him £829, including £200 from the Club. The same year Bobby Abel's benefit raised £621, including 50 guineas from the county.

Walter Read retired in 1897 having scored 22,349 runs for Surrey. At the Club's Annual General Meeting three years later he stood for election to the Committee but finished last in the poll. However, by 1905 he was employed by the Club as cricket coach. His two rivals for the position were William Attewell of Notts and Walter Wright of Notts and Kent, both former professionals.

'Walla Walla', as he was affectionately known, died of pneumonia in January 1907. *Cricket*'s obituary echoed 'the regret universally felt for the loss of a cricketer of such unique and commanding abilities'. Later that year Lords Alverstone, Harris and Hawke, and Mr C. E. Green, launched an appeal on behalf of Read's widow and four children who were living on a 'small income'. A total of £157 was raised. Walter Read may have batted like an amateur and been considered one socially, but he was paid as a professional.

A. C. MACLAREN

In 1902 the cricket public was surprised to read that Archie MacLaren had resigned from Lancashire due to his wife's illness. MacLaren added that he would not be lost to cricket as under the residential qualification he would be available for Hampshire's home fixtures. Under the circumstances he was keen not to be 'away from home so much' and had accepted the position of 'assistant treasurer' with Hampshire.

The Lancashire minutes tell a different story. In March 1902 a special Committee meeting was convened solely to discuss the MacLaren question. It was agreed to offer Archie a five-year contract at £450 per annum but not the captaincy which went to Alexander Eccles. Further, the Committee expressed the 'strong hope' that MacLaren would move house and reside in Lancashire. Two months later the minutes record that Archie accepted the salary but insisted on being skipper. The Committee acceded and offered Eccles their gratitude and life membership.

This was not the first time that the Lancashire Committee had been forced to negotiate for MacLaren's services. In 1895, after it was announced Archie was taking up a position at a prep school, they offered him £60 for a 20-week season. By 1899 the figure had increased to £100 and in January 1900 the minutes state that 'the sum offered shall not exceed £400 per annum and that any agreement entered into shall not be of more than three years duration.' In 1900 Archie was allegedly assistant secretary and in 1902 cricket coach, although it was stipulated he must play in all first-class matches.

A. C. MacLaren, the most notable Lancashire amateur, was the only cricketer at Old Trafford honoured with a 'star' contract and it was worth twice the annual earnings of the club's leading professionals.

In *Fifty Years Reminiscences of a Non-Player* William Howard remembers MacLaren's 'egotistical manner' and his penchant for money-making schemes which never came to fruition. At one time he considered starting a bat-making business, but lacked the capital, while at another moment he thought about marketing inflatable leg-guards!

In 1903 MacLaren joined a firm of London wine merchants; five years later he was Ranji's secretary; in 1909 he was employed by a Manchester motor engineering business and in 1914 he became the editor of the doomed *World of Cricket* which made a heavy loss. After the War MacLaren found employment as cricket manager to the Australian stockbroker Lionel Robinson at Old Buckenham Hall, a 2000 acre estate near Norwich.

During the 1922 season MacLaren was employed by the Lancashire Club as coach for which he received a salary of £550 but four months prior to commencing his appointment he had received advances totalling £350. In August 1922 the Lancashire Committee voted by the narrow margin of seven to five to re-engage MacLaren, albeit on the reduced terms of £500, however the following May Archie accepted £105 to terminate the contract. The new cricket instructor appointed immediately was the leading professional batsman J. T. Tyldesley who was offered and accepted the salary of £300.

A. C. MacLaren's testimonial in 1906 grossed more than £1000. This included a donation of £250 from the Lancashire Committee. Apart from a hall clock and a diamond necklace for his wife Kathleen (née Power, the daughter of a wealthy director of the Australian Dalgety pastoral empire) Archie used the money to buy a car.

S. M. J. WOODS

Australian-born Sammy Woods was captain and secretary of Somerset from 1894 to 1906 on a salary of £200 per annum. After his retirement from first-class cricket he remained secretary until 1923. Sir Home Gordon, a good friend of Woods, commented that 'grey matter was not predominant in his powerful physique'. He recalled Woods telling him that 'there is one thing I have steadily tried to do: to drink more beer for the years I have lived than any other man who has ever come down from Cambridge.'

As in the case of the appointment of Mr V. F. S. Crawford as Leicestershire secretary in 1903, Somerset were keen that Woods would be in a position to play for the county on a permanent basis. In May 1907 Sammy Woods was rewarded with a testimonial which exceeded £1600.

C. P. MCGAHEY

'Cheerful Charlie' McGahey played 400 times for Essex from 1893 until 1921, captained the eleven from 1907 to 1910 and for some years euphemistically occupied the post of assistant secretary. According to *Scores and Biographies*, McGahey was a 'rough and ready hitter' who learnt his cricket in East London.

In March 1914 Essex dispatched a circular 'to promote a Testimonial Fund, the proceeds of which the Committee will invest or utilise for Mr McGahey's benefit'. From 1930 McGahey was employed as the county scorer. McGahey also played soccer for Tottenham Hotspur, Arsenal and Sheffield United and lived for many years at the Three Blackbirds public house in Leyton. Circumstantial evidence points to McGahey being a professional in amateur clothing.

J. J. FERRIS

Jack Ferris was one of the great Australian successes on the 1888 and 1890 tours of England. On those two trips the left-arm bowler captured 199 and 186 wickets respectively. During the 1890 tour he agreed to qualify by residence for Gloucestershire but immediately returned to Sydney. Gloucestershire, being short of good bowlers, were keen to expedite Ferris's qualification and rented a house in his name despite his absence in Australia. This ruse should have disqualified Ferris playing as an amateur but, as *Cricket* commented in 1891, nobody was 'so ungracious as to question Mr Ferris's position'.

In Sydney Ferris worked as a bank clerk in the same office as C. T. B. 'Terror' Turner and Percy McDonnell. In Bristol work was found for him with a firm of stockbrokers. For his adopted county Jack Ferris never recaptured his Australian form and in 1895, after 63 appearances, he returned home. He died in Durban during the Boer War where he served with the Imperial Light Horse.

M. P. BOWDEN

'Monty' Bowden represented Surrey in 72 matches between 1883 and 1888 as an amateur but in 1884 the Committee minutes record that his entrance fee to the Stock Exchange was to be paid by the Club; a maximum expenditure of £50 was set. In the English winter of 1888-89 Bowden toured South Africa with Major Warton's party and when C. A. 'Round-the-Corner' Smith contracted fever he captained the England side in the second Test. Bowden and Smith received £100 plus expenses in payment, just as the professionals did. 'Monty' Bowden remained in South Africa, joined Rhodes' Pioneer Column in its attempt to occupy Mashonaland, became a liquor runner and died at Umtali in February 1892.

GIFTS AND TESTIMONIALS

As the examples of Grace, Read, MacLaren and McGahey show, notable amateurs expected to receive a substantial one-off payment in the form of a testimonial. Invariably the sums raised were at least as large as the professionals' benefits (see Table 7 in the previous Chapter). Other cases were:

* A 400 guinea pair of candelabra to Lord Harris in 1882.
* In 1894, following John Shuter's decision to relinquish the Surrey captaincy, the Club launched his testimonial and opened the list with 200 guineas. Eventually Shuter received a grand piano from the proceeds.

* A 'handsome testimonial', according to *Scores and Biographies,* was given to William Newham in 1897. The Committee headed the list with £100. Newham played for Sussex as well as being Club secretary.
* In 1904 the Sussex Committee and members presented C.B.Fry with a 12hp motor car in recognition of his services to the county.
* In 1907 L. G. Wright of Derbyshire received £576, an illuminated address as well as pearls and a pendant for his wife. This testimonial far exceeded the value of any professional's benefit at Derbyshire.
* A. O. Jones, the Notts captain from 1900 to 1914, was the recipient of £1578 in 1908, the year after Notts won the county championship. That amount was larger than any benefit awarded to a Notts professional prior to the First World War.
* In 1908 the Lord Hawke testimonial fund reached £1842 which he received in the form of six heirlooms including jewelry and old china.
* J. R. Mason of Kent accepted £755 in 1912.

Cricketers of the stature mentioned above also expected a substantial wedding present. For example, Mason was given a silver tray and candelabra; Jones a cheque for £100 and Walter Brearley, the Lancashire fast bowler, accepted £200 and £40 of silverware. When Gilbert Jessop married in 1902 Gloucestershire presented him with a 'handsome cheque'. Since 1900 Jessop had been the county captain but could play full-time only because the Committee paid him substantial expenses for several months of the year. In 1909 he became Gloucestershire secretary.

EXPENSES

In 1897 both the Lancashire and Surrey Committees began to express concern about the possible abuse of the arrangement whereby amateurs' expenses were paid. At Old Trafford the Committee deemed the situation 'unsatisfactory' and added that there was 'no proper manner of checking amateur expenses'. At the Oval it was decided to limit such payments to £1 per day.

Two years later the Lancashire Committee was still unhappy and minuted that 'amateur expenses incurred during the southern tour have been excessive'. In January 1900 a new scale was established which fixed amateur expenses at 30 shillings per day plus first-class rail travel for away games and 10 shillings per day for home matches. So for an away fixture a Lancashire amateur would receive £4 5 shillings plus free first-class travel, while a professional was paid £6 but had to meet his travel costs. Surrey were a little less generous than Lancashire and in 1903 decided that amateurs would be given daily expenses of 25 shillings and the first-class rail fare for 'out' matches, but only their travel expenses for games at the Oval, Lord's, Crystal Palace and Leyton.

For Test matches at the turn of the century amateurs received 30 shillings per day plus first-class rail fares. However, at these rates of remuneration an amateur could make a profit from playing cricket and contravened the traditional definition of an amateur.

FROM AMATEUR TO PROFESSIONAL

Major Philip Trevor in *The Problems of Cricket,* published in 1907, considered that two of the most significant reasons why an amateur would be reluctant to turn professional were the friendships they might lose and the marked fall in their social status. The disguised professional was created by social and class pressures on middle-class cricketers who lacked the independent financial means to play as true amateurs and who could not accept the stigma of being a professional.

Despite these disincentives a small number of amateurs did turn professional. At the start of the 1886 season E. J. Diver of Surrey and W. R. Gilbert of Gloucestershire made that choice. *Cricket* commented that such a move involved 'no small amount of courage' as relations between amateurs and professionals, although pleasant, were 'well-defined and strictly kept'.

Edwin Diver had played as an amateur for Surrey from 1881 until 1885, although his status is questionable given that in September 1884 the Committee agreed that he was to be paid £2 per week in winter 'as long as he remains in the county'. Around this time Wimbledon College, the school at which Diver taught, had gone bankrupt.

In August 1885 the Club gave Diver £75 to mark his retirement, but during the winter he made the decision to turn professional. On 19 April 1886 he wrote to the Committee commenting that he was 'heartily sick of office work and extremely fond of cricket but not having private means to allow me to continue playing as an amateur' and asked to join the Oval ground staff. The Committee concurred with the rider that they could 'not pledge themselves to play you continuously'. Diver's father was not amused and the Committee had to write to assure him that 'no encouragement had been given to E. J. Diver to become a professional'.

After the 1886 season Diver left the Oval and returned to his home town of Cambridge where he opened a school. He became joint secretary and treasurer of the Cambridgeshire County Cricket Club, before in 1891 keeping goal professionally for Aston Villa. Under the residential qualification Diver appeared for Warwickshire from 1894 until 1901 and during that period was the first professional to captain Warwickshire. During this match at Leyton in August 1899 Diver led his players along the boundary edge to the amateurs' gate and only then on to the field of play. Essex lodged a complaint.

After leaving Edgbaston Diver had professional engagements in South Wales with Newport and Pontardawe. He died of pneumonia in the latter town, without kin, alone in his lodgings on Boxing Day 1924.

The list of other Victorian amateurs who turned professional includes V. A. Titchmarsh (MCC and Herefordshire); Sydney Santall (who played as an amateur with Northants although at the time they did not have first-class status, and as a professional for Warwickshire); George Spillman (Middlesex); C. J. B. Wood (Leicestershire, but only for one season); William Wood-Sims (Derbyshire); H. B. Daft (Notts) and, of course, his father Richard Daft.

Richard Daft's amateur career was restricted to the 1857-58 seasons, two matches in 1881, and remarkably, three appearances in 1891 at the age of 55, including the clash with Surrey at the Oval. Harry Butler Daft followed the same path as his father, representing Notts as an amateur from 1885-90 and then as a professional until 1899.

Richard Daft and Edwin Diver share the distinction of having played for the Gentlemen and also for the Players.

A few other players possessed the necessary social and class credentials to have appeared as amateurs, but prefered to turn professional. For example, George Lohmann's father worked on the Stock Exchange, while Arthur Paul of Lancashire, who in later years was the coach at Old Trafford, was the son of an army colonel who became Chief Constable on the Isle of Man. At 17 Arthur captained the Victoria College and Douglas elevens. He trained as a civil engineer but in 1887 agreed terms with Nelson as a professional. Two years later Arthur Paul joined the Old Trafford ground staff.

The case of Charlie Llewellyn shows the ludicrous nature of the amateur-professional divide. As a professional with Hampshire, Llewellyn, born in South Africa, used the players' entrance and facilities, but when he toured England (1904 and 1912) and Australia (1910-11) he was considered to be an amateur with all the privileges of such status. However he might have wished it otherwise. According to Rowland Bowen in his book *Cricket*, Llewellyn:

> was tormented by his white fellow tourists to such an extent that for peace and quiet in the hotels where the team stayed, he had to take refuge in the WCs and lock himself in. His chief tormentor was J. H. Sinclair, the leading Transvaal batsman.

After the First World War Charlie Llewellyn was to be found playing league cricket in Lancashire and working for the East Lancs Paper Mill.

The small number of cricketers who crossed the amateur-professional divide indicates how rigidly the class separation was maintained. Like every other Victorian worker the professional cricketer knew his place, and was reminded of it by innumerable everyday distinctions.

SECOND-CLASS CITIZENS

The players in the 1880s and 1890s may have been some of the first popular sports' stars but within the cricket world they remained second-class citizens. Their subordinate position was perpetuated by a combination of paternalism, dependence, deference and strict discipline. Again in this respect they were no different from any other Victorian workers.

Deference from the players was not only expected (from an early age children were told and made to understand their place) but was reinforced by a myriad of minor distinctions. And this moral order was validated by the players' active acceptance of it and their self-subordination. It should not be forgotten that these rigid class divisions within cricket were a reflection of the larger ideological whole – the British class system. It was this point that Major Philip Trevor failed to comprehend when he wrote in 1907 about these 'irritating little restrictions and petty official distinctions which would be laughable did not so many excellent people, for old associations' sake, regard them as vitally necessary.'

The 'irritating restrictions' and 'petty distinctions' which segregated the professionals from the amateurs included:

* separate dressing rooms;
* separate entrances on to the field of play – the amateurs used the pavilion's centre gate;
* separate travel arrangements to away matches – first-class for the amateur and third-class for the professional;
* different hotels or lodging houses for away games and
* if the professionals were invited into the luncheon room, separate tables and menu.

At Old Trafford the professionals did not always enjoy the 'luxury' of changing in the pavilion. For many years they had a very small room on the popular side of the ground. When the new pavilion was built in 1895 the players were even discriminated against by the provision of three bathrooms for the amateurs as opposed to only one for them. In an interview in *Cricket* in July 1896 George Lohmann was asked about the changes in the game since his career began. He replied that:

> In fact, cricket has improved all round, except in the matter of the Players' dressing rooms. In many places they are so arranged that if a player wants to watch a match he has to go out among the crowd.

Lohmann continued that on another 'very important item' – luncheon arrangements – Australian grounds were far superior. Until the 1890s the professionals either arranged for their wives to deliver their lunch (Mrs Barlow's pies were held in high regard by the other Lancashire professionals) or they went to the beer tent. Wilfred Rhodes explained to Sidney Rogerson the problems that could occur:

> So it was easy to come off at lunchtime, sweating hot after a long spell, and make straight for the bar. The pro would buy himself a pint, down that and as he started to leave to eat his sandwiches or find a bit of food someone would recognize him and offer another pint, then a third would press one on him and so on.

As late as 1893 the Warwickshire professionals were still eating their lunch with the spectators, but on the occasion of the Australian visit they were invited into the pavilion to eat with the amateurs and the tourists. After being led to side tables and served meat pies, instead of the salmon which was on offer to everybody else in the room, Edwin Diver led his fellow professionals out in disgust.

This amateur-professional segregation was known to the public but usually it occurred behind the closed doors of the pavilion. However, there were other more open manifestations of the same phenomena:

* amateurs were addressed as either sir or Mr, the professionals were addressed by their surname only;
* match reports distinguished between amateurs and professionals by either adding the amateurs' initials before the surname but simply printing the professionals' surname, or by including all the cricketers' initials, but adding Mr for the amateurs;
* from the 1880s it became the rule that only an amateur could captain the county eleven. In their treatment of the players some amateurs' behaviour left much to be desired. Joe Darling, the Australian captain, recalls hearing 'some English captains speak to their professionals like dogs . . . no Australian would stand it for one moment'.

At the turn of the century it was by their style of dress that a spectator could most easily pick out an amateur. Multi-coloured club blazers, quartered caps, boaters with club hatbands and club ties around their waists were standard attire for well-dressed amateurs. Most professionals can be seen in photographs either in their shirts, usually lightly starched, and flannels, or in a county blazer and cap, although boaters did become widely fashionable prior to 1914. Gone are the spotted or striped shirts favoured by the All-England Eleven, the dark ties, the snake-clasp belts, the brown boots, the check caps or the brightly striped blazers of Shaw, Shrewsbury and Lillywhite's touring parties. During the 1890s the professionals had been made to accept a drab uniformity while the amateurs expressed their individuality through their dazzling caps and blazers.

In *Adorned in Dreams – Fashion and Modernity,* Elizabeth Wilson makes the point that:

> The (private) railway companies were the first to introduce uniforms for their employees; these clothes were intended to give them authority with the public. They were a mark of official status and dignity, yet at the same time signalled that the officials were 'servants of the public' and hence liveried for public service.

Lancashire 1894; Back row, left to right, Mold, Paul, Lunt (scorer), Baker, Smith (A); Middle row, Ward (A), Tindall, MacLaren, Bardswell, Sugg; Front row, Briggs, Smith (C), Tinsley

The standardisation of the professional cricketers' attire into a uniform represented a similar development. Lord Hawke, who along with Lord Harris was keen to raise the professional to new heights of working-class respectability, quickly introduced the Yorkshire white-rose cap after he became captain. The only difference from the railway employees was the players' caps and blazers marked them as servants of the county club – not the general public.

A new style of professional was being fashioned in the 1890s. They were respectable men who took a pride in their appearance and provided the rest of the working class with role models worthy of aspiration. William Bates, the Yorkshire player whose career was tragically ruined when he was hit in the eye in Melbourne in 1887, was known as 'the Duke' because of his sartorial elegance. His son, who played for Yorkshire and Glamorgan, maintained the family style and was nicknamed 'the Marquis'. As a schoolboy Sidney Rogerson remembers sharing a train carriage in 1907 or 1908 with Wilfred Rhodes:

> Every detail of his appearance remains etched on my mind. He was wearing a well-cut grey flannel suit. His brown shoes shone with much polishing and his straw hat had the scarlet and yellow band of MCC, or else he was wearing an MCC tie, I forget which. With his deeply tanned face he looked, I remember thinking, almost exactly like the young captain in the 60th Rifles who used when on leave from India to attend the parish church.

Lord Harris would have delighted in that description.

CHAPTER 8

Disputes and Discipline

A carrot and a stick provides an apt description of the environment inhabited by the players in the late-Victorian and Edwardian years. On the one hand they strove after the carrot of match fees, bonuses and a benefit, while on the other hand they trod carefully to avoid the stick of harsh discipline which was occasionally meted out to any recalcitrant professional.

In that era the press rarely disclosed a player's misdemeanour or punishment, although the news quickly passed around the professional dressing rooms. Every player knew the strict standards by which the MCC and the county Committees ran the game. On two occasions a handful of leading professionals withdrew their labour in an effort to win better pay and conditions. Ultimately, like any other workers, strike action was their only effective course of action.

In 1881 seven Notts professionals, and in 1896 five England stars, refused to play. On both occasions the Notts and Surrey Committees stood firm and forced the professionals to concede and apologise.

Remarkably, from 1873 until the First World War these were the only two disputes of national significance. The fact that the players lost on each occasion is in itself part of the explanation as to why there were so few confrontations.

However, it must be remembered that, in general, these were years of unprecedented trade union growth and socialist political activity. The success of the 1889 Dock strike in London preceded a rash of 'new unionism' amongst unskilled and semi-skilled workers. The following year at the Trades Union Congress these new unions claimed impressive memberships – for example, 60,000 in the Gasworkers' and General Labourers Union; 56,000 in the Dock, Wharf, Riverside and General Workers' Union; 50,000 in the National Union of Dock Labourers and 40,000 in the Amalgamated Union of Labour.

In 1881 H. M. Hyndman helped found the Social Democratic Federation, a small but influential marxist organisation. Hyndman lived near Hampstead Heath, worked in the City, was a member of the MCC and had played for Sussex between 1863 and 1868. Twelve years later, in 1893, the Independent Labour Party was formed with more substantial working-class support, while throughout the 1890s the widely-read weekly, the *Clarion*, edited by Robert Blatchford, vigorously denounced capitalism and advocated socialism. Blatchford was also a cricket-lover and the *Clarion* carried regular profiles of players such as Ephriam Lockwood, Arthur Shrewsbury and George Lohmann. In the issue of 23 July 1892 Lohmann commented that 'he admires the *Clarion* very much'. The article continued that he 'has evidently read it, and assimilated its motto, "You cannot be too careful".'

But why did this upsurge in trade union and socialist politics have such an insignificant effect on professional cricketers?

THE 1881 NOTTS STRIKE

The defeat of the strike by seven leading Notts professionals in 1881 had far-reaching consequences. This action by Arthur Shrewsbury, Alfred Shaw, Fred Morley, John Selby, William Scotton, William Barnes and Wilfred Flowers raised two major issues. First, who could make fixtures, and second, the players' desire for greater security.

The dispute was precipitated by Shaw and Shrewsbury's acceptance of Bradford's offer to take a Notts side to the town to play a Yorkshire eleven. The Notts Committee took exception and seized the opportunity to settle decisively the question of who arranged matches. Today it may seem extraordinary that Shaw and Shrewsbury could select a so-called Notts side but it has to be remembered that until at least 1879, professional touring elevens, such as All-England, W. G. Grace's United South and the United North, were still seen regularly throughout England. Furthermore, as Shaw and Shrewsbury were quick to point out, in 1873 Richard Daft had organised a similar fixture without comment from the Notts Committee and in 1880 arranged a match at Bestwood Park between a Notts eleven and the MCC and Ground.

After the dispute over the Bradford fixture had begun, Jack Holden, the Notts secretary and Nottingham's Chief Constable, introduced the issue of the Notts players' contractual agreements and demanded that the players make themselves available for all county matches in 1881. In response the seven sought greater security of employment by asking to be contracted for the entire season and the guarantee of a benefit after 10 years.

A confrontation was inevitable. In *A Short History of Nottinghamshire Cricket*, published in 1887, Edwin Browne, the assistant secretary at Trent Bridge, wrote that 'a number of ambitious proposals were developed which no Committee could sanction'. In retrospect that argument cannot be accepted. Hindsight would suggest that it was not unreasonable for the leading professionals to expect some security of employment, such as five months in summer, and a benefit after 10 years.

Despite the intervention of intermediaries such as William Denison, Conservative MP for Nottingham from 1874 to 1880, and Henry Perkins, the MCC secretary, Captain Holden rejected any compromise. Five of the seven strikers were members of the Lord's ground staff and, according to Perkins' correspondence, 'the seven Notts

Nottinghamshire 1884; Back row, left to right, Bromley (secretary), Rowbotham (umpire), Wright (W), Shrewsbury, Coward (umpire), Browne (asst secretary); Middle row, Wright (C.W.), Attewell, Shaw, Barnes, Gunn, Flowers; Front row; Selby, Scotton, Sherwin players had placed the matter in his hands and agreed to abide by his decision'. In a letter to Charles Alcock, the Surrey secretary, Perkins added that the MCC men had 'placed themselves in a right position with our club'. Holden urged Alcock not to select any of the seven in the Players side to meet the Gentlemen at the Oval, but Perkins, when asked by Alcock, raised no objection to any of the seven being chosen.

In the latter part of the 1881 season Flowers, followed by Selby, Barnes, Scotton and Morley, conceded defeat and returned to the Notts side. Shaw and Shrewsbury remained intransigent, but in May 1882 the Committee accepted Shaw's 'apology' and Shrewsbury's 'expression of regret'. Having signed an 'agreement to play in any Notts county match', Shaw, Shrewsbury and the other five were asked to play for the county.

The potential repercussions of this dispute were considerable. If, for example, the seven had won the right to a seasonal contract and a guaranteed benefit it would have been a landmark decision for all first-class professionals. As with the introduction of winter pay in the mid-1890s, such concessions would have been forced on every county Committee if they wished to retain their top professionals. No doubt every county secretary was relieved to see the strike collapse. The 1882 edition of *James Lillywhite's Cricketers' Annual* echoed that sentiment when it accused the seven of being guilty of 'misconduct' in forming 'a deliberate combination against a recognised administration'.

Further, Nottinghamshire was seen as the professional heart of the game with a few hundred players going out 'proing' every season. For the county's leading professionals to have suffered a humiliating setback indicated to the rest of the cricket world that strike action would not pay.

The dispute highlighted the inherent weakness of the professionals' bargaining position. The seven's withdrawal from the county eleven did not stop Notts from fulfilling their programme of fixtures. Young local players, such as William Gunn and William Attewell, grasped the opportunity of breaking into the county side, while older professionals, such as William Oscroft, with his benefit scheduled for 1882, declined to join the strike, and previously discarded men such as Fred Wild were happy to be recalled.

The seven strikers could not count on the support of their fellow Notts professionals or of their county brothers elsewhere in the country. In contemporary parlance they lacked 'solidarity' and, of course, a union organisation. The 1881 strike could have set an important precedent; instead it turned into a sobering defeat for the players. As Edwin Browne wrote,'an elected Committee must rule' – and, he might have added, be seen to do so.

THE 1896 ENGLAND STRIKE

The second dispute of national significance occurred prior to the third Test at the Oval against Australia in August 1896. On 3 August William Gunn (Notts), George Lohmann, Tom Richardson, Bobby Abel and Tom Hayward (all Surrey) wrote to the Surrey Committee as follows:

> We the following players having been asked to represent England v Australia on August 10 and two following days do hereby take the liberty to ask for increased terms viz. twenty pounds. The importance of such fixture entitles us to make this demand.

Three days later George Lohmann sent another letter which repeated the basic demand for £20 instead of the usual £10 match fee. In response the Surrey Committee sent a telegram to the four Surrey professionals who were playing at Leyton which stated 'fee for playing against Australians ten pounds and expenses or they will be out of match'. William Gunn was simply told his 'terms were not accepted'.

The four Surrey players were called before a special Committee meeting on Monday 10 August only hours before the start of the Test match. Richardson, Hayward and Abel backed down and signed a letter which included:

> The Australians have made and are making large sums by these fixtures and it seemed to us only reasonable that we should beneficiate in a small way out of the large

> amount of money received . . . but after further consideration we desire to withdraw our refusal to play.

Having apologised the Surrey trio were reinstated in the England eleven. George Lohmann declined to sign the statement until he had spoken with William Gunn and both were omitted from the side. Further, Lohmann was told he would not be chosen for Surrey until the matter was resolved. On Wednesday 12 August, the last day of the Test which England won by 66 runs, at another specially convened Committee meeting, George Lohmann's 'apology was accepted' and he agreed to the following letter being sent to the press:

> . . . express my sincere apologies for my refusal to sign the document placing myself unreservedly in the hands of the Committee (in company with Abel, Hayward and Richardson) on Monday morning . . . having associated myself with him (Gunn), merely desired to wait until his arrival before taking any action . . . my idea was that a request was being being prefered instead of a demand being made, and that the expression 'demand', which I now see to have been so unfortunate, was inserted against my wish and better judgement.

And so the matter ended. The criticisms of the players were summed up in *Wisden* in 1897 – 'right in principle, but their action was ill-judged and inopportune'. Or, as A. A. Lilley, the England wicket-keeper in the third Test, wrote in his memoirs *Twenty Four Years of Cricket*, the request was 'perfectly justifiable' but he could not accept the means. Like all the other professionals, Lilley resented the amount of money the so-called amateur Australians were making from Test matches.

The final selection for the England side had been made only seven days before the Test commenced and the five broached the matter as quickly as possible with the Surrey Committee, and as Charles Alcock conceded in *Surrey Cricket*, a similar suggestion had been mooted at Manchester and Lord's 'but without success'. Alcock was more concerned by the fact that it was 'a peremptory demand and not a request for consideration'.

In any negotiations the five were weakened by the fact that not all the professionals selected had signed the original claim – Peel and Lilley were the absentees – and that once their demand had been rejected they could not stop Mold, Hirst and Pougher from agreeing to act as reserves. From the players' point of view the same problems arose as had occurred in 1881, namely, a lack of organisation and solidarity.

In *The Trent Bridge Battery* Basil Haynes and John Lucas comment on why William Gunn became involved. They conclude that 'Gunn was not a greedy man. We have seen that by this stage in his career he did not need the money. What he did expect was proper recognition of his worth.' Seven years earlier Gunn had moved into 'The Park', an exclusive residential area close to the centre of Nottingham and there his neighbours were 'captains of industry and commerce'.

Players such as Gunn and Lohmann wanted recognition not just in comparison with the Australian tourists but also with the amateurs whose behind-the-scenes payments were widely known. During the dispute Lohmann had bitterly remarked that the amateurs would receive in expenses twice the amount the professionals would be paid. Accusations were made in the press about Grace and Stoddart's expenses and the latter chose to withdraw from the Test.

Although the players had suffered another setback in their efforts to improve the professional's lot, the strike did bring the issue before the public and to the cricket authorities' attention. The legitimacy of the claim was widely accepted, including by Lord Hawke, and two seasons later in 1898 the professionals' Test match payment was increased to £20.

DISMISSALS AND THE BOBBY PEEL CASE

Lord Hawke established an infamous record for instant

dismissal with no second chance or right of appeal. Among Hawke's victims from the ranks of the Yorkshire professionals were Edmund Peate in 1887 – in *Recollections and Reminiscences* Hawke claims that it had been his 'saddest task to dismiss him' but Peate has 'borne no grudge'; Joe Preston in 1889, who Hawke felt was 'irresponsible', lacking in 'self-restraint' and 'had too many friends' (that is, who were publicans); and Robert Moorhouse in 1898 for allegedly not attempting to take a catch in a match against Middlesex at Lord's. Moorhouse did play on one more occasion for Yorkshire in May 1899 against Worcestershire although Hawke did not captain the side.

Finally there was the case of Bobby Peel, dismissed by Hawke in 1897 in the 'most decisive action of my whole career (which) . . . had to be done for the sake of discipline and for the good of cricket'. Again Hawke claims that the player 'never bore me malice for my decision to dismiss him'.

The events surrounding Bobby Peel's dismissal are part of cricket folklore. The story which first appeared in A. A. Thomson's *Hirst and Rhodes,* was included in Rogerson's *Wilfred Rhodes* (although Rhodes wasn't there as he made his debut the following season) and has been repeated in David Frith's *The Slow Men* as follows:

> His friend, the yeoman all-rounder George Hirst, had tried to cover for him, telling HIs Lordship that Peel was ill and would not be down to the ground for some time. As the team, with substitute, took the field, a swaying Robert Peel appeared, red-faced, cap askew. To impress his captain of his fitness, he grabbed the ball and bowled it. He thought he was bowling at the stumps; the ball actually careered off and thudded against the sight-screen. The final disaster, which may or may not be accepted as fact, was Peel's decision to pass water on the pitch.

The match report in *Cricket* cannot be made to fit this wonderful scenario. The incident occurred at Bramall Lane, Sheffield (not Chesterfield as Hirst and Thomson claimed) in the match against Middlesex in August 1897. This was Peel's first game after an injury he received in July at Bradford. In Yorkshire's first innings Peel hit 40 and was not required in the county's second knock. When Middlesex batted for a second time on the last day they were left three and a quarter hours to score 302. However in that innings Bobby Peel bowled seven overs, conceded 30 runs and took no wickets.

The first important point to note is that Peel was on the field on the third day and obviously bowled more than one ball at a sightscreen. Equally implausible is George Hirst's story about Peel being drunk at breakfast. What could be possible is that Bobby Peel took his lunch in the beer tent, although the player denied that.

In *Cricket*'s report of Yorkshire's next match against Derbyshire it is stated that Peel had been suspended by the Committee for the rest of the season due to a 'contretemps' in Sheffield. Three years later Peel spoke about the incident to *Cricket:*

> I have never been called before the county Committee during the course of my career. I had been in bed for three weeks as a result of a blow which I received when batting, and after I recovered I played in a match for Yorkshire, in which I took five wickets and made about 40 runs. The next thing that I knew was that I was not to play again for Yorkshire. No reason was ever given to me.

The following season Bobby Peel played for Accrington in the Lancashire League. Other county Committees were not as harsh as Yorkshire. Notts, for example, gave William Barnes a severe caution in 1889 after 'he admitted he had a good deal of champagne but was not drunk' during a match in Brighton, while in 1897 Surrey gave William Lockwood another chance 'on condition that he should keep the pledge of total abstinence'.

DIFFERENT STANDARDS FOR THE AMATEURS?

While it might be assumed that there was one code of discipline for the professionals and another for the amateurs, the limited evidence available does not substantiate that view. For example, the Surrey minutes from 1890 to 1914 contain two instances where disciplinary action was taken against amateurs.

The first incident involved the Middlesex amateur and one-off England captain Sir Timothy Carew O'Brien. In August 1896 the Middlesex Committee apologised for O'Brien's bad language during a match at the Oval. The letter contained an 'expression of regret' and their 'strong disapprobation' over Sir Timothy's behaviour in speaking roughly to one of the Surrey professionals. The following July the Surrey Committee again complained to Middlesex about O'Brien and stated that they would be 'compelled to decline to play the county of Middlesex again if Sir T. C. O'Brien is one of the eleven'. Middlesex replied by confirming that O'Brien would not be chosen for the fixture against Surrey.

The second occasion when a Surrey amateur incurred the Committee's wrath occurred in August 1909 after J. N. Crawford declined to captain the county against the Australians and was 'not invited again to play for Surrey'. John Crawford, brother of V. F. S. Crawford the Leicestershire amateur and secretary, made his Surrey debut in 1904 while still at Repton school and his first England appearance in South Africa on the 1905-06 tour. He remains the youngest Surrey cricketer to score a century (18 years and 257 days) and 1000 runs in a season (19 years and 270 days).

The dispute with Surrey arose because Crawford objected to being given a side for the return match against Australia which lacked Davis, Lees and particularly Tom Rushby. Crawford was not told by Leveson-Gower, the official captain, why he had dropped the three professionals. The rancour between Crawford, Leveson-Gower and Lord Alverstone, the Surrey President and Lord Chief Justice of England, reached such a low that Leveson-Gower wrote on 29 July that 'I must cancel my invitation to you for Scarborough' and the MCC 'have asked me to let you know that under the circumstances they will not now require your services' for the tour of South Africa. The following week Leveson-Gower concluded that 'Either you or I must give up playing for Surrey.'

After being told that he would not be invited to play for Surrey again John Crawford replied bitterly of 'the awful example made of me to every amateur in the United Kingdom' and in *Cricket* complained of being 'practically branded as a criminal'. To avoid such a stigma Crawford emigrated to South Australia and joined the teaching staff of St Peter's College in Adelaide. Representing South Australia he hit two centuries and 110 for an Australian eleven against the 1911-12 MCC tourists.

During the War Crawford returned to England and in 1919, time apparently having healed the breach, he reappeared at the Oval. Crawford suggested that the Club might help him find suitable employment to which the Committee countered by proposing that he turn professional. The offer was declined when he found 'a billet in Rochdale' and in 1920 Crawford played as an amateur in the Central Lancashire League. His final first-class appearance was for the Gentlemen against the Players at the Oval in 1921.

SYDNEY BARNES

In the introduction to Wilfred White's short biography, *Sydney Barnes,* Pelham Warner wrote that Barnes was the best bowler, on all wickets, he had ever played against. In that absorbing, but ultimately futile endeavour to discover the greatest bowler of all time, Barnes remains a sure favourite.

To the cricket establishment in the 'golden age' Barnes proved a truculent enigma. Leslie Duckworth in *S. F. Barnes – Master Bowler* explains why:

> Barnes certainly knew his own mind, but it is not surprising that some people found him difficult, one reason, perhaps, being that it was unusual in those days for a professional to speak so firmly and, indeed, bluntly, but

Barnes was never one for mincing words when he felt strongly about anything.

In 1896, after four games with Warwickshire, Barnes joined Rishton in the Lancashire League where, also working as groundsman, he received 70 shillings per week plus performance bonuses. Five years later, during his second season with Burnley, Lancashire paid the League Club £100 to release Barnes from his contract.

Throughout his life Sydney Barnes expressed concern about the insecurity of the professional's life and lack of prospects once he had retired from the first-class game. His disagreement with the Lancashire Committee, which resulted in him returning to the Lancashire League in 1904 to play with Church, arose because of Barnes' desire to make his position more contractually and financially secure.

In his negotiations with Samuel Swire, the secretary at Old Trafford and a cotton manufacturer, Sydney Barnes raised two issues. First, that the Club should find him winter employment rather than pay him winter wages and second, that he should receive a benefit match after eight years against a county side of his choice. Swire rejected the first point, countering with £1 per week as pay in winter. Barnes suggested £2, which he never received. On the second point the Club agreed to a benefit after eight years, instead of the usual 10, but would not accept the player choosing any match; in other words, he could not have the Bank Holiday fixture against Yorkshire.

An impasse was reached. Barnes, the man of principle, refused to re-sign for the county. The Committee responded by withholding Barnes's talent money for the season but eventually agreed to pay it over. On 30 October 1903 the Club minutes record they were 'finally disposing of Barnes'. However, aware of the gifted bowler they were losing, the Committee made another approach to Barnes in February 1904 and suggested he should play 'on his merits on the same scale of pay' as the other Old Trafford professionals. This proposal still failed to address Barnes's desire

Sydney Barnes

for greater security and he prefered to accept the £8 per week from Church.

For the sake of a few hundred pounds Sydney Barnes was lost to county cricket, but the Lancashire Committee did not want to be seen making concessions to a strident player which would set a precedent that other professionals could follow. Generally the county authorities recognised the leagues as a potential competitor for their players' services. In part the threat from the leagues ensured that the county professionals' wages and bonuses could not be reduced. As A. W. Pullin wrote in a *History of Yorkshire County Cricket 1903-23*:

> Yorkshire, like other counties, could not regard it as consistent with their position and reputation that any of their players should find league cricket more financially attractive than that of the county game.

Sydney Barnes was exceptional among the leading professionals in the 'golden age' in turning his back on the first-class game to play in the leagues. Other lesser players, who failed to gain a regular place in a county side, willingly made such a move but invariably the public recognition that went with county cricket, and the possibility of Test selection, proved too attractive for first eleven players. A place in the England side at home or on tour offered a small number of professionals relatively big rewards. It was the hope to which many aspired.

THE LACK OF UNIONS AND MILITANCY

In 1907, after failures in 1893 and 1898, the Association Football Players Union was established. By December 1908 the AFPU had 1300 members playing for 70 soccer clubs. A reaction common amongst the cricket authorities was stated by the Middlesex hitter and writer William Ford in *A Cricketer on Cricket* when he asserted, 'Heaven defend us from the time when cricketers form "unions".'

Despite the general growth of unions and the landmark passage of the Trade Disputes Act in 1906 which left workers relatively free to undertake industrial action, there is no record of professional cricketers attempting to form their own union or to join general unions prior to the First World War. A number of related reasons explain this situation:

* Players' individualism, inevitably fostered by the very nature of cricket, led them to seek personal achievements and the financial benefits which went to a few top stars.
* Leading county players, whose involvement would have been crucial for the success of a union, were well rewarded during their short careers in comparison to other workers and most professional sports people.
* Beyond the county sides, there were plenty of players who were only too keen to forsake the boredom of factory life for the chance to play professional cricket. 'There's lots willing to take your place' would have been the obvious catch-cry.
* Many professionals used their time in the game's limelight to open a small business or run a public house. Some succeeded, notably William Gunn, who when he died in 1921 left an estate valued at £57,392, although many failed. Bobby Abel's business was sold in 1927, and an appeal was launched by the *Daily Mail*, which raised £1010. The proceeds were used to pay off Abel's debts and mortgage, while Surrey began to pay their former professional a regular supplementary grant of £1 per week as well as meeting the cost of his parish rates and taxes. Also, many players used cricket as a means to better themselves socially, which created a lower middle-class attitude that unions were unnecessary if you wanted to get on in life.
* The county Clubs provided paternalistic support for professionals who maintained a good disciplinary record. Most notably this took the form of a benefit, while other welfare provisions were available via the Cricketers' Fund Friendly Society.
* Finally, the county Committees had gained a reputation for stern discipline and as the 1881 and 1896

strikes had shown, the authorities would stand firm against any 'militant' action.

These six reasons when taken together led to the creation of a community of interest between the players and the county Committees, rather than a sense of solidarity between the Victorian professionals against their employers.

PART THREE

The Inter-War Years

CHAPTER 9

A Sense of Security

THE ROLL OF HONOUR

ON 31 August 1914, four days after W. G. Grace's appeal to arms had been published in the *Sportsman*, Gloucestershire fielded only 10 men against Surrey at the Oval. Alf Dipper had abandoned his colleagues and signed up. In 1915 *Wisden* reported that there had been a 'splendid response to the call to the colours' from the nation's cricketers.

By the end of 1914 one million men had responded for 'King and Country', but by the middle of the following year recruitment had waned as jingoism was tempered by more than 380,000 casualties which included 75,000 dead. As part of the drive to persuade more men to enlist Captain Jessop of the 14th Manchester Regiment and Lieutenant MacLaren of the Royal Army Service Corps spoke at numerous public gatherings. The county Committees expected and encouraged their professionals to join up or engage in war work. Any Kent player who volunteered for the armed forces received the difference between their army and ground staff pay from the county, while Yorkshire made it 'a strict condition of their continued engagement' that the county's professionals enlist or find war work. In 1917 Lancashire proudly announced that 'nearly all' their 1914 side were at the front or in training.

Colin Blythe

The wartime Army and Navy elevens included Corporals Makepeace and Ernest Tyldesley, Lt-Corporals George Gunn and Sandham, Sgt-Major Hardinge, Lieutenant Astill, Coxswain Woolley, Air Mechanic Hobbs and Privates Hendren and Lee. Harry Lee had left the Lord's ground staff and joined the County of London Regiment before being wounded and captured in March 1915. Despite still being alive, Lee's death was announced and a memorial service held! He was repatriated and discharged the following year.

The cost of the War in human terms was immense. Almost 750,000 men from Britain lost their lives, but there were relatively few casualities from the world of professional cricket. The roll of honour reads:

* Corporal Atherton, for six years a member of the Old Trafford ground staff and later employed as a professional with Lowerhouse;
* Sergeant S. H. Bates, a member of the Lord's ground staff who played for Warwickshire, having been born at the Edgbaston ground;
* Sergeant Colin Blythe of Kent and England, the most significant loss to English cricket, he was killed in action near Passchendaele in 1917. Apart from 1901 when ill-health restricted his performances, in each of the 15 seasons from 1900 Blythe captured more than 100 wickets. He had represented England on 19 occasions and vied with Wilfred Rhodes for the accolade of the greatest left-arm spinner of the Edwardian era.
* 2nd Lieutenant Major Booth ('Major' being Booth's first name) was one of a notable line of Yorkshire professionals from Pudsey. In 1913 he performed the 'double' including 158 wickets for his county and although in the following season he failed to repeat that achievement he did capture 141 wickets for Yorkshire. Booth toured South Africa in 1913-14 and made two appearances for England. This popular player was mourned in the Pudsey newspaper with this verse:

Cricket field, or battle plain,
He e'er went in might and main!
Things going hard, smooth or rough,
Made of good old Yorkshire stuff,
Major, he was e'er the same,
Kept his end up, 'played the game!'
Good old Major.

* Staff-Sergeant C. G. A. Collier of Worcestershire and formerly employed on the Warwickshire ground staff;
* Percy Jeeves, immortalised by P. G. Wodehouse, was born in Yorkshire but qualified for Warwickshire in 1912. The following season he took 106 wickets with his right-arm medium-fast bowling and shortly before the War broke out had been selected to represent the Players at the Oval. Jeeves was considered one of England's most promising professionals.
* Corporal David Jennings represented Kent 35 times from 1909 onwards. Like Colin Blythe he served in the Kent Fortress Engineers.
* Alan Marshal, the former Surrey player who had been sacked in 1910 and returned to his native Australia, served with the 15th AIF Battalion at Gallipoli but died of enteric fever at Imtarfa Military Hospital in Malta. In three of his four seasons at the Oval he hit more than 1000 runs; *Wisden* mourned Marshal as a player of 'unfulfilled promise . . a hitter of great, natural powers'.
* William Tyldesley, the eldest of four brothers who all played for Lancashire – the most famous was the youngest, Richard – and who all died relatively young.

County cricket stopped for the duration of the First World War. The Oval ground staff had declined from 25 in 1914 to four by February 1916. Fifteen shillings per week was paid to Freeman, Goatly, Myers and Sandham being 'actually engaged on the ground'. Seven months later this quartet had been joined by Hobbs and Sullivan, although that year Hobbs joined the fledgling Air Force. Eight years later in his first autobiography, *My Cricket Memories,* Hobbs felt it was necessary to justify his late departure for the armed forces by explaining his circumstances: he was a 32-year-old father of four young children, with a widowed mother and a financial position that 'left room for improvement'. During the first two years of the War Jack Hobbs was employed in a London munitions factory and, like many other professionals, played cricket on Saturdays in the Bradford League.

The Bradford League sides during the First World War were packed with cricketing talent. For example, the Undercliffe eleven included Cecil Parkin, who worked as a fuel overseer at Oswaldtwistle, Charlie Llewellyn, the South African and ex-Hampshire all-rounder, George Gunn and Thomas Oates, both from Notts. Other sides secured the services of Jack Hobbs, Frank Woolley, Ernest Tyldesley, Schofield Haigh, 'Topsy' Wass, Jack Hearne, Sydney Barnes, Wally Hardinge and Bill Hitch.

The young Herbert Sutcliffe, who did not make his Yorkshire debut until 1919, was also playing in the wartime Bradford League for his home-town Pudsey St Lawrence, albeit under a false name. Sutcliffe, a Corporal in the Sherwood Foresters based at York, absented himself without leave every Saturday afternoon. His pseudonymous Bradford League career ended when he was transfered to Salisbury as a 2nd Lieutenant with the Green Howards.

As the War dragged on and became what *Wisden*, in 1918, called 'a normal condition', the ban on cricket appeared 'illogical', especially as other sports such as boxing and professional billiards played on. But what did the future hold? The prevailing opinion within the cricket establishment, articulated by Lord Harris, was that once cricket resumed 'we must all be prepared for at least a temporary falling off in public support'. Guided by that perspective, Ludford Docker, the Warwickshire President, advocated a programme of two-day county fixtures. Such a proposal was endorsed by the Advisory County Cricket Committee in 1918 by an 11-5 margin. In its 1919 editorial *Wisden* correctly considered this to have been a 'sad blunder', predicting that nine out of ten matches would end in draws.

The first post-War season was far from easy for the professionals. Jack Hobbs, in *My Cricket Memories*, recalled:

> It was hard work, and both players and public soon got fed up with the new arrangement. After a 7.30 finish, by the time one had dressed and dined, it was too late to go anywhere.

In his biography by Sidney Rogerson Wilfred Rhodes remembered that 'we had to dash away to catch the train and snatch what sleep we could'. To everybody's relief, half way through the 1919 season it was agreed to revert to the normal three-day programme for the following year.

Two other discussions at the Advisory County Cricket Committee threatened the players' future. First, in July 1919, it was recommended that the Clubs not pay their staff winter wages. Since its introduction in the mid-1890s many Committee members had sought to abolish winter pay; for example, during the War the matter had been re-opened at the Hampshire Annual General Meetings. Surrey opposed the ACCC decision arguing that their 'leading professionals would accept league engagements' and decided to pay a bonus on 1 October 1919 and 1 January 1920 equivalent to the winter wages of 1914-15. In practice the ACCC's decision was unrealistic if the counties wanted to retain their professionals, and it seems to have been ignored.

Second, a resolution was defeated at the ACCC which suggested that each county should limit the number of professionals in its eleven to three! *Wisden*, applauding the demise of this naive proposition, remarked that cricket was now 'never so dependent' on its professional talent and continued by doubting if there were three amateurs worth a place in the England side.

There was also a more serious problem confronting the professional cricketer. During the 1919 season, despite a doubling of admission charges and larger crowds than pre-War, the players' basic rate of pay remained as it had been in 1914. Wilfred Rhodes recalled that 'by the end of the season, living as carefully as I knew how, I finished all square and just made ends meet'. This was hardly surprising given that retail prices had more than doubled between 1913 and 1919. Lord's and the counties were forced to respond. The MCC ground staff accepted a 60 per cent increase on their 1914 rates and in 1920 Yorkshire began to pay their capped players £11 for a home match and £15 for an away fixture as compared to the previous £5 and £6, although only £8 against the Universities and the MCC. As usual it was the Surrey Committee who showed most understanding of their players' plight and in March 1919 awarded them a 50 per cent rise on the pre-War pay rates. Deliberations over wages continued at the Oval during 1920 and a new pay scale was implemented in November, backdated to September. Under this agreement for the first time the senior professionals – Hobbs, Strudwick, Hitch, Ducat, Rushby, Sandham, Peach and Harrison – were guaranteed an annual income which in the case of the first three was £400, while the other four received a guarantee of £300. The leading Surrey professionals had achieved the important goal of financial security.

THE NEW GENERATION

The inter-war county championship was completely dominated by the northern professionally-based elevens. After 1921 Yorkshire won the title in 1922-25, 1931-33, 1935 and 1937-39; Lancashire carried it off in 1926-28, 1930 and 1934; Nottinghamshire in 1929 and Derbyshire in 1936. Throughout this period these county sides rarely included more than one amateur, who in many cases was a titular captain. Commenting on those successful years Maurice Leyland said, 'I never counted the captain in the Yorkshire side – but we won a few championships with the handicap of one.' At other counties, where often a large number of amateurs might play in a few games each season, a professional nucleus proved essential. John Arlott, for example, writing in *Hampshire County Cricket* about the inter-war years, states, 'the major playing strength was always professional'.

Among the new generation of post-War professionals two interesting trends can be discerned. First, a group of players emerged who had been educated at grammar schools and who in subsequent years further enhanced the professionals' respectable image; and second, a number of ex-miners brought not only their undoubted physical and cricketing skills but also great character to the game.

The 1918 Fisher Education Act established universal compulsory education for all children until the age of 14, but even more fundamental changes were envisaged by the Hadow Report published in December 1926. It proposed extending the school leaving age to 15 – a measure not implemented until after the Second World War – and creating in the secondary sector a division between more academic grammar schools and modern schools. To attend a grammar school the pupil either had to pay a fee or gain a scholarship. Under those circumstances the local grammar became a middle-class imitation of the establishment public schools with all the trappings of houses, prefects, corporal punishment, tailored uniforms, prizes and sporting colours.

Of the small percentage of children educated in the grammar schools, there were a few who found professional fame on the cricket field. Among them were Les Ames of the Harvey Grammar School, Folkestone. Ames left school at 17 and was apprenticed into his cousin's grocery business; his father's intention being that Leslie would eventually open his own concern. George Cox junior, like his father a Sussex professional, attended Collier's Grammar in Horsham. On his death in 1985 his estate was valued at £138,000. George Duckworth, born in a Warrington backstreet, one of nine children, won a free scholarship to Botler Grammar in his home town. He left school at 15 to follow his father's trade as a wire-drawer. Walter Hammond, the son of an army officer spent much of his early life in Hong Kong and Malta before being sent to Cirencester Grammar in April 1918. One month later Major Hammond was killed in the War. Cyril Washbrook, whose father ran a calico printing business, went to Bridgnorth Grammar. His parents intended that he should go to university and eventually become a teacher. Stan Worthington, having been educated at Netherthorpe Grammar, went to work as an electrician at the Bolsover colliery before making his Derbyshire debut in 1924. In various ways, on and off the field, these players were destined to raise further the status of the professional cricketer.

Life for the young Harold Larwood was very different from that of his future England colleagues Les Ames and Wally Hammond. In *The Larwood Story* he recalled:

> There was little ahead of you except a life of hard work. No parents in Nuncargate could afford to send their children to school beyond the primary level unless they won a scholarship . . . At 13, in order to get my mind more on the business of earning a living, my parents set me to work in the colliery co-operative stores.

A year later, against his parents' wishes, the frail Harold Larwood became a pony pit-boy at Annesley colliery, a three-mile walk from his home. At 17 Harold took a night-shift job at the Langton coal-face. He described the work in his autobiography:

> Night after long night I tore skin off my back knocking against the jagged coal edges as I reached and dug and shovelled and half-straightened up, my back screaming, my sides aching. I got used to it. I had to.

As he dug coal Harold Larwood 'dreamed of cricket'. He, and a few other Derbyshire, Lancashire and Nottinghamshire miners, realised that dream and escaped from the pits. Prior to the First World War distinguished Notts professionals, like Fred Barratt, Thomas Oates and 'Topsy' Wass, had beaten a path to Trent Bridge from the local collieries. By 1936, of the 12 Notts players receiving winter pay, an obvious indication of their seniority, six – Charlie Harris, Walter Keeton, Harold Larwood, Arthur Staples, Bill Voce and Arthur Wheat – were former miners. And during the inter-war years several other miners represented the county in first-class matches.

Arthur Wheat joined the Trent Bridge staff in 1922 although he did not gain a regular place as the county's wicket-keeper until 1937, due to the presence of Ben Lilley. After initially offering Wheat 50 shillings per week for the summer the county agreed to match his £3 per week wage as a miner. During the winter months he returned to the pits.

In 1926 Bill Voce was taken by the manager of Annesley colliery to Trent Bridge for a trial. Afterwards Voce remembered:

> I had to go before the Committee who were seated round the central table in the Committee room – J. A. Dixon was at the head of table . . . I was feeling very nervous . . . J. A. Dixon said he could offer me a 20 week engagement at 30 shillings plus travelling expenses between Annesley and Trent Bridge. I said that 30 shillings was not enough and turned and walked straight out of the room. I don't know how I had the nerve to do it, especially as I was only earning 18 shillings in the pit.

The next day the Committee raised the offer to £2 and Voce accepted: 'The colliery owners were very keen on cricket and kitted me out with flannels'. And when he went back to the pit in winter they promoted him to the position of under-deputy with the remark that 'We've got to look after those hands.' The connections between the local colliery owners and the County Cricket Club were strong; for example, the Barber family, one of whom sat on the Notts Committee, were part-owners of the Annesley colliery.

A glance down the list of clubs playing in the local Bassetlaw League during the inter-war years confirms the mining influence on the county's cricket. By 1936 16 of the 21 Bassetlaw sides were colliery elevens. In John Shawcroft's *A History of Derbyshire County Cricket Club 1870-1970*, the author makes a similar point:

> In the final analysis, however, it is not the big leagues of Lancashire and Yorkshire, or even the Bassetlaw, to which Derbyshire owes its allegiance. Rather, it is the colliery sides of the Chesterfield area, the Blackwells,

Mortons, Bolsovers, Glapwells, Tibshelfs, Whitwells, Pilsleys and Creswells, the Derbyshire Alliance and the Notts and Derbyshire Border League, with their Butterley, Heage, Heanor, Denby and Marehay clubs.

For season after season prior to the First World War the Derbyshire attack had been led by the formidable combination of Bill Bestwick and Arnold Warren. Shawcroft described Bestwick as 'one of the greatest fast-medium bowlers the county had ever possessed and certainly the richest character'. Bill Bestwick, a miner from Heanor, made his county debut in 1898. In 1909 the county foolishly dispensed with his services, but 10 years later he returned to be Derbyshire's leading wicket taker. Aged 46, in the 1921 season he claimed 147 wickets, including 10 for 40 in an innings against Glamorgan at Cardiff. Four years later Bill Bestwick played his final match for Derbyshire. His partner, Arnold Warren, came from the mining area of Codnor, one of five sons of a prosperous local builder. In his only Test appearance in 1905 Warren took Victor Trumper's wicket in both innings – a feat matched only by Sydney Barnes, Wilfred Rhodes, J. N. Crawford and Walter Brearley. Warren retired in 1920 aged 45.

The nine-day 1926 General Strike, from 3 to 12 May, in support of a million miners already on strike struggling to oppose a cut in wages, made little impact on county cricket. In the absence of trains teams undertook long, cold journeys by char-a-banc, but the only mishap seems to have been when Hampshire found themselves three players short when they met Warwickshire at Edgbaston. The replacements did not arrive in time to play on Saturday and when rain washed out the rest of the match their journey proved fruitless.

For the future of Derbyshire cricket the General Strike produced two valuable bi-products – Bill Copson and Tommy Mitchell. As a boy Bill Copson had shown no interest in cricket but during the Strike the young miner from Morton Colliery was persuaded to join in a game. The consequence was his immediate inclusion in the local side and six years later he made his Derbyshire debut. With his first ball in first-class cricket Copson claimed the wicket of Andrew Sandham, the Surrey and England opener.

Tommy Mitchell's story is similar. Seen bowling during the General Strike, Mitchell, a face worker at Creswell Colliery, was recommended to the local Bassetlaw League side. Two years later he was in the county side at £4 per week – orginally he rejected the Committee's offer of £3 on the basis that he could earn more underground. Mitchell, a leg-break and googly bowler, was commended by R. C. Robertson-Glasgow in *Cricket Prints* because he took 'pomposity and convention by their noses and tweaked them sharply', although his comment to Bob Wyatt during a Test match that 'You couldn't captain a box of bloody lead soldiers' ended his England career.

Copson (who played three times for England) and Mitchell were important members of the championship-winning Derbyshire side in 1936, as were Denis Smith and Stan Worthington, both of whom had mining backgrounds.

Lancashire had reason to be grateful to the local mining village of Westhougton for producing the four Tyldesley brothers, Dick Pollard and William Farrimond. Even Yorkshire's Herbert Sutcliffe had a brief career working for a colliery, albeit in the sales office. Immediately after the War Sutcliffe was contracted to play for Allerton Bywater in the Yorkshire Council and a job was arranged with the local pit. However, the request to represent Yorkshire came shortly afterwards.

Harold Larwood calls chapter three of his autobiography 'Into the Sunlight' which seems to express the relief of a young coal-face worker escaping from the pits. In *The Militancy of British Miners* Professor V. L. Allen, writing about these years, commented:

> Uncertainty entered the lives of miners in different ways. Once for all pit closures was one way. Another was partial and temporary closure relating in indecently high unemployment levels . . . There was uncertainty in the

very process of mining coal, reflected in the high accident and disease rates.

Fred Newton was a 'promising' batsman who never quite made the first-class grade. He represented Derbyshire 20 times between 1909 and 1919. Born in the Yorkshire mining community of Denaby Main, Newton returned to the pit and was killed in a roof fall at Warsop Main on 8 August 1924.

EARNINGS

Little changed in the make-up of a professional's earnings during the inter-war years. A player's income continued to come from a combination of ground staff wages, a winter retainer and various payments dependent on selection and performance, such as match fees, win bonuses and talent money. The only important development occurred when several counties began to provide their leading professionals with an annual guaranteed income.

Harry Lee made 401 appearances for Middlesex before and after the War. In *Forty Years of English Cricket* he wrote that 'payment by the match was a cruel system . . . A cricketer who was sick, or out of form, often had nothing to fall back upon except charity.' He continued that having 'a sense of security was a fine thing', while the loss of pay due to poor form was always 'a source of worry', not an incentive.

Within the first two seasons of post-War cricket the county clubs had increased their professionals' rates of pay to compensate for the substantial rise in prices that had occurred during the War. Once that allowance had been made very little changed until after the Second World War. Overall, however, the cost of living fell by more than a third between 1920 and 1938. In fact, during the 1930s prices fell faster than wages so that provided a person was in work he could maintain or slightly improve his standard of living, as compared to the early 1920s.

Table 8 provides details of the payment arrangements for capped players with Hampshire, Kent, Lancashire, Nottinghamshire, Surrey and Yorkshire in this period. The significant difference between the counties was whether they provided their leading players with a higher weekly rate and overall guarantee, as Surrey did, or expected them to earn a larger proportion of their income from match fees.

Table 8: Basic payments to capped players in the inter-war years (£)

	Hants	Kent	Lancs	Notts	Surrey	Yorks
Summer weekly wage	4	3	5	3	4-10s	
Winter weekly wage	2-5s	2	2	2	4-10s	2-2s
Annual guarantee	200		315	250	400	
Home match	8	8	9-10s	9	4	11
Away match	10	11-10s	14-5s	11	8	15

TALENT MONEY

All counties paid a £1 win bonus and some form of talent money. While Surrey and Notts had followed the pre-War Yorkshire lead and adopted the mark system (see Chapter 5), others such as Glamorgan, Hampshire and Somerset persisted with a scale of payments whereby 50 runs was worth £1, a century £2, five wickets £1, etc. As Hampshire's Phil Mead scored a further 50 he is reputed to have chuckled, 'That's another ton of coal for the winter.'

At a meeting in June 1925 between Yorkshire's Lord Hawke and the Club secretary F. C. Toone and Lancashire's T. A. Higson and secretary H. Rylance it was decided to put a limit of £200 on any season's total talent money. An exception was made for championship-winning years, although even in 1927 and 1930 when Lancashire topped the table they distributed only £194 and £200 respectively among their leading professionals in talent money. In 1927 Hallows (2119 runs) and McDonald (150 wickets) headed the list receiving £31 each, while three seasons later McDonald (108 wickets) was given £30, Richard Tyldesley (133 wickets), Iddon (1352 runs), Ernest Tyldesley (1904 runs) and Watson (2031 runs) £25. From 1932 onwards the Notts Committee also imposed a £200 ceiling on total talent money – a figure substantially exceeded during the previous seven seasons. For example, in 1927, 1928 and 1929 when the county finished second, third and first in the championship the total talent money distribution had been £295, £330 and £337 respectively.

CHAMPIONSHIP BONUS

Players with winning sides, such as Lancashire and Nottinghamshire, could also expect bonuses if the county won the championship. In 1926, 1927 and 1928 the Lancashire Committee awarded their leading professionals an end-of-season bonus of £40 plus momentoes such as silver cigarette cases or salvers. After a series of very profitable seasons – in 1926 the annual profit was £10,283 – Lancashire's overall balance in 1928 stood at £42,479 and in that light the championship bonuses appear mean.

In an interview in 1981 Bill Voce commented rather cynically about the Notts players' reward for winning the 1929 championship. 'We were given a civic reception at the city hall, and a dinner – oh yes, and we each got a silver cigarette case. That was it.' However, it should be added that a local 'Shilling Championship Fund' raised £893 for the professionals and in the Committee's defence the Club made an annual loss in at least eight of the 11 seasons between 1923 and 1933. Even in 1929 the club recorded a deficit of £1400. In 1936 Notts were forced to launch an appeal for £6000 to cover the overdraft and outstanding debts of £3793. Times were hard at Trent Bridge and would have been much worse but for the unstinting generosity of Sir Julien Cahn, the local furniture retailer.

COUNTY EARNINGS

Excluding winter pay, bonuses and talent money, the leading 12 Notts professionals in 1936 could, according to the Committee records, expect to earn £300 per annum from ground staff money and match fees. The actual figures for the previous season show that although Harris, Staples and Walker received £310, Voce £307 and Larwood £306, the average was only £280. The addition of winter pay, bonuses and talent money raised the 1935 average to £408 with Voce drawing £444 and Lilley, Larwood, Harris, Staples and Walker £439.

Despite facing financial difficulties, Notts remained one of the 'big six' and paid their staff accordingly. In *A Cricket Pro's Lot*, published in 1937, Fred Root paints a rather different picture of the player's life at a less fashionable club such as Worcestershire. Between 1920 and 1929 Worcestershire's best performance in the championship was 14th; they finished bottom in 1922, 1926, 1927 and 1928. Fred Root proved the mainstay of this losing side taking more than 100 wickets every season from 1923 until 1931, including the 'double' in 1928. In his autobiography he wrote:

> Let me correct a mistaken impression that a cricket professional's life is a joyous combination of thrills, plaudits at the instigation of hero-worshipping crowds, talent money and banking accounts which place one beyond the cares of the financial troubles so closely associated with this life.

Root continued that cricket 'is the worst paid of all the professional games' and highlighted the point by stating that each season he bowled 1500 overs and played 47 innings for a reward of less than £300. Furthermore, he knew that four counties were paying less than Worcestershire and several the same.

In comparison with the rest of the working class, however, a professional cricketer's earnings were good. In 1935 skilled workers such as a coalface worker or an engine driver were paid £149 (a decline from £180 in 1924) and £258 respectively; a semi-skilled London bus or tram driver £218; white-collar railway clerks £224 and bank clerks £368 per annum. Three years later only 12 per cent of the working population earned more than £250. At least during their cricketing careers capped players in the inter-war years maintained the professionals' financial status as part of the labour aristocracy, although, of course, a professional cricketer incurred considerable expense in earning his income. Players had to meet the cost of bats, flannels, boots and other equipment as well as cover train and hotel expenses for away games. Bill Voce remarked 'The county really only provided the wicket and the ball, you had to look after everything else.' In 1934 the cost of an average hotel breakfast was three shillings, although players often sought out cheaper lodgings. In his biography by David Foot, Harold Gimblett reminisced that when they visited London 'Mother Nye's was a favourite establishment for impecunious cricketers'. Bed and breakfast could be obtained for three shillings and sixpence, while Mother Nye did not mind if three of her guests slept in the same bed.'

TEST MATCH PAY

In 1925 Fred Root established a new Worcestershire record when he claimed 207 wickets and a subscription list raised nearly £200 in his honour. Nevertheless Root could never be classed with the 'select few professionals . . . in the very front rank . . . who enjoy incomes that are far beyond the dreams of the average county cricketer.'

Just as in the so-called golden age, during the inter-war years a handful of star players distanced themselves financially from the average county professional. The first step was to attain selection for England. The rates for a Test appearance in England varied with the opponents. Against Australia in 1930 the England professionals received £40 plus a third-class return railway ticket. The 12th man was paid £30 and the reserves £20. Against South Africa the rate was £27, while against India, New Zealand and the West Indies £20. The lower rates are a reflection primarily of the shorter match duration, but also the status of the opposition in the Test hierarchy. England's first home Test matches were played against the West Indies in 1928, New Zealand in 1931 and India in 1932.

Clearly, being selected for a home Test series provided lucrative additional income. For example, Jack Hobbs,

Walter Hammond, Maurice Tate and George Duckworth played in all five Tests against Australia in 1930 for which they received £200 plus a £50 bonus; £10 per Test was retrospectively paid to each professional as a consequence of the tremendous success of the series. Test receipts exceeded £75,000.

Having established himself as a Test performer a leading professional could expect to be selected for Test trials, the Players against the Gentlemen and in end-of-season festival matches, all of which commanded higher match fees than an ordinary county fixture.

AUSTRALIAN TOURS

It was the four-yearly tours to Australia which proved to be the big money earners. For the 1928-29 and 1932-33 tours the MCC paid the professionals a basic £400 with the added possibility of being awarded a bonus of £300 in 1928-29 and £350 in 1932-33. The latter was divided into two equal parts for discipline and merit. In 1933 after the party had returned home all 12 professionals, on Jardine's recommendation, were given £175 for discipline, while the merit money was allocated as follows: Hammond, Larwood and Sutcliffe £175 each; Ames, Duckworth, Leyland, Paynter, Verity and Voce £125 each; Bowes, Mitchell and Tate £75 each.

During such a tour each professional's hotel and travel expenses were paid by the MCC. The player had only to cover drinks, cigarettes, parties and his own entertaining. Les Ames remembers saving enough money from the 1928 tour to buy a house, and at that time a semi-detached house with a bathroom and a garage cost around £450. Of course such tours were not all cricket. In an interview in 1974 Charles Barnett of Gloucestershire, who made the trip in 1936-37, recalled:

> the sight-seeing, the ship and train travel and hotel comforts for seven months, and you had wonderful conditions . . . in the winter months at home unemployment queues were very common sights.

The 'amateur' Australian tourists in 1930 were paid £600 by the Australian Cricket Board of Control, again making a mockery of the amateur-professional distinction. The final £150 was handed over on the tourists' return home, subject to the manager's discipline report. On this occasion the Board deducted a £50 fine from Don Bradman for contravening his contract by writing for the *Star*.

A successful tour occasionally led to a special subscription list or fund being raised in the player's home county. After the 1924-25 MCC tour to Australia, during which Herbert Sutcliffe hit four centuries in nine Test innings, a shilling testimonial fund was launched in Pudsey. Maurice Tate, who captured 38 wickets in that series, was similarly honoured with a testimonial fund backed by Sussex and the local newspapers. Likewise after the 1932-33 bodyline tour a shilling fund in Nottingham raised £776 for Harold Larwood and Bill Voce. The presentation was made by Douglas Jardine on Whit Monday 1933 during the Notts versus Surrey encounter at Trent Bridge.

ENDORSEMENTS AND SPONSORSHIPS

During the inter-war years the endorsement of cricket equipment by leading players became more widespread. Prior to the First World War W. G. Grace and Tom Hayward had endorsed particular bats but in the 1920s and 1930s the cricket consumer had a choice of bats bearing the approval of Hobbs, Mead, Macartney, Leyland, Bradman, Sandham, Kilner, Sutcliffe, Ames and Hutton; of Woolley leg guards and of gauntlets bearing the endorsement of Dolphin, 'Tiger' Smith, A. A. Lilley and Stedman (Fred Stedman's name continued to be used even though he had been accidentally killed in 1918 while walking on the railway at Bray in County Wicklow, Ireland).

For the first time too notable players were being used to market products with only a peripheral cricket connection. Jack Hobbs put his name to Reid's Ovalba White; Fred Root appeared in adverts for Elliman's Athletic Rub and Maurice Tate endorsed Hovis and Shredded Wheat. And while today it is commonplace to see county players driving a sponsor's car, in the 1930s it was very rare. The first professional to be so 'honoured' was Wally Hammond who in 1929 took the wheel of a Saloon Graham Paige. At that time the more down-market Austin Seven or Ford Eight would have cost £100.

Taking into account other occasional work, such as engagements at major stores like Gammages or Harrods, an England player could expect to earn £6-800 per annum from cricket, excluding overseas tours. As Les Ames said in a recent interview, it was 'a comfortable living'.

CONTRACTS

During the inter-war years more and more counties began to issue contracts to their capped players, although there were some surprising exceptions. Harry Lee recalled that he never had a written contract from Middlesex, nor did Herbert Sutcliffe with Yorkshire.

Sutcliffe wrote in *For England and Yorkshire* that his cap was his agreement. Rather than a contract Yorkshire issued a booklet entitled 'Regulations relating to Players'. These rules stated that a player must not write for the press; that as soon as a professional received his cap he was to join the Cricketers' Fund Friendly Society, and that the Committee reserved the right to withhold permission for a player to undertake an overseas tour in winter.

After outlining rates of pay and duties point 10 in the standard Notts contract also stated that the player was 'not to write any article or sign his name to any article dealing with cricket'. The document concluded that in the event of 'serious misconduct' the Club could 'terminate this Agreement at any time'.

STAR CONTRACTS – JACK HOBBS AND TED MCDONALD

Before the First World War George Lohmann, Tom Richardson and Tom Hayward successfully negotiated a better deal with the Oval authorities on the basis of their 'star' status.

Jack Hobbs was accorded the same privilege after the War, as was Ted McDonald, the former Australian Test player who joined Lancashire.

Jack Hobbs – 'The Master' – scored 35,107 of his 61,237 runs and 131 of his 197 centuries after the First World War. John Arlott wrote in his biography, *Jack Hobbs*, that:

> For those amazing fifteen years after he was thirty-six, he was, apart from Bradman, the most consistently heavy run-scorer the game has ever known. Unlike Bradman, he scored his runs in all conditions . . . His eminence at this time – indeed, for his entire passage along his high plateau – lay in his ability to make runs against all kinds of bowling on all types of wickets.

In May 1919 the Surrey Committee recognised Jack Hobbs' pre-eminent status amongst the professional staff and gave him the additional security of a contract until April 1924. In the various discussions with the Oval authorities Jack Hobbs represented the players and in November 1920 new terms were agreed. Jack Hobbs, Herbert Strudwick and Bill Hitch, the three Surrey professionals chosen for the 1920-21 tour of Australia, were given a weekly wage of £4 10 shillings and an annual guarantee of £400.

An operation for appendicitis disrupted Hobbs' performances in 1921, although the Surrey Committee made him a special grant of £200 to compensate for 'the loss and disappointment resulting from his illness', but in the following season, despite not being fully fit, 'The Master' hit 10 centuries. Jack Hobbs was approaching his 40th birthday but the Surrey Committee were so confident of his talents that they renegotiated a new five-year contract worth £440 per annum, excluding talent money and win bonuses. Financially this deal set Hobbs apart from the rest of the Oval staff and made him the best-paid professional in England. In September 1927 the contract was renewed for a further five years.

'The poorest season of his maturity' is how John Arlott describes Hobbs' 1923 performance, despite a career landmark in May at Bath when he became the third batsman (after W. G. Grace and Tom Hayward) to score a century of centuries. The Committee immediately awarded Hobbs 100 guineas to mark the occasion. Seven months later the astute Tom Hayward requested similar treatment; when he passed that milestone in the 'golden age' the Committee had not been so generous. Initially the Committee refused, but to their credit relented in March 1924 and Hayward received a belated 100 guineas.

Two seasons later, again in the away fixture against Somerset, although on this occasion played in Taunton, Jack Hobbs hit 101 not out to equal Grace's record of 126 centuries and in the second innings, before a small crowd and one journalist, added another 101 to set a new record. The Committee rewarded him with 250 guineas and a second benefit the following season which totalled £2670. The Committee led the subscription list with £100, instead of the usual £50, and guaranteed £1000 from the gate receipts, as opposed to the normal £750. This was a benefit that could not fail.

Jack Hobbs had wisely invested the proceeds (£1671) from his war-delayed first benefit in 1919 in a sports goods shop at 59 Fleet Street. John Arlott has commented:

> As soon as his shop prospered – which was almost at once – he stood in a changed position. He was a professional cricketer who earnt more from another source than from cricket . . . This simple fact . . . was a major step in the elevation of the professional cricketer – indeed the professional games player in Britain – above dependence.

England's leading batsman was assured of other income during his playing career. He endorsed various products; he 'wrote' books (*My Cricket Memories*, published in 1924, was ghosted by Jack Ingham, *Playing for England*! appeared seven years later with the help of Thomas Moult and *My Life Story* in 1935, thanks to the work of J. T. Bolton); he covered the bodyline tour and other Test matches (again with Jack Ingham's help) for the *Star*; and in winter when he was not on tour with the MCC or running his business he accepted an overseas engagement such as that in 1930-31 when, at the invitation of the Maharaj Kumar of Vizianagram, he accompanied Herbert Sutcliffe to India. His Yorkshire partner recalled that they were 'fêted in royal fashion' and entertained, by among others, the Viceroy – Lord Irwin, the Governor of Bengal, who at the time was Sir Stanley Jackson, and the Governor of Madras.

It is impossible to assess accurately what Jack Hobbs might have earned in a year from all sources, but as John Arlott wrote in his biography it was 'a most handsome' living. Ian Peebles in *'Patsy' Hendren* claimed that the former orphan who became a hero at Lord's was guaranteed £500 per season and from all sources (press articles, books, the Acton cricket school and Warsop bat endorsements) had an income of about £1500. It is doubtful if Jack Hobbs' earnings were inferior and by way of comparison it should be remembered that a General Practioner's annual income in 1935 was £1094. As Peebles said of Hendren, he was 'comfortably off without being affluent'.

Ted McDonald's return to England to play for Nelson in the Lancashire League in 1922 did not find favour with *Wisden*. An editorial 'objected strongly to the importation of Australian players'. McDonald played in only 11 Tests for Australia, but in the space of five matches during the 1921 tour of England he established himself as one of the great fast bowlers by claiming 27 wickets and, in combination with Jack Gregory, tore the heart out of the English batting. For the first time in a Test series sustained pace bowling had been used from both ends.

Bert Oldfield in *Behind the Wicket* made some interesting observations about Ted McDonald's bowling:

> It is notable that throughout their association in Test cricket, Gregory always had the advantage of bowling with the wind. I found McDonald's approach to the wicket rhythmical and graceful by comparison to the bounding and somewhat ungainly run and delivery of Gregory . . .
>
> McDonald was able to turn the ball back from the off

> even at his fastest speed . . . Nothing in cricket was prettier than the action of the late E. A. McDonald . . . All his energy went into flinging the ball down and none into superfluous pounding of the earth or waving of the arms.

While this may not be the most eloquent prose ever written about Ted McDonald – Neville Cardus after comparing him to a 'panther' described McDonald as 'a satanic bowler, menacing but princely' and R.C.Robertson-Glasgow was moved to employ adjectives such as 'saturnine and mahogany-grim' – it derived from the experience of observation at close quarters.

Edgar Arthur McDonald was born in Launceston, Tasmania in 1891, the son of a tinsmith. In *A History of Tasmanian Cricket* Roger Page records that the youthful, bespectacled McDonald went to work for an insurance company, bowled round-arm and slogged. He represented his native island in 1909-10 before making a 'hurried exit from Launceston early in 1911' – the exact nature of his misdemeanour remains a mystery. After settling in Melbourne Ted McDonald won a place in the Victorian Sheffield Shield side before finally graduating to the Australian eleven for the third Test against England in Adelaide on 14 January 1921.

While McDonald played for Nelson he was fulfilling a residential qualification for Lancashire and in July 1924 T. A. Higson opened negotiations with the Lancashire League Club and McDonald for his 'transfer' to the county side. The deal which was struck contained four major points. First, Nelson were paid £500 as compensation for bringing McDonald to England; second, they were accorded one first-class match in 1925 and one in 1926 and given 10 per cent of the net gate receipts; third, McDonald was released by Nelson at the end of 1924, but in the interim he was made available for the clash with Yorkshire at Old Trafford in August; and, finally, Ted McDonald was to be paid £500 per annum and awarded a benefit after only five seasons.

Ted McDonald had superceded Jack Hobbs as the best paid professional in England. Compared to other employees at Old Trafford he was earning £200 more than J. T. Tyldesley, the county coach, and even £50 more than the Club secretary, while 11 years later the England wicket-keeper George Duckworth was being offered a guarantee of only £315. The other important aspect of the McDonald deal was that he was to be allowed a benefit after five years instead of the usual minimum of ten. Despite terrible weather his benefit realised £1920 in 1929.

The Committee continued to be generous to their 'star' player. Ted McDonald moved into a club house at 23 Queens Avenue, Old Trafford, paying a rent of only £40 a year on a property which had cost £750 to purchase. Lancashire even paid the £18 removal expenses. However the county were well-rewarded – in his first full season McDonald took 205 wickets at an average of 18.67. The *Cricketer* recognised that Ted McDonald was 'the best fast bowler in the world'. In September the Committee paid their destructive fast bowler a further £80 towards his 'season's expenses'.

Between 1924 and 1931 Ted McDonald took 1053 wickets for his adopted county and played a crucial role in four of Lancashire's championship victories. In Lancashire's 1000th match in the county championship McDonald hit his only first-class century. Batting at number seven in the first week of August 1926 against Middlesex at Old Trafford he hit 100 not out in exactly 100 minutes. The Committee minutes record that in March 1926 the Club advanced McDonald a loan of £150 at 5 per cent interest to start a business and in October of the following year, when it was 'imperative' that he go overseas, another loan and a gift of £100.

In July 1927 Ted McDonald's contract had been renewed for a further two years but when the issue rearose in September 1929 it became the subject of considerable controversy on the Committee. Ted McDonald asked for a three-year extension after a season's haul of 142 wickets.

However, in the context of a need for staff economies, the Committee voted by nine votes to six to offer him only a one-year extension. At the next meeting the matter was re-opened and by a margin of seven to six it was decided to award McDonald a four-year contract! Due to the close vote the issue reappeared on the agenda of the following meeting and a totally different package was arranged. McDonald was given £200 in cash and his outstanding debt of £300 was cancelled; the county was to have a two-year option on his services at the previous rate of £500 per annum plus £80 expenses and the player was to be allowed to visit Australia with his wife and children during the winter of 1929-30.

During the 1930 season Ted McDonald again took more than 100 wickets, including those of Don Bradman and Archie Jackson when the Australian tourists visited Liverpool. Bert Oldfield remembered 'McDonald amazed me by his speed, which was particularly disconcerting', given the fast bowler was now 39 years old.

In the following season McDonald played in only half of Lancashire's championship matches and claimed just 26 wickets. The county slumped to sixth in the table, their worst position since the championship was recommenced after the War. Although Ted McDonald's contract had one year to run it was terminated by mutual agreement. McDonald returned to the Lancashire League with Bacup, where he succeeded his fellow Australian Arthur Richardson as the professional and in 1932 captured more than 90 wickets at an average of nine runs. During the ensuing seasons Ted McDonald represented the 'star-studded' Blackpool eleven in the Ribbleswade League, albeit by 1934 as an amateur. Also in the side were C. S. Dempster and K. C. James, two outstanding New Zealand Test players, and Peter Fairclough, the former Lancashire professional.

Ted McDonald died tragically on 22 July 1937, killed by a passing vehicle on the side of the Manchester-Chorley road after his own car had been involved in an accident. In *More Cricket Prints* R. C. Robertson-Glasgow wrote that in Lancashire Ted McDonald:

> found those who were only too ready to play up to his swashbuckling and devil-may-care nature. He loved to be thought the 'tough-baby', and he fell into ways that foreshadowed tragedy.

Richard Tyldesley endeavoured to follow the precedent set by Ted McDonald in arranging a special contract with the Lancashire Committee. Having joined the ground staff in August 1919 at the minimum of £150 for the season, Tyldesley, a right-arm slow bowler who frequently opened the bowling, had progressed by 1924 to the top rate of £5 in summer and £2 in winter. And there, like all the other leading Lancashire professionals with the exception of McDonald, he remained. In 10 successive seasons from 1922 Dick Tyldesley claimed 100 or more wickets for his native county. In 1929 Tyldesley grabbed 154 wickets and in the following season a further 133 justifying his selection for the first and third Tests against Australia. From what appeared a position of strength Dick Tyldelsey met the Lancashire chairman in Blackpool in September 1930 and outlined his terms. He asked for a five-year contract, an annual guarantee of £400 plus £80 expenses and after five years two-thirds of a benefit match or £1000.

Dick Tyldesley threatened to leave the Club. The Committee stated they could not entertain such terms. The player backed down and signed the usual one-year contract with a sweetner that there might be a bonus at the end of the next season, albeit at the Committee's discretion.

In 1931 Tyldesley's 116 wickets cost him less than 16 runs apiece and *Wisden* acknowledged that he was 'essential to the success of the county', but by July the Committee had already decided 'unanimously' against retaining the player's services. *Wisden* lamented the prospect of Lancashire without either McDonald or Dick Tyldesley and hoped for reconciliation, but to no avail. The Committee was in no mood for compromise. Tyldesley went to play for Nantwich in the North Staffs and District League – they won the championship both seasons he was their professional – before returning to play in the Lancashire League for Accrington in 1934.

Dick Tyldesley's departure from Old Trafford brought to an end the family connection with the county. All four brothers had represented Lancashire but William was killed in the War and James died under anaesthetic in January 1923. Lancashire launched a testimonial for the widow and family of James Tyldesley which reached £422. In November 1922 Harry Tyldesley was not re-engaged at Old Trafford and after many successful seasons of Lancashire League cricket died in 1935 aged 42. Dick was only four years older than Harry had been when he died in 1943. The fate of the Tyldesley brothers was reminiscent of the three McIntyre brothers born in Nottinghamshire 50 years earlier.

UNCAPPED PLAYERS

Being awarded a county cap represented more than a recognition of cricketing talent; it had important financial consequences. Yorkshire and Lancashire paid uncapped players £2 less than their capped brethren for first team appearances, while differentials also existed in ground staff pay. An uncapped member of the staff would be lucky to receive £3 per week for the 20-week summer season and even more fortunate if he was given a winter retainer of between 10 and 20 shillings.

In 1925 the Old Trafford staff numbered 21 of whom nine were first team regulars receiving the £2 winter maximum. Of the other 12, three players were granted £1 and one 10 shillings as winter pay. Three years later, by which time the staff had grown to 28, there were still eight players receiving no winter pay.

The contracts with all the staff at Trent Bridge, including the leading professionals, stipulated that they had to attend each weekday at Trent Bridge, unless they were selected for an away fixture, put up the practice nets, help roll the wicket and in the event of their non-inclusion in the side for a home match, work as a gate-keeper or ticket-collector. Practise with the rest of the staff ran from 10.30 a.m. for two hours and was followed in the afternoon by three hours of bowling in the nets to members. Writing about life on the staff at Lord's Frank Lee in *Cricket, Lovely Cricket* added that it 'mattered little' that he had to sweep the stands or sell score cards because he had achieved his ambition of becoming a professional cricketer.

SUMMARY

In comparison to the pre-War years the capped county professionals and the handful of star players had managed to maintain their earnings and purchasing power. Like the rest of the working class between 1913 and 1930 their wages had doubled. This cannot be said for an ordinary member of a county ground staff. During the so-called golden age they would have been paid between £70 and £100 per year. In the inter-war years their earnings had barely increased, although prices had almost doubled by 1930. An agricultural labourer's annual income in 1935 was estimated to be £89. The ground staff bowler fared little better.

CHAPTER 10

'Hired Labourers of the Game'

THE DEPRESSION, THE DOLE AND WINTER WORK

UNEMPLOYMENT dominated the inter-war years. Coincidentally, a high point was reached during the body-line winter of 1932-33 when three million workers were on the dole. In *Defending the Ashes* Maurice Leyland commented to R. W. E. Wilmot that he was 'a lucky lad' – playing cricket was 'better than being a carpenter. And 'Ducky' and Harold Larwood, and Bill Voce and Tommy Mitchell; they're coal miners. They're better playing cricket.'

For these former miners it was not just that they were better paid, but that they had work. In 1932 the rate of unemployment reached 22.9 per cent but it was the old staple industries that were hit hardest with more than 41 per cent of miners out of work. Hunger marches, dole queues and the despised means testing of unemployment benefits became part of everyday life. A Home Office report in the 1930s stated that on average two unemployed men were committing suicide every day.

In these circumstances it is hardly surprising that public interest in county cricket fell away, a situation made worse by two wet summers in 1930 and 1931. When the 1937 Findlay Commission reported to the MCC on the state of county finances it concluded that only Kent, Middlesex and Yorkshire were in a position to raise substantial sums without recourse to appeals or borrowing. The report continued that some counties were 'not in a position to stand the financial strain'. In *Dai Davies Not Out . . 78* the Glamorgan professional recalled that the county Club 'faced extinction at the end of every season'.

Like several other counties Leicestershire consistently lost money in the 1930s – for example, £1500 in 1933, £5000 in 1935 and £3000 in 1936. Sir Julien Cahn, already a very substantial benefactor at Trent Bridge, came to the rescue. Worcestershire was not so fortunate and in 1933 made an appeal for funds through the pages of the *Cricketer* in order to ensure their continued participation in the county championship. Two years earlier the *Cricketer* astutely recognised that many county treasurers were 'waiting for that leap year which now comes once in four' (that is, the visit of the Australian tourists) or being 'granted a windfall from the profits made by the MCC overseas'.

A National Government composed of members of the three main political parties had been formed in August 1931 with Ramsay McDonald, the former leader of the Labour Party, as Prime Minister. The following month, in an emergency budget, unemployment benefit was cut by 10 per cent and teachers' salaries by 15 per cent. The county cricket authorities were quick to follow this lead and by March 1932 had pushed through wage cuts of 10 per cent.

In this climate of cost cutting, at the end of the 1931 season the Surrey Committee decided not to re-engage Andy Ducat and Bert Peach, two of their leading professionals. While both players were more than 40 years old Percy Fender, the Club captain, thought the move 'premature', but the times were such that even Fender's expenses were being queried by the Committee.

The depression and high inter-war unemployment rates exacerbated the difficulty that the professional cricketer had in finding winter work. And there were the traditional seasonal fluctuations. From October to March the growing leisure industry marked time, the shorter daylight hours restricted construction work and even the car plants put workers on short-time because of seasonal demand. It has been estimated that unemployment rose by at least 10 per cent during the winter months in most industrial towns.

Frank Lee in *Cricket, Lovely Cricket* calls the search for winter work the 'biggest bugbear' of being a professional cricketer. One winter he washed and painted the seats at Lord's. Les Ames had his own sports outfitting business or was on tour with the MCC, but he remembers that 'life was hard' for many players, especially as the county did not see it as their responsibility to help find the staff winter work.

The number of places on overseas tours either with the MCC or privately organised affairs was limited and inevitably restricted to the leading players. Similarly the overseas coaching jobs, particularly in South Africa, tended to be the prerogative of the senior professionals. From the 1920s several players coached regularly in South Africa – Harry Lee was there most winters, Maurice Tate in 1922-23 and Bill Hitch, Dick Tyldesley and Charlie Hallows two seasons later, while in 1929-30 Andy Ducat successfully answered the advertisement in the *Cricketer* for an all-round professional to coach in Queensland for £550 inclusive of return fares and expenses.

For the less illustrious professionals it was either work or the dole. A number of the former Notts miners who were on the staff at Trent Bridge returned to the pits, while the young Bill Bowes in Yorkshire sold electric lamps.

Another option, at least for those with the talent, was to play professional soccer – those were the days when the football season did not occupy most of the year! At the time there were some notable double internationals including Lancashire's Harry Makepeace who also gained League championship and FA Cup winners medals with Everton; Wally Hardinge, capped for England at soccer in 1910, and Andy Ducat who led Aston Villa to an FA Cup victory in 1920, played six times for England and left the Oval staff in June 1924 to become the manager of Fulham. Other noted cricketing-footballers were Harry Storer (Derbyshire), Les

Berry and Maurice Tompkin (Leicestershire), Pat Hendren (Middlesex), Syd Copley, Arthur Jepson, Walter Keeton, Arthur Staples and Willis Walker (Notts), Jack Lee (Somerset) and Laurie Fishlock (Surrey).

Arthur Jepson, by trade a baker, accepted a place on the Trent Bridge staff in 1938. He agreed despite the fact that the terms of 30 shillings a week for the summer only were half the rate he received as non-League Grantham's goalkeeper. When he pointed out this fact to a member of the Committee he was told, 'My lad, 'tis an honour to walk through those gates.' The authorities' attitude of 'there's plenty of others only too keen to take your place', which was so strong before the War, showed no signs of diminishing.

The 1920s and 1930s were years of tremendous social and political turmoil. The Russian Revolution, the 1926 General Strike, the 1929 Wall Street Crash, the Depression, the Spanish Civil War and the rise of fascism were profoundly important events which seem to have left the world of professional cricket untouched, at least overtly. The sole exception appears to have been Charlie Parker whose 'admiration for the Bolshevik triumph was never disguised', according to David Foot in *Cricket's Unholy Trinity*. There were still no moves to 'unionise' the players; a professional survived through his own prowess on the field, and the Committees' paternalism. The turbulent decades between the Wars intensified the view expressed by Harold Gimblett in David Foot's biography:

> Professional sportsmen are a defensive and insecure breed; they become lop-sided from habitually looking over their shoulders to see who is coming up to take their contract in a couple of years time.

DISCIPLINE

The payments-by-result carrot, combined with a firm, disciplinary stick continued to guide the thinking of the county Committees in their treatment of the professionals. Lancashire was, apart from Yorkshire, the most successful side in the inter-war years, winning the championship on five occasions and their side often included great characters such as 'Ciss' Parkin and Dick Tyldesley. These players did not always see eye-to-eye with the Old Trafford Committee.

Cecil Parkin finally joined the Lancashire staff in 1922 at the age of 36. Although born in County Durham he had made his first-class debut for Yorkshire in 1906 when Lord Hawke conveniently overlooked his lack of birth qualification with the famous remark, 'We are not particular about a few yards.' Parkin's move to Church in the Lancashire League, on the recommendation of Sydney Barnes, eventually gave him a residential qualification for the red-rose county and he duly made his debut in 1914. After the War an offer from Rochdale of £15 per week, a £20 signing-on fee and a guaranteed £100 benefit proved too tempting and Parkin remained in the leagues, although he did occasionally represent Lancashire. Like Sydney Barnes before him, 'Ciss' Parkin played for England and went on tour to Australia as a league professional. In 1921 the *Cricketer* acknowledged that Parkin was 'the best bowler in England today, on all wickets' but warned, he is 'a man of moods and requires careful supervision'.

Parkin had been suspended from the Lancashire League in 1920 after he walked off the field, having been told by the umpires that he could not obtain LBW decisions if he continued to bowl around the wicket. Rochdale supported their professional and withdrew from the League, although due to the intervention of the town's mayor a face-saving compromise was reached and the club's resignation was withdrawn.

In his first full season for Lancashire 'Ciss' Parkin showed his worth by capturing 181 wickets but in December 1922, in company with Dick Tyldesley, he was 'censured' for his attitude in not re-signing his agreement with the county. Both players were told they faced 'instant dismissal' in the event of any subsequent complaints. In future the Committee decided that players would be paid only from the date they signed their contracts. Clearly the Old Trafford authorities

Cecil Parkin, Richard Tyldesley and Ted McDonald

ruled out any negotiations or discussions about terms. It was a case of take it, or leave.

The following season Parkin's haul was 186 wickets but again the question of his continued employment with Lancashire was on the Committee's agenda. In October 'Ciss' applied to sever the connection but was persuaded to change his mind by a £100 bonus and an agreement that he could have a benefit 'not later than 1926' provided he 'remains in the service of the club as long as the Committee desires'.

With a tally of 194 wickets 1924 proved to be Parkin's best-ever season with Lancashire but it also marked the beginning of the end. Dick Tyldesley (167 wickets) and Parkin achieved some remarkable successes bowling out Glamorgan at Liverpool for 22, Derbyshire at Chesterfield for 40 and Yorkshire at Leeds for 33. Of the last-mentioned performance Neville Cardus wrote, 'We have been led out of the wilderness; we have entered the promised land.' Within a few weeks the same could not be said of Parkin; the cricket establishment had banished him.

In June 1924 Parkin was top of the national averages and a certain choice for the first Test against South Africa at Edgbaston. The tourists first were dismissed for 30 in their first innings but reached 390 in the second. In his regular column in the *Weekly Dispatch* on 22 June, Parkin wrote:

> I was standing all the time at mid-off wondering what on earth I had done to be overlooked. I can say that I never felt so humiliated in the whole course of my cricket career. Mr Gilligan bowled himself; he used Tate; he called up Frank Woolley; he went on again himself; he called back Tate; he asked Roy Kilner to bowl . . . I feel that I should not be fair to myself if I accepted an invitation to play in any further Test match.

The story, headlined 'Cecil Parkin refuses to play for England again', caused a sensation. Not only had he dared to criticise England's amateur captain but he had taken it upon himself to decline to play Test cricket. The fact that a journalist friend had ghosted the story on Parkin's behalf proved a flimsy defence. Pelham Warner was incensed and through the columns of the *Cricketer* demanded:

> Something more than a private apology is necessary for the health of the cricket body politic . . . A frank public apology, and he will earn the respect of cricketers. Otherwise the cricket world will regard him as the first cricketing Bolshevist, and will have none of him.

In July 'Ciss' Parkin apologised to the Board of Control and although Warner considered he had been 'a long time taking the only, and obvious course' the matter was closed. However, Warner had already made it clear that Parkin had 'now put himself outside the pale of any more representative cricket'. Parkin had played his last Test, although Arthur Gilligan bore him no malice and provided the foreword for *Cricket Triumphs and Troubles*.

Before the Lancashire Committee Parkin refused to name his ghost but did promise to stop writing in the press. The issue of leading players writing for the newspapers was to become contentious over the next few years. The Notts professionals' contract categorically excluded it. Yorkshire were equally adamant and the only exception made to this 'definite rule' was Herbert Sutcliffe's 'How to play' column. In October 1929 the Lancashire Committee passed a resolution which stated that 'No professional playing for Lancashire will be permitted in the future to write for the press during the cricket season'. In the close season they would be allowed to do so provided the articles were 'submitted and approved by the Committee'. The Surrey Committee did not resolve this question until July 1935, by which time Jack Hobbs had retired. A clause was added to the Surrey players' contracts which stated they 'shall not write any articles on cricket during the currency of their contract without the permission of the Committee.'

'Ciss' Parkin's benefit in 1925 raised £1880, a slightly disappointing outcome which Parkin attributed to the fact that a number of prominent Lancashire supporters refused to subscribe. The following June Parkin asked to be released and the Committee agreed, granting him an additional £150 bonus. 'Ciss' Parkin returned to the leagues, initially with Blackpool in the Ribblesdale as an amateur (he kept a hotel in the seaside town), then as a professional with East Lancashire in the Lancashire League, Tonge in the Bolton League and finally Levenshulme in the Lancashire and Cheshire. Gout brought his career to an end in 1935, at the age of 49.

Other Lancashire players had fallen foul of the Old Trafford Committee. Lol Cook, who played for the county on more than 200 occasions between 1907 and 1923, was dismissed after the Manchester versus Stockport match and banned from the professionals' dressing room and the pavilion in June 1924. Five years later Frank Watson, the county's opening batsman, caused grave consternation to the Committee when he declined an invitation from the MCC to tour New Zealand. He was instructed to 'write to MCC expressing his regret and that similar behaviour in such matters would never happen again'. The matter never had occasion to arise, he was not selected again. In 1930, when Watson applied for a benefit during the 1931 season, the Committee minutes stated it was 'not desirable', although they did subsequently agree.

The decision to grant a player a benefit remained at the discretion of a county Committee. Given the financial importance to the professional of his benefit it inevitably ensured that players were careful to avoid jeopardising their prospects. In October 1926 when the Lancashire Committee agreed that Hallows could have his benefit in 1928, McDonald in 1929 and Dick Tyldesley in 1930 they added 'subject to their general conduct and services to the Club being in every way satisfactory'.

BENEFITS AND THE SEYMOUR CASE

In the 1920s a new threat, far worse than inclement weather, appeared to blight any player's benefit – tax. The Inland Revenue claimed that benefit monies were derived from employment and therefore subject to taxation. The test case was fought over the proceeds of James Seymour's 1920 benefit of £939. Seymour had joined the Kent nursery in 1899 and represented Kent on 536 occasions between 1902 and 1926. His relatively small return, given his service to the county, was invested in a fruit farm.

The Seymour case, no doubt anxiously watched by all the leading professionals, progressed through the courts after the Commissioners for Income Tax had rejected the arguments of the Inland Revenue. The Crown appealed to the High Court, where Mr Justice Rowlatt upheld the view of the Commissioners. On 13 May 1926 the Crown appealed to a higher court and Seymour lost. The Master of the Rolls, backed by Lord Justice Warrington, ruled the sum taxable, although Lord Justice Sargant dissented and stated that the benefit was 'a personal gift from the public in recognition of Seymour's brilliant achievements'. Finally the case was resolved in Seymour's favour by the House of Lords. *Wisden* recorded that the Seymour case 'established the right of the cricket benefit, unless guaranteed by contract, to be free from tax'. Sadly, James Seymour did not live to reap the full rewards of this legal battle; he died in September 1930, aged 50.

County Committees had rallied to assist James Seymour and Kent in this protracted but crucial case. Both Lancashire and Surrey agreed to meet 10 per cent of the legal costs. The consequence for the players was that no professional could be guaranteed a benefit in his contract; pre-War benefit paternalism reasserted itself more strongly than ever.

The basic formula determining a player's benefit changed little during the inter-war years. A county Committee would not consider granting a professional a benefit unless he had completed at least 10 years of satisfactory service (the only exception being for 'star' players such as Parkin and McDonald at Old Trafford); all home and away expenses for the match against the nominated county were deducted; the restrictions on the choice of fixture continued (Jack Hobbs was a notable exception in being allowed the Bank Holiday encounter against Notts), and a large part of the proceeds were invested by trustees on the beneficiary's behalf (one of the rare exceptions being Les Ames who convinced the Kent Committee in 1938 that his benefit money would be better used if he invested it in his own business).

Benefit returns continued to vary substantially between counties. Table 9 lists the inter-war benefits of Hampshire, Lancashire, Notts and Yorkshire players. During the two inter-war decades the record established by George Hirst in 1904 of £3703 was exceeded on only one occasion, by fellow Yorkshireman Roy Kilner. In 1925 when Yorkshire entertained Middlesex at Headingley a crowd of 71,000 helped swell Kilner's benefit to £4016. Of course, in real terms, when inflation is taken into account Hirst's total was still unsurpassed. As usual Yorkshire was also generous in their support for non-professional testimonials. In 1926 F. C. Toone, the Club secretary, received £3500; a figure bettered in this period only by Kilner and Maurice Leyland (1934, £3648).

Table 9: Benefit returns 1920-39, Hampshire, Lancashire, Nottinghamshire and Yorkshire

	Hampshire	Amt	Lancashire	Amt	Notts	Amt	Yorkshire	Amt
1920	Mead	1000			Hardstaff	588		
1921			Heap	1804	Payton	825		
1922			Makepeace	2110	Gunn J	992	Dolphin	1891
1923			Cook	1657	Oates	753		
1924	Newman	1000	Tyldesley E	2458				
1925			Parkin	1880	Gunn G	948	Kilner	4016
1926	Kennedy	1095	Howard	1609	Whysall	628		
1927					Richmond	1126	Oldroyd	1700
1928	Brown G	1000	Hallows	2906	Barratt	1371	Holmes	2620
1929	Livsey	750	McDonald	1947			Sutcliffe	3057
1930	Mead	640	Tyldesley R	2027	Payton	800	Robinson	3255
1931							Macauley	1633
1932			Watson	1268	Staples S	1334		
1933			Tyldesley E	802	Walker	889		
1934			Duckworth	1257			Leyland	3648
1935					Lilley	1138		
1936	Boyes	764	Iddon	1266	Larwood	2098		
1937			Sibbles	1229	Staples A	1212	Mitchell	2227
1938			Hopwood	1105				
1939			Farrimond	1000	Voce	980	Wood	2563

However Yorkshire, as a Club, did take seriously the task of ensuring that a benefit would be a success. The Committee guaranteed that every benefit would realise a minimum of £1000; a secretary was appointed in each large town to organise the raising of funds; numerous collecting boxes were issued and the gate receipts were insured against rain. The target of £2000 was invariably reached.

Yorkshire players also knew that if they failed to retain a place in the side for the necessary 10 seasons their efforts would still be recognised. A professional of five years standing was given a grant of £250 with a bonus of £50 for each additional year. The only proviso, which highlights the way such payments were used by the county to enforce loyalty, was that if a player took an engagement elsewhere without the Committee's approval they would forfeit the right to such a bonus.

Surrey implemented a similar system to Yorkshire and guaranteed a beneficiary £750, albeit in lieu of all the gate receipts. Again, Hobbs was an exception, being given £1000. The Oval Committee also demanded that the player sign an agreement that he would remain with the Club for a further five years after his benefit.

As Table 9 indicates Lancashire benefits, on average, dropped significantly after the First World War. Nobody bettered J. T. Tyldesley's record return of more than £3000 in 1906; the nearest challenger was Charlie Hallows with £2906 in 1928. Hallows, who first requested a benefit in 1925, subsequently showed better timing by completing 1000 runs in May during the home match preceding his benefit game. Success was assured.

The Notts figures show that only Harold Larwood managed to exceed the pre-War record testimonial of the amateur A. O. Jones who received £1578 in 1907. Larwood's deserved return was the product of considerable organisation with 18 local matches being arranged in the city and county as well as a benefit dance. In Larwood's case he was permitted collections at his benefit game against Yorkshire and at the fixtures against Surrey and Derbyshire. In comparison Bill Voce must have been a disappointed man receiving only £980 in 1939. Similarly, William Farrimond, the England and for many years Lancashire understudy to George Duckworth, received only £1000 for his loyalty to the red rose. The second eleven wicket-keeper at Old Trafford had rejected several tempting offers to qualify for other counties.

What is striking about the Hampshire benefits is how few there were in the 1920s and 1930s and, of course, the low returns. The first point is explained by the presence of a large number of amateurs in the Hampshire side, albeit with a small nucleus of loyal professionals. And for stalwarts – like Mead, Newman, Kennedy, Brown and Livsey – it must have been galling to know their benefits would never match those achieved in the more prosperous and densely-populated counties.

The case of Phil Mead highlights the inadequacies of the benefit system. Mead was a player who represented his county on 700 occasions from 1905 to 1936 and scored a total of 55,061 first-class runs; his aggregate for Hampshire remains the greatest number of runs ever made by one cricketer for one team. Yet from his two benefits Phil Mead received only £1640, or an additional £2.34 per Hampshire match, whereas Jack Hobbs was rewarded with an extra £7.26 for each Surrey appearance; Lancashire's Ernest Tyldesley with £5.69 and Herbert Sutcliffe by £5.08. The ever-considerate Sutcliffe may have recalled his luck in later life for after the Second World War, when it was announced that Phil Mead had gone blind and Len Braund, whose 1908 Somerset benefit had been a financial disaster, had undergone surgery to amputate both his legs, the Yorkshire star turned successful businessman launched an appeal fund which raised more than £7000.

A number of long-serving professionals received second benefits, for example, Leicestershire's J. H. King after 28 years of first-class cricket, although the 1937 Findlay Commission Report to the MCC warned that 'counties should consider carefully before awarding a second benefit to a player . . . made the position of the smaller counties difficult.'

Throughout the inter-war years a voice of reason was occasionally heard which questioned the benefit as a means of rewarding players. In 1929 the *Cricketer* wrote, 'There must ever be that dread of a bad benefit in the minds of those playing. Remove the uncertainty and better cricket would be seen.' That appeal went unheard.

SHABBY TREATMENT – THE CASE OF MAURICE TATE

'If one of their serfs wanted to leave, who cared?' was Harold Gimblett's retrospective comment on Jack Lee's departure from Somerset. Jack Lee, the younger brother of Frank and Harry, had qualified by residence for Somerset and played 241 times between 1925 and 1936. Lee's benefit was imminent when the offer of a £300 per year job came up at Mill Hill school and when he sought advice from the county, the Club secretary Brigadier Lancaster told him 'Take it'. As a consequence Jack Lee did not receive a benefit.

A similar fate befell George Hunt, a Somerset professional from 1921 to 1931, who was sacked by the Club and despite the length of his service the only compensation granted was a collection during the following season.

Even notable England players, like Maurice Tate, could be treated in a disgracefully high-handed manner by their county Committee. On 3 August 1937 Tate was summoned before the Sussex Chairman Brigadier-General D'Arcy Brownlow and secretary W. L. Knowles and told that the Committee was not seeking his re-engagement for the following season and that he would be asked to play during the remainder of the 1937 season only in the event of an emergency.

Although Maurice Tate was 42 years old he wrote in his column in the *Hastings and St Leonards Observer* four days later that 'I have never felt fitter than I do at present.' More significantly, Maurice Tate was one of the best-known

England players of his generation and a player who had been with his county since 1912, representing them on more than 500 occasions, while his father Fred Tate first played for Sussex in 1887. Thus 50 years of family loyalty came to an abrupt end.

In the event, due to injuries Sussex were forced to call on Maurice Tate and he played in every match until the end of the season. In those eight games he added another 25 wickets to his enormous tally of wickets. After five against Surrey, including a first innings performance of 4 for 116 off 39.4 overs, Tate concluded with a total of 2784 wickets at an average of only 18.16. On 18 October the Committee confirmed its decision and bade farewell to Tate with a gift of £250 which they considered 'in view of our financial situation is certainly generous'.

Maurice Tate would have liked to continue playing county cricket but the two-year residential qualification made this impossible. This case shows the fallacious nature of this rule which kept a player of Tate's stature out of the first-class game when his own county did not require his services. In the event a poisoned foot stopped Tate playing in 1938 but the following season he appeared for Walsall in the Birmingham League. After the Second World War Maurice Tate coached at Tonbridge, kept a public house and in the spring of 1956 was employed at the Butlin's camp in Clacton. A few months later he died at his home in Wadhurst, Sussex aged 61.

ANOTHER CAREER?

After his 'retirement' from the first-class game Maurice Tate followed a path well established by hundreds of former professionals – league cricket, coaching and a public house. Potentially the job as a professional with a league club offered the players alternative employment, although very few took that option while they were at the height of their on-field powers. Len Hopwood, who failed to agree terms at Old Trafford in 1925 and spent the next two seasons playing for Wallasey, was one notable exception.

Subsequently he returned to the Lancashire staff and made an outstanding all-round contribution. In the championship-winning season of 1934 Hopwood became the first Lancashire player to achieve the 'double' since 1904. 'Nobby' Clark, the Northants and England left-arm fast bowler, was another to seek a short respite in the leagues during his county career.

In 1920 *Wisden* voiced the opinion of the cricket establishment when it stated, 'The menace of the Lancashire and Yorkshire Leagues cannot be ignored . . . leading professionals constantly receive from League clubs offers of better terms.' The previous year a resolution moved by Yorkshire was carried at the Advisory County Cricket Committee which asserted that players who did not pledge themselves to assist their counties when required would be barred from representative matches, overseas tours and festival games. This was part of a general move to tighten the counties' hold on their professionals. Nevertheless throughout the inter-war years league clubs continued to approach leading professionals. Fred Root turned down £600 for a 20-week season, while after the bodyline tour Harold Larwood was at pains to deny a rumour that he had been offered £40 per week in summer and £10 per week in winter to play for Burnley. However, such sums were definitely available to Test stars, for example, Accrington offered Don Bradman a guarantee of £1000 plus lucrative performance bonuses to play in the Lancashire League.

A number of fine Australian cricketers did make the trip to play league cricket in the North of England. Apart from Ted McDonald they included Arthur Richardson, who hit a Test century against England at Headingley in 1926; Bill Hunt, who made one Test appearance against South Africa in 1931-32; and Frank O'Keefe, considered one of the best batsmen in Australia, who moved to the Lancashire League in 1922. The colder climate never suited O'Keefe and, tragically, three months before he would have qualified for Lancashire, he died of peritonitis at the age of 27.

Sir Julien Cahn's side also provided an alternative source of employment for a few professionals, particularly from overseas. Ginty Lush, disappointed after missing selection for the 1938 tour of England, signed up with Cahn at £600 per year – at the time he was earning £5 per week as a cadet journalist in Sydney! Similarly Harold Mudge, Vic Jackson and Jack Walsh all emigrated from Australia and qualified for Leicestershire while playing for Cahn.

The county Committees, however, and all their professionals realised that the only way to be really financially successful was to gain a Test place. As *Wisden* commented in 1920, a player had to 'sacrifice a little so as to keep in the public eye' and, it should be added, that of the England selectors.

Few professionals, once retired from the first-class game, returned to their original trades. Most either maintained an involvement with cricket via coaching and umpiring or they sought to cash in on their brief notoriety by opening a shop or becoming a publican. Of the 54 professionals who played for Notts during the inter-war years the subsequent occupations of 43 are known. The most popular careers were coaching (12), umpiring (5), the police force (5), sports and other shops (5) and publicans (3). Those five occupations cover 70 per cent of the total. The only difference from the position of pre-War Notts players was the recruitment of former professionals into the local police force. The most notable was A. W. Oates, a former miner who played only seven times for Notts before he joined the Nottingham City Police in 1933 and retired as an Inspector 31 years later.

Of the better known Trent Bridge professionals George Gunn, Wilf Paynton and Bill Voce became coaches; Charlie Harris, Arthur Jepson, Thomas Oates and Sam Staples umpires (Staples also occupied the post of coach to Hampshire in 1939); 'Dodge' Whysall, Walter Keeton and Willis Walker ran sports shops, while at one time Harold Larwood opened a confectionary shop in Blackpool; and Ben Lilley kept a public house.

Harold Larwood in his Blackpool shop *(Photo: Nottinghamshire CCC)*

This pattern was typical of virtually all professional cricketers in the inter-war years. It had changed very little from pre-War days.

The first moves towards the creation of a national old-age pension scheme began in 1908 with a non-contributory system for those over 70, subject to a means test. Seventeen years later this was followed by the Widows', Orphans' and Old Age Contibutory Pensions Act which provided an insured worker with a pension of 10 shillings between the ages of 65 and 70. These arrangements were made more complex by the existence of company and private insurance schemes; however, after the Second World War the Labour Government implemented an old-age pension of 16 shillings per week.

Professional cricketers could also still seek support from the Cricketers' Fund Friendly Society which on payment of an annual subscription of one guinea and after a two-year eligibility period provided temporary (30 shillings in summer and 18 shillings in winter for one year) and permanent (seven shillings and sixpence) disability pensions as well as a £20 payment on the member's death.

One consequence of the increased provision of pensions was the decline in the numbers of destitute professional cricketers and the virtual end to players committing suicide. A. E. Relf, the popular Sussex and England all-rounder, shot himself in March 1937, but his decision was apparently the consequence of poor health and depression, rather than destitution. According to *Wisden* he died 'a wealthy man'.

Two players who died while still in their cricketing prime were 'Dodge' Whysall, the Notts opening batsman, and Roy Kilner of Yorkshire. Whysall fell on a dance floor and subsequently died of blood-poisoning, while Kilner contracted enteric fever on the way home from India where he had spent the winter coaching.

In 1919 there were about 100,000 cars on the English roads and even more motor-cycles. Inevitably road deaths increased and by 1934 the annual total exceeded 7300. Several cricketers were among the grisly statistics. George Street, the Sussex wicket-keeper who had represented England on one occasion in South Africa during the 1922-23 tour, was killed instantly at Portslade on 24 April 1924 when his motor-cycle hit a wall after avoiding a lorry. A fund was launched for his widow and children. Ten years later Dudley Pope, the dour Essex opener, died in a car smash. Ted McDonald was the most famous player to die on the road; however the previous year, 1936, two amateurs – R. P. Northway (Northants) and D. A. C. Page (the Gloucestershire captain) – also became car-accident fatalities.

Although several cricketers, particularly amateurs, liked to motor to matches the county Committees began to forbid it after the first road accidents. Arthur Carr, the Notts captain, was a notoriously reckless driver. One of his motoring exploits is recounted in *The Trent Bridge Battery*: 'He nearly killed himself and five Nottinghamshire players when he swung his three-wheeler round a particularly sharp bend on the way back from Mansfield.' A few seasons later Harold Larwood and three other Notts players were involved in a car crash which kept Larwood out of the side for a month.

THE FIRST CRACKS IN THE HIERARCHY

Throughout the inter-war years the obvious manifestations of the 'snobberies of the first-class game', as Harold Gimblett called them, continued. The amateurs and professionals were still segregated in their dressing rooms, through their entrances on to the field of play, in hotels and railway compartments and by the status accorded them on the score-card. Jack Lee conveyed his forthright opinion on this state of affairs to Harold Gimblett:

> Don't you bother yourself, Harold, about them going out of a different gate. Just you think that we're good enough in our own right to be playing this game and getting paid for it. All the amateurs have to do is put on a pretty hat.

Percy Fender and Lionel Lord Tennyson, two amateur captains with reputations for bold tactics, on separate occasions decided to overturn tradition and lead their amateurs and professionals together as a team out of the centre gate at Lord's. The MCC authorities were not amused. Lord Harris summoned Fender to the Committee room and informed him, 'We do not want that sort of thing at Lord's, Fender', while Tennyson recalled that he 'got it in the neck from one of the old MCC Presidents'.

At a number of county grounds amateurs and professional did change together; for example, in Yorkshire, Glamorgan and Kent (except Dover). Percy Fender, who often had a large dressing room to himself, tried to implement such a reform at the Oval, but was dissuaded by Hobbs and Strudwick. Predictably, it was at Lord's that rigid segregation was *de rigueur.*

According to Les Ames the England side did much to break down the amateur-professional barriers. The England eleven, and the MCC tourists abroad, invariably changed together and stayed in the same hotels and, as Sir Gubby Allen commented in an interview, 'on a tour you got to know the professionals'. However, that also depended on the amateur in question. Douglas Jardine, for example, an aloof and shy man, rarely spoke to the professionals on the 1928-29 tour of Australia. The difference between Jardine and Allen as captains was quite pronounced. In 1932-33 it was always 'Mr Jardine', whereas four years later 'skipper' was perfectly acceptable. Nevertheless, on both trips the on-tour selection Committee of five included two senior professionals. During the bodyline tour of 1932-33 the inclusion of Herbert Sutcliffe and Wally Hammond as selectors was known and accepted by the MCC Committee. In 1936-37 Sir Stanley Jackson vetoed the idea, but Gubby Allen was unperturbed and once the side reached Australia he established an 'unofficial' selection Committee including his two senior professionals. In fact, it was this unofficial Committee which over-ruled Allen and chose Bill Voce, despite his being unfit, for the decisive fourth Test in Adelaide which Australia won by 148 runs.

England players like Jack Hobbs, Wally Hammond and Herbert Sutcliffe were not only internationally-renowned batsmen but, in their own right, were socially accepted in the most illustrious circles. On an MCC tour they were invited to many functions along with the amateurs.

For the most part the 'snobberies' continued in the 1920s and 1930s but minor encroachments were being made around the edge of cricket's citadel. Similarly, the hierarchies between the leading professionals and the rest of the ground staff were slowly being eroded. Until invited to do otherwise the rest of the staff addressed the senior professionals as 'mister' or 'sir'. In a recent interview Alf Gover recalled the difficulty he had in making the transition from 'sir' to 'Jack', despite encouragement from Hobbs.

At Lord's and the Oval there were two professional dressing rooms which demarcated the division between the senior players and the rest of the staff. At Taunton, with its smaller staff, the young Harold Gimblett was told, 'There's two pegs. That's where you change. And speak when you're spoken to.' This advice 'given in a kindly way . . . was the best advice I was ever given.' Although Frank Lee had been given the same advice by his elder brother when he joined the Lord's staff he inadvertently ignored it on one occasion and was 'soon made to realise the crime I had committed by the ensuing silence'.

After the First World War when many of the players who had been 'educated' in cricket's class-conscious so-called golden age returned as senior professionals, the hierarchy and formalities were adhered to rigidly. J. T. Hearne, who had made his debut for Middlesex in 1888 and played until 1923, was known as 'The Squire of Chalfont St Giles' because of his immaculate dress-sense and manners. In *Forty Years of English Cricket* Harry Lee recounted the etiquette that was followed during away matches when Hearne was the senior professional:

> J.T. set the hour for us to be at meals or in bed. When we came to sit down, the juniors stood back until the seniors had chosen their places. Then J.T. would take his seat at

> the head of the table and carve the joint, handing round the plates in proper order of seniority, and giving himself the carver's portion last of all.

As the inter-war years passed these formalities and traditions began to wane. Harry Lee commented that increasingly there was less respect. On every front cracks in tradition were beginning to appear but the issue which divided the cricket world more than any other in those two decades was whether a professional was fit to captain his county or, ultimately, England.

THE PROFESSIONAL CAPTAIN

In 1925 'Ciss' Parkin suggested in a newspaper article that if England could not find a suitable amateur to captain the eleven then why not select a professional such as Jack Hobbs or Herbert Sutcliffe? Once again Parkin's pen placed him at the centre of a controversy. At the Yorkshire Annual General Meeting Lord Hawke responded and made the famous statement 'Pray God no professional will ever captain England.'

Lines were drawn even within amateur circles. Lord Forster, the Governor General of Australia and former Kent captain, supported Parkin by commenting that he would 'never hesitate to play under the captaincy of a man like Jack Hobbs'. Percy Fender was even more forthright in an interview given to the *Daily Herald* in which he began by calling Lord Hawke's assertion:

> a gratuitous insult to the main body of professional cricketers . . . My experience of professional cricketers does not teach me that cricket would necessarily go to the dogs if a professional should happen to be in charge . . . I, personally, have played under a professional captain before and should not hesitate to do so again, if it were in the best interests of the side.

In the *Cricketer* Lord Harris and Plum Warner gave Lord Hawke their wholehearted support. Warner attacked Parkin's article as 'an effusion in equally bad taste' and the man himself as one of those 'mischief-makers who seem bent on creating a class warfare in the cricket world'. On the advice of Sir Edwin Stockton, the Lancashire President, 'Ciss' Parkin adopted a low profile and did not respond.

The following season, 1926, Hawke's prayers went momentarily unanswered when Jack Hobbs took over the England captaincy during the fourth Test against Australia at Old Trafford after Arthur Carr had succumbed to tonsilitis. A professional had last captained England when Arthur Shrewsbury led the side in 1877 in Sydney. Hobbs was subsequently offered the England captaincy but declined the honour. Herbert Sutcliffe was 'deeply disappointed . . . for the sake of the professional cricketer he should have accepted.' However, according to Percy Fender, Jack Hobbs disliked the responsibility of the Surrey captaincy and if Fender ever left the field Hobbs preferred Herbert Strudwick to take command.

Given Sutcliffe's views on Hobbs and the England captaincy it seems remarkable that he himself chose to decline the Yorkshire captaincy when it was offered to him in November 1929. The Committee decision, achieved by a two-vote majority, immediately caused a sensation. For some it was out of the question that a professional could lead the county, while others claimed the job should have been offered to the senior professional, Wilfred Rhodes. According to Leslie Duckworth's *Holmes and Sutcliffe*, the Committee decided to end the controversy by cabling Sutcliffe in South Africa, where he was on tour, and asking him to withdraw his acceptance. Herbert Sutcliffe agreed. According to Leslie Duckworth, in retrospect Herbert Sutcliffe regretted that he had succumbed to the Committee's pressure.

Eight years later, over the Pennines, a debate arose on the Lancashire Committee about who should succeed Peter Eckersley as the county captain. Eckersley had won the parliamentary seat of Manchester Exchange and the choice lay between 24-year-old amateur W. H. L. Lister and the 46-year-old senior professional Ernest Tyldesley. The Committee voted 11-6 in favour of Lister and after a few matches in 1936 Tyldesley retired. One of Ernest Tyldesley's pre-War professional colleagues, John Sharp, did captain Lancashire for three seasons from 1923, but as an amateur. Sharp was a professional from 1899 to 1914 and during that period also played soccer for Everton as a professional. In his post-War amateur years *Wisden* described Sharp as a 'very capable leader' and in 1924 he became an England selector.

During the 1920s and early 1930s a number of senior professionals led their counties in emergencies or when no amateurs were available. The short list reads:

Derbyshire: Elliott
Glamorgan: Bates
Gloucestershire: Goddard, Hammond and Parker
Hampshire: Brown, Kennedy and Mead
Lancashire: J. T. and E. Tyldesley
Leicestershire: Astill and King
Middlesex: Hendren
Nottinghamshire: J. and G. Gunn
Surrey: Ducat, Hobbs and Sandham
Sussex: Cornford
Warwickshire: Bates and W. G. Quaife
Worcestershire: Root
Yorkshire: Hirst and Rhodes.

To Leicestershire's Ewart Astill belongs the honour of being the first professional captain appointed by his county Committee for a full season in the twentieth century. Astill led Leicestershire in 1935 to sixth spot in the county championship – their best position since 1905 – and their tally of 11 wins was not bettered until 1975. *Wisden* wrote:

> 1935 must be regarded as the most successful season in the history of the Club . . . the presence of a regular and first-class leader undoubtedly led to a strong will-to-win spirit and provided just the fillip needed to set the Club on its feet once more.

Ewart Astill was a perfect choice as county captain. He made his debut in 1906 and topped the Leicestershire bowling averages the following season when he took 80 wickets. In four successive seasons he did not miss a match. During the First World War Astill gained a commission with the Machine Gun Corps, and between 1921 and 1930 he achieved the 'double' every season except 1927. Four MCC tours no doubt ensured that his handsome face retained a healthy tan, as well as putting his skills as a pianist and vocalist to good use. As E. E. Snow wrote in *A History of Leicestershire Cricket*, for Ewart Astill 'the captaincy, leadership and demeanour presented no problems'.

Remarkably, after such a fine season, the county Committee gave the captaincy in 1936 to the newly-qualified New Zealand amateur C. S. Dempster who had been playing in the leagues and with Sir Julien Cahn. Despite the presence of Dempster, considered at the time to be one of the best batsmen in the world, the county slumped to 15th in the championship and won a meagre two games. The following season, again under Dempster, they fared even worse and finished 16th after winning only one match.

Cricket's dominant individuals, and Committees with their conservative values, could not cope with the idea of professional captains. The Second World War would change that and many other out-dated ideas in British society. In the interim, ridiculous face-saving compromises were reached whereby Wally Hammond became an amateur in November 1937 to enable him to be acceptable as the England captain. The deal was possible only because certain MCC members arranged for Hammond to be given a £2000 salary as Director of Marsham Tyres, part of the Dunlop group of companies.

THE DECLINE OF THE AMATEUR

Between the wars the amateur steadily disappeared from the first-class scene. In 1928 205 amateurs appeared for their counties, but nine seasons later the figure had fallen by 35 per cent to 133. Similarly, the number of amateurs who played in 10 or more county matches fell by 22 per cent from 46 to 36.

By the end of the 1920s Lancashire, Leicestershire, Nottinghamshire and Yorkshire rarely put a side into the field which contained more than two amateurs and usually it was 10 professionals plus the obligatory amateur captain. During the following decade this quartet were joined by Derbyshire, Surrey and Sussex in selecting sides predominantly composed of professionals.

Ultimately the decline of the amateur was a consequence of economic changes in society at large. The landed gentry, with their country estates, were on the wane. Between the 1870s and the early 1950s two-thirds of the gentry in Essex, Oxfordshire and Shropshire lost their country seats. The material conditions for the so-called golden age were well and truly over. In *Sticky Wickets* Lionel Lord Tennyson remembered the Edwardian years as 'pleasant and gay'. He continued:

> During the London season for night after night doors were open wide in Mayfair, and throughout the West-End, until the small hours of the morning. There was an abundance of champagne and the loveliest girls in England to be danced with.

Tennyson's parents owned two houses in the country and often rented a third in London during 'the season' and parliamentary sittings. By the time *Sticky Wickets* was published in 1950 Tennyson considered himself 'impoverished', although that, of course, is a relative term! An indication of the change in the distribution of wealth in Britain in the inter-war years was that the three largest fortunes in that period were left by a shipowner, a brewer and a linoleum manufacturer. According to John Stevenson in *British Society 1914-45*, almost 40 per cent of all millionaires and 50 per cent of half-millionaires originated in the commercial and financial sector where they were merchants, bankers, shipowners, merchant bankers, stockbrokers and insurers.

Commerce and finance proved an attractive career for many talented amateur cricketers. Errol Holmes and Gubby Allen worked on the Stock Exchange, while Douglas Jardine, although qualified as a solicitor, went into banking. In 1928 Jardine played only six times for Surrey, Allom on three occasions and Holmes just once. A similar trend was evident at Lord's with Middlesex – Allen made a solitary appearance and Peebles only two, while Greville Stevens, who had represented the Gentlemen against the Players in 1919 while still at school, did not play at all in 1928. Stevens had virtually abandoned first-class cricket because of the pressure of his business career as a stockbroker.

The only way a number of prominent amateurs could give the game their full attention was if they were employed as the county secretary and club captain. Strictly speaking this contravened the definition of an amateur, but continued the well-established pre-War practice of 'gentlemen professionals'. In the 1920s and 1930s the three most notable examples were Vallance Jupp at Northants, C. F. Walters with Worcestershire and Maurice Turnbull at Glamorgan.

Jupp had been educated privately and at St John's school, Burgess Hill, but played cricket as a professional for Sussex before the War. In 1919 he became an amateur, qualified by residence for Northants, and assumed the post of secretary in October 1921. Six years later he was appointed county captain. Jupp made a tremendous contribution to Northants' on-field performance achieving the 'double' eight times for his adopted county. By 1935, when Jupp missed the entire season due to illness, he was no longer listed as Club secretary. According to *Wisden* it was an 'irreparable' blow for Northants who lost 17 games, their worst-ever championship season.

C. F. Walters had represented Glamorgan irregularly between 1923 and 1928, but having accepted the secretary's job at Worcestershire and fulfilled the necessary two-year residential qualification, he became a permament fixture in the county side. In the absence of the Hon. J. Coventry he captained the eleven in 1931, a position which was formalised the following season. In 1935 Walters resigned as secretary and also asked to be relieved of the captaincy and despite stating that he would play as often as possible, his career was at an end.

Maurice Turnbull's acceptance of the Glamorgan secretaryship also solved the continuing problem of the lack of a regular amateur captain. In 1929 the job had been shared. Turnbull captained the side until 1939; five years later he was killed in action at Normandy.

The position of assistant secretary was still open to abuse as a means to ensure that a particular 'amateur' was paid. After Bob Wyatt told the Warwickshire Committee that he could not afford to take time off work to play for the county they immediately offered him the position of assistant secretary, as well as saying they 'would see to it that I got a good job in engineering'. Similarly, in June 1936 the Gloucestershire Committee offered Wally Hammond the assistant secretaryship and joint captaincy if he turned 'amateur'. Hammond declined because the remuneration would still have been less than the £450 he earned as senior professional.

The issue that annoyed the professionals was not the 'shamateurism' of cricketers like Jupp, Walters and Turnbull, but the sudden availability of amateurs for certain plum fixtures. Les Ames expressed the players 'disappointment' over the large numbers of amateurs selected to play in Canterbury week; Bill Andrews in *The Hand That Bowled Bradman* commented, 'With the sun shining at Weston there was no shortage of amateurs who wanted to play'; and Harry Lee added in *Forty Years of English Cricket* that Middlesex amateurs were always 'popping up from nowhere' for the away fixture against Sussex, lured by the prospect of a weekend by the sea. For the professionals who were asked to stand down to make way for the intermittent amateurs their chagrin was, in part, caused by the loss of their match fee.

The hard-headed professionals also complained about the amateurs' lack of interest in playing in the season's tougher fixtures. Bill Andrews reckoned that the Somerset amateurs avoided the northern tour, Trent Bridge and the Oval, while Fred Root felt the Worcestershire amateurs were reluctant to play against Yorkshire.

By the end of the 1930s the future of the amateur in first-class cricket was in doubt. Of course the MCC, still under the influence of the thinking of men like Lord Harris, Lord Hawke and Sir Stanley Jackson, felt otherwise, but they were eventually to be proved wrong. In the 1943 edition of *Wisden* the former Somerset amateur and prominent journalist R. C. Robertson-Glasgow made a strong case for the abolition of the amateur. He felt that 'the hour is ripe, indeed over-ripe, for the sweeping away of anachronisms and the exploding of humbug.'

WHO WERE THE MCC COMMITTEE?

The regime at Lord's often came in for criticism from the professionals. In general, according to Fred Root, Lord's was 'not popular' because the 'rules are so stringent, decorum so necessary, the atmosphere too stiff and starchy'. Even Jack Hobbs disliked it – 'there was nowhere to sit and watch . . . the lunch was always one of the worst in England till 1922 when they took us up to lunch with the amateurs.' Frank Lee, who began his career on the MCC staff, recalled being called into the secretary's office and reprimanded by Francis Lacey for not leaving the field more promptly after he was given out; if the incident was repeated Lee was told he faced instant dismissal.

In *A Cricket Pro's Lot* Fred Root quoted an unnamed but leading Lord's official who told him that 'professional bowlers are nothing more nor less than the hired labourers of the game'. And so they were, particularly in the mind of a 70-year-old aristocrat and member of the MCC Committee.

Despite the fundamental changes occurring within the British ruling class and society at large, the MCC Committee remained a bastion of the Conservative, imperialist, landed gentry throughout the inter-war years. The MCC Committee of 16, plus the five trustees, held unprecedented influence over English and world cricket and, indirectly, over the lives of hundreds of county professionals. So who were these men, what were their backgrounds and what values did they share?

By way of an example it is interesting to look at the MCC Committee of 1933 which handled the bodyline crisis. The average age of the 21 Committee members and trustees was 65; all had been educated at public schools with Eton (eight) and Harrow (five) being the most heavily represented; 18 of the 21 then went up to Oxford or Cambridge. The majority of members were titled – three Lords (Aberdare, Hampden and Hawke); three Viscounts (Bridgeman, Lewisham and Ullswater); one Duke (Buccleuch); two Earls (Dartmouth and Lucan) and four Knights (Jackson, Lacey, Sanderson and Studd).

Politically the group was staunchly Conservative, with seven of the 21 men having previously represented the Party in the House of Commons. Bridgeman attained the position of Home Secretary (1922-24), while Ullswater was Speaker in the House (1905-21). Most of the Committee listed the Carlton as their club, reflecting their attachment to the Conservative Party. Access to the highest in the land was assured via Brigadier-General the Earl of Lucan and Lord Hampden – both had been Lords in Waiting to King George V. Such political prestige and connections were awesome and standards were more than maintained by the incoming President in 1933, Lord Hailsham, the Secretary of State for War and Leader of the Government in the House of Lords.

The wealth and power of the Committee members emanated from the land. It is striking that commerce, banking and manufacturing were not represented. To a man they identified with the Empire (Jackson was Governor of Bengal from 1927 until 1932) and championed the conservative virtues of the Victorian and Edwardian eras. Interestingly, at least two (Sir Kynaston Studd, a former Lord Mayor of London, and the Earl of Dartmouth) were prominent Freemasons.

The Committee was leavened by a number of men with cricketing rather than political or aristocratic backgrounds: for example, Percy Chapman, a recent England captain; 'Shrimp' Leveson-Gower, the Surrey President; Lt-Colonel Heseltine, the Hampshire President; Dick Palairet, the former Surrey secretary; Pelham Warner, and Sir Francis 'Ben' Lacey, the MCC secretary from 1898 to 1926.

Lionel Lord Tennyson was never approached to seek election to the MCC Committee. According to his memoirs they were 'the biggest autocrats in the world, and as I have always spoken my mind to some of them and always will do, I stand no chance whatsoever of ever being asked.' Similarly C. B. Fry, Archie MacLaren, Percy Fender and Gilbert Jessop, despite being great amateur cricketers and tacticians, were not approached. All suffered from being too outspoken and occasionally crossing influential Committee members. Fry and MacLaren were known as eccentrics; MacLaren and Jessop as paid amateurs; all worked as journalists and Fender was also a wine merchant. As Richard Streeton wrote in his biography *P. G. H. Fender*, 'Fender's face often failed to fit in the circles that mattered.' Thirty years earlier Robertson-Glasgow, commenting on Fry's ommission from the MCC Committee, wrote that at Lord's 'birth and convention have always ranked higher than originality and knowledge'.

This, then, was the MCC Committee in 1933 – drawn from the best aristocratic families, educated at the finest public schools and universities, closely involved with the Conservative Party and strongly loyal to the Empire. The Committee was a mirror image of the landed British ruling class and to be a member was to display the social and cultural credentials of that class. It is hardly surprising that such men saw the professionals as paid servants of the MCC or their respective county clubs. The Committee stood for the continued amateur domination of the game.

UPWARDLY MOBILE PROFESSIONALS

The inter-war years saw the professional cricketer reach even greater heights of social acceptability – a handful were nominated for membership of their county Committees or given honorary life memberships. This new respectability was, in large measure, a consequence of the lead provided by Jack Hobbs, Pat Hendren, Wally Hammond and Herbert

Sutcliffe. Not only were they players of the highest distinction, but off the field they were erudite, assured, polite, middle-class and successful. They set the standards for all professionals to follow.

Jack Hobbs by his manner advocated the temperate and ecclesiastical life. He celebrated his century of centuries with ginger ale and regularly attended church on Sunday mornings. Similarly, Pat Hendren was a devout Roman Catholic, happily married and always neatly and meticously dressed. Herbert Sutcliffe, spotlessly attired, not a hair out of place, like Jack Hobbs established a successful sports outfitters and after the Second World War became a prominent businessman in Yorkshire with a paper manufacturer. In its obituary of Sutcliffe *Wisden* wrote that he had been 'as successful in commerce as in cricket'.

The Times, in 1937, said of Wally Hammond, 'He is cricket himself' while Neville Cardus once compared Hammond to the Elgin Marbles! Good-looking, with an attractive character, the sociable Hammond had married into a Yorkshire textile family. It was typical of a man who sought friendships in a class above his own, but who nevertheless was always readily accepted.

As children Hobbs, Hendren, Hammond and Sutcliffe had all known difficult times either emotionally or financially. In *My Life Story* Jack Hobbs recalled his 'humble' background and 'inferiority complex'; Pat Hendren's Irish working-class parents had died when he was still young and his elder brother assumed the responsibility of heading the family; similarly, Wally Hammond's father had been killed in the First World War, while by the age of six Herbert Sutcliffe had lost both his parents and was brought up by three of his aunts. All four had something to prove to the world and succeeded admirably.

Hobbs, Hammond, Hendren and Sutcliffe became national figures and heroes in a way that would have been impossible in previous decades. Newspapers continued to extend their circulation; by 1930 the *Express, Herald, Mail* and *Mirror* all exceeded a million copies daily, while seven

Jack Hobbs and Herbert Sutcliffe

years later the *People* and the *News of the World* topped three million, and from the late 1920s radio was booming. The media had begun to fashion the people's heroes. It is not surprising that cricketers were popular choices on cigarette cards, and in turn this marketing technique helped boost cigarette sales. Shortly after the Second World War 80 per cent of men and 41 per cent of women in Britain smoked.

Hammond always hankered after becoming an amateur provided the money was right, but Hobbs, Hendren and Sutcliffe were proud to be professional cricketers. In *Express Deliveries* Bill Bowes recounted Sutcliffe telling him:

> 'Lord Hawke lifted professional cricket from there to there,' said Herbert, raising his hand from knee to shoulder level. 'Professional cricketers lifted it to there,' he continued, raising his hand above his head, '– and even Lord Hawke always wanted it back again.'

PART FOUR

The Modern Era

CHAPTER 11

The Abolition of the Amateur

THE SECOND WORLD WAR

DURING the worst of the blitz in London in 1941, George Orwell wrote a short book called *The Lion and the Unicorn* in which he said:

> People who at any other time would cling like glue to their miserable scraps of privilege, will surrender them fast enough when their country is in danger. War is the greatest of all agents of change. It speeds up all processes, wipes out minor distinctions, brings realities to the surface.

How prophetic these lines turned out to be in post-War Britain. In July 1945 the Labour Party achieved a landslide victory in the general election. With a margin of 180 seats over the Tories, the Labour Government began to implement its election promises. In 1946 the National Coal Board was created and the mines nationalised, while the Transport Act led to the nationalisation of the railways, the canals and most long-distance road haulage. The following year the school-leaving age was raised to 15 and in July 1948 the National Health Service was established.

A welfare state was being fashioned along the lines proposed by the 1942 Beveridge Report. Sir William Beveridge's Report on Social Insurance and Allied Services had been widely acclaimed during the War and, remarkably for a government publication, sold in excess of 600,000 copies. Beveridge argued that the state should provide all individuals and families with public health care, pensions, family allowances, insurance against unemployment, improved housing and public education; care 'from the cradle to the grave'.

Beveridge urged the 'abolition of want before the enjoyment of comfort' and opinion polls showed that 90 per cent of the British population endorsed his views. The war years of collective sacrifice and service, evacuation, air-raids and rationing strengthened the post-War push for egalitarianism.

Cricket could not shield itself from such social pressures. Although it was to take until 1962 for the amateur-professional distinction to be abolished, most of the amateur privileges and trappings began to disappear in the immediate post-War years. In 1952 Len Hutton, the Yorkshire professional, was asked to captain England. Fifteen years earlier the implementation of such a proposition was unthinkable, but as Hutton wrote in *Just My Story*:

> If someone who had risen from the ranks was good enough to lead an army regiment in the field of battle, professional cricketers could be good enough to lead England in the field of sport.

As in the First World War, professional cricketers had responded to the call to arms in 1939. By 1942 Derbyshire, like all the other counties, could claim that all their former playing staff were in the armed forces, doing munitions work or employed in the mines. Several players held commissions and had distinguished war records. Les Ames, Bill Edrich and Wally Hammond finished their service in the RAF as Squadron Leaders; Edrich was awarded the Distinguished Flying Cross after a low-level attack on a power station near Cologne. Among the other players-turned-officer were Major Herbert Sutcliffe, Captains Hedley Verity and Stan Worthington, and Lieutentants Bill Bowes, Alf Gover and Maurice Leyland. Many professional cricketers and footballers were enlisted as physical training instructors and in this group were Sergeants Len Hutton and Cyril Washbrook. Hutton was discharged in 1942 after he broke his left arm in the gym.

In comparison to the First World War, and combatant nations such as the Soviet Union, Germany and Japan, British casualties were relatively small: 303,000 members of the armed forces killed, 60,000 civilians died in air raids and 30,000 deaths in the merchant navy. Again, the loss of life among former professional cricketers was slight. The roll of honour reads:

* Walter Hawtin, who played four times for Northamptonshire between 1929 and 1934, died in an accident in a munitions factory.
* Jack Lee, brother of Frank and Harry Lee, was killed in action in Normandy. He represented Somerset in 241 matches over 12 seasons and hit 1000 runs on three occasions.
* George Macauley, the Yorkshire right-arm medium pace spin bowler, always retained the fire from his youthful days as a fast bowler. From 1920 to 1935 he was a regular member of the county side and in ten of those seasons claimed more than 100 wickets, including 211 in 1925. In the 1933 Old Trafford roses clash, Macauley helped Yorkshire to an innings victory by capturing 7 for 28 and 5 for 21, including four wickets in five balls. After that victory, Neville Cardus caught the spirit of the man when he wrote that Macauley 'created their weakness of resolution, not so much by skill as by his tremendous power of will'. George Macauley, who had fought in the First World War with the Royal Field Artillery, died on active service with the RAF in 1940, aged 43.
* Hedley Verity, a Captain in the Green Howards, was the most notable professional casualty of the Second World War. He died of wounds, a prisoner of war in Italy, on 31 July 1943. Verity did not make his Yorkshire debut until 1930, when he was 25, due to the presence of Wilfred Rhodes in the county side as the slow left-

Yorkshire players in uniform; left to right, Verity, Smailes, Sutcliffe, Leyland and Hutton

arm bowler. Prior to his first-class career he had played league cricket on both sides of the Pennines. In each of his nine full county seasons he claimed more than 150 wickets, including 216 in 1936. Verity's most astonishing performance occurred against Notts, at Headingley in 1932, when he produced a world-record spell of 10 wickets for 10 runs off 19.4 overs. The previous season against Warwickshire, also at Headingley, he had 10 for 36. In 40 Test appearances Verity captured 144 wickets and even opened the batting against Australia in the fourth Test in Adelaide during the 1936-37 tour. R.C.Robertson-Glasgow, in the *Wisden* obituary, wrote of Verity that 'whereas his bowling included grace, his batting had only style. The former was nature embellished by art; the latter was art improved by imitation.' As a token of their respect for Verity the Yorkshire Committee donated £1000 to the Leeds General Infirmary for a memorial bed and a further £1000 to a trust fund for the player's family. The latter eventually reached £8233.

Cricket, like soccer, had continued during the Second World War, albeit in a slightly haphazard way. While there was no county championship several counties met on a regular basis, for example, in 1942 a Notts side played against Derbyshire and Leicestershire, home and away. The most frequent matches played on the county grounds were against the Army, the RAF, the National Fire Service and the British Empire XI. On 23 July 1942 the game between the Surrey and Sussex Home Guards at Lord's was abandoned after Andy Ducat, the former Surrey professional and Eton coach, died at the wicket, bat in hand, following a heart attack.

Provided that cricket and soccer matches did not interfere with recruitment or industrial production the war-time governments considered them as important means to maintain civilian morale. The Lancashire League cancelled the contracts of all their professionals as soon as War was declared, but numerous leading players were paid to appear in the Birmingham and Bradford Leagues. The latter, at various times, included such well-known county professionals as Barber, Bowes, Hutton, Macauley and Wood from Yorkshire; Oldfield and Paynter of Lancashire; Keeton, Harris and George Gunn from Nottinghamshire; and Copson, Mitchell, Alfred and George Pope, Denis Smith and Townsend of Derbyshire.

During the War the amateur-professional distinction had come under severe attack in *Wisden*. In the 'notes of the season' in the 1943 edition R. C. Robertson-Glasgow had launched a broadside against 'humbug'. He argued that in 1939 there were 'very few amateurs who earned no money, directly or indirectly, from the playing of their game', and continued that the true amateur was a 'survivor of an almost lost society'. Robertson-Glasgow concluded that he would 'welcome the total deletion of all distinction', but it was an appeal that the cricket authorities were not yet ready to countenance.

Lord Hawke had died in October 1938 but Sir Stanley Jackson remained an influential figure until his death in March 1947. The social composition of the post-War MCC Committee had, however, changed markedly from its aristocratic majority of the 1930s. In 1950 the MCC Committee included only one Duke (Edinburgh), one Lord (Cornwallis), two Earls (Dartmouth and Gowrie) and five Knights (Abell, Adam, Browne, Warner and Worsley).

In March 1944 an MCC select committee report on county cricket after the cessation of hostilities was published. This committee, under the chairmanship of Sir Stanley Jackson, had a strong amateur cricketing presence including Gubby Allen, Walter Hammond, Errol Holmes, Walter Robins, Brian Sellers, Maurice Turnbull and Bob Wyatt. The report was cautious in its proposals, no doubt wary after the calamity of two-day matches which had followed the First World War, although the recommendation of a new ball after 55 overs resulted in far-reaching changes which encouraged fast and medium-paced bowling. From 1949 the new ball law was altered to 65 overs.

The select committee urged the resumption of county cricket as soon as possible after the War ended particularly as 'entertainment' would be an 'essential feature of the post-War social structure'. To facilitate the return of first-class cricket it was agreed that there would be a temporary relaxation of the qualification criterion for amateurs and professionals during the 'emergency season'. Under 'special registration' a player not required by the county for which he was qualified or by the county in which he resided could transfer to another county without fulfilling the usual two-year residential qualification. In 1953 the rules were tightened to insist that counties did not have more than 10 specially registered cricketers on their books, of which only eight could be professionals. Further, a county could make only two such signings per year and each player had to be given a three-year contract. Despite these conditions special registration did entail a freeing of the labour market for professional cricketers.

Finally, as part of an attempt to put the county clubs on a more secure financial footing, it was agreed to lobby the government to repeal the entertainments tax on ground takings. The entertainments tax on cricket was finally abolished on 14 April 1953. R. A. Butler, the Conservative Chancellor of the Exchequer, decided that the amount of revenue generated by such a tax on cricket was 'so small' that an exception could be made. In the financial year 1952-53 it contributed a mere £36,000 to government coffers, although according to *Wisden* 'this added burden cannot be met from the present resources of the greater majority of the clubs'.

Two important proposals were rejected, indicative of the committee's caution. First, the Lancashire suggestion, backed by Surrey, that a knock-out competition should be inaugurated was considered to involve 'many practical difficulties', and second, Sunday cricket was unanimously rejected for unspecified 'obvious reasons'.

The select committee also discussed means to ensure a high public interest in cricket. Ideas canvassed included free passes for school children, better amenities and positive media coverage. In the event none of these suggestions was necessary. The public was eager to watch post-War cricket and soccer. In 1946 George Orwell wrote:

> Everyone is intent on having a good time, so far as our reduced circumstances permit. Football matches are attended by enormous crowds, pubs and picture houses always packed, and motoring has revived to a surprising extent considering that petrol is still theoretically rationed.

Total attendances at soccer matches peaked in 1947-48 and 1948-49, exceeding 41 million. Cricket crowds were smaller but counties such as Yorkshire and Kent recorded their highest-ever attendance figures in 1947. That season, excluding members, 2,300,910 people paid to watch first-class cricket. Three years later attendance at county championship matches still exceeded two million, but the trend from 1950 onwards was downhill fast. In 1960 the figure was just over one million but by 1981 it had slumped to below 200,000, or an average daily attendance of 323.

John Arlott's *Vintage Summer: 1947* was aptly titled. The tremendous batting exploits of Middlesex's Denis Compton (3816 runs including 18 centuries – both records) and Bill Edrich (3539 runs including 12 centuries) thrilled thousands of spectators. John Arlott concluded that 1947 was 'a happy record-breaking, historic and gloriously sunny summer' with huge crowds 'forgetting rationing, revelling in the simplicity of cricket played in peace'.

Denis Compton became the nation's sporting hero, promoted through a print media which had expanded enormously in the post-War years. In 1947 daily newspaper sales exceeded 15 million, while on Sunday the figure topped 29 million. The *News of the World* had a circulation of just under 8 million; it had been 4 million in 1937.

According to Ian Peebles' biography, *Denis Compton*, the Middlesex professional had a growing problem with fan mail. 'Denis was delighted, but also dismayed, at the vast number of letters he received daily.' The solution came in the form of Bagnall Harvey who offered to 'relieve him of all the problems his fame had brought him'; Denis Compton became the first player to appoint an agent. The relationship flourished and Harvey secured an advertising contract for Denis Compton to promote Brylcreem. The message was obvious for the club cricketer – grease your hair and you too will bat like Compton.

POST-WAR EARNINGS

Despite the tremendous popularity of post-War cricket, and the gate receipts this produced, the cricket authorities' immediate reaction to players' earnings had been to try to restrict them to the 1939 seasonal maximum of £440. Such a position was untenable, not only because players were aware of increased match attendance figures, but also because war-time price increases of more than 30 per cent and the doubling of manufacturing wages meant that professional cricketers were being asked to accept a drastic cut in their standard of living. The Football League showed a similar reluctance to improve soccer players' wages, but after the Professional Footballers Association threatened strike action and to take their case to the National Arbitration Tribunal, a new deal was negotiated. In 1946 a professional footballer was paid £10 per week in winter (a 20 per cent rise) and £7 10 shillings in summer (a 25 per cent improvement). Professional cricketers, still lacking a union or association, began the process of discussing pay and conditions on a county by county basis.

As usual the Surrey and Lancashire Committees recognised their responsibilities towards their playing staff and opened negotiations in 1945. In August the Oval Committee accepted that the pre-War wage bill of £4500 would have to be substantially increased. Two proposals were considered – the majority view was for a total wage bill of £7095, while Percy Fender advocated a more generous total of £8326.

By July 1946 Fender's salary plan had been accepted. The staff was divided into three groups. The first grade, comprising nine capped, first eleven players, were paid £6 10 shillings weekly with a guarantee of £450; the second grade, predominantly members of the second eleven, received £5 10 shillings weekly with a guarantee of £350; and the third grade, that is the rest of the staff, earned £4 10 shillings, but lacked a guarantee. For the players in the first and second grades this new pay structure represented an increase of £2 per week on the 1939 rates, but only the first grade received an improvement (£50) in their guaranteed income.

Match fees rose from the pre-War levels of £3 10 shillings for a home match and £6 10 shillings (with an extra £1 for an away weekend fixture) to £5 and £10 respectively. Finally, the win bonus was doubled and was now worth £2, while £200 was set aside as talent money.

In 1947 Surrey finished sixth in the county championship, winning 10 of their 26 matches. Leaving aside income from other sources, a regular Surrey first eleven professional would have earned between £500 and £550 from the county, as compared to £350 to £400 before the War, while the average male annual earnings in the manufacturing sector in 1948 were £370.

At Old Trafford the capped players, led by Cyril Washbrook and Eddie Phillipson, initially rejected the Lancashire Committee's post-War wages proposal. The Committee suggested two grades of £6 and £5; £12 for a home match and £16 for an away fixture; a £5 win bonus and £300 in talent money. The professionals argued that in the event of 30 games their total earnings would not be any higher than in 1939 and that a £5 win bonus put 'so much at stake'. Instead their representatives put the case for a £500 guarantee with the possibility of earning an extra 20 per cent; a £2 win bonus and no weekly differentials between capped players.

The compromise reached in September 1945, to take effect in the 1946 season, gave all capped players a guarantee of £416 (the equivalent of £8 per week); a 25 per cent increase on the pre-War home and away match fees to £12 10 shillings and £18 15 shillings; a £3 win bonus and talent money. In the Committee's opinion a successful player could earn £600 from the county.

At the end of the 1946, 1947 and 1948 seasons, when Lancashire finished third, third and fifth respectively, the Committee made £1000 available in talent money, which was considerably more generous than their Oval counterparts, even in the years when Surrey won the county championship. Cyril Washbrook, who featured prominently in the national batting averages with totals of 2400, 2662 and 1900, received well in excess of £100 in each of those three seasons.

Cyril Washbrook's pre-eminent status at Lancashire was also recognised when the Committee agreed to grant him one of the fixtures against the 1948 Australian tourists for his benefit. Washbrook was the first Lancashire player ever to be given such a concession. Don Bradman supported the Lancashire and England opening batsman by breaking his rule of appearing only once against each county and then declined to enforce the follow-on to ensure the match ran its full course. Out of the match receipts of £8648, Washbrook received £4270 after the deduction of entertainments tax, the payment to the tourists and the match expenses. The Lancashire public gave generously to collections during the match – on the second day the total was £400, and the Committee headed the subscription list with £100.

Cyril Washbrook's benefit of £14,200 set a new record, eclipsing Bill Bowes' £8083 in 1946, and was not surpassed until the 1970s. In his autobiography, *Cricket – The Silver Lining*, Cyril Washbrook reckons that, 'I am certain that my benefit would not have been the success it was without the novel idea to form a Benefit Committee.' He continues:

> Altogether nearly £10,000 came to me from subscriptions, collections on the ground, through evening and weekend club matches played on my behalf, raffles and the rest of the many functions run specially to raise funds for the benefit.

Cyril Washbrook had set the precedent for the future organisation of contemporary professionals' benefits.

However most professionals in the 1950s received between £1500 and £4500. Among the notable exceptions were Middlesex's Denis Compton (£12,258 in 1949), Lancashire's Dick Pollard (£8035 in 1949), Yorkshire's Len Hutton (£9713 in 1950) and Surrey's Arthur McIntyre (£8500 in 1955). But in real terms the professionals' benefits were not improving. George Hirst's 1904 benefit of £3703 would have been worth almost £15,000 in 1950.

In line with the post-War cost of living increases the fees for Test appearances and tours were increased. For example, the players on the 1946-47 tour of Australia received £550 (a £150 increase on the 1930s) and a potential maximum bonus of £275 plus weekly expenses in Australia and on board ship. As before, Tests against other nations, such as South Africa, paid less well. The fee for the 1948-49 South African tour was only £450, the bonus of £75 was a gift of the South African Board, not the MCC, and no expenses were paid. The fee for a home Test against Australia was £75.

While these Test and tour rates had increased with inflation they were hardly generous given that, according to *Wisden*, Test profits in the nine series played in England between 1946 and 1954 were an enormous £465,900 and that figure excludes the £280,600 paid to the tourists. The profit to 'English cricket' from the 1953 Australian tour was £130,000, but the England professionals received less than £6000 in match fees, railway fares and hotel expenses. As a momento of the series the participants were given a silver mug.

1953 – A MOMENTOUS SEASON

In 1953 the inevitable finally happened. For the first time in the twentieth century a professional was asked to lead the England side in a Test series against Australia. Even Lord Hawke might have gained some satisfaction from the choice of Yorkshire's Len Hutton for the job.

England's post-War record against Australia, under the amateur captaincy of Hammond, Yardley and Brown, had resulted in only one win and 11 defeats in 15 encounters. A professional captain could hardly do worse!

In the summer of 1952, against the Indians, the predominantly amateur England selectors of Yardley, Brown, Wyatt and Ames had to their credit chosen Hutton to lead the side and he retained the position after a comfortable three-nil series victory. Len Hutton made it clear to the selectors that he would captain England only as a professional; there was no question of him 'turning amateur'. As Charlie Harris, the droll Notts opening batsman used to say, 'Once a pro', always a pro'.' In 1953 England regained the Ashes and successfully defended them, again under Hutton's leadership, in 1954-55 in Australia. In 23 Tests with Len Hutton as captain, England won 11 times and lost on only four occasions.

The 1953 season was also notable for the knighthood accorded to Jack Hobbs, the first professional cricketer ever to receive such an accolade. The ever-modest Hobbs, according to John Arlott's biography, 'was genuinely surprised, even flustered' and sought an interview with Sir Walter Monckton, the Surrey President, to ask 'Sir Walter most pressingly to use his influence to stop what he called "all this" which, he felt was extravagant, embarrassing, even worrying.' As *Wisden* wrote in 1954, 'cricket and particularly the professional player was honoured'.

RECOGNITION FOR THE PROFESSIONALS

Four years before the historic events of 1953 the MCC had finally recognised the tremendous contribution of the professionals to cricket by bestowing honorary life membership of the Marylebone Cricket Club on 26 former England players. The list read Barnes, Barnett, Bowes, Braund, Duckworth, Freeman, Geary, Gunn (George, senior), Hearne (J. W.), Hendren, Hirst, Hobbs, Larwood, Leyland, Mead, Paynter, Rhodes, Russell, Sandham, Smith (E. J.), Strudwick, Sutcliffe, Tate, Tyldesley (E.), Voce and Woolley.

Two years later, in 1951, Warwickshire's Tom Dollery became the first professional this century to lead a championship-winning side. *Wisden* applauded Dollery, saying he 'has raised the status of the professional just as Hobbs did'. Speaking at a Cricket Society gathering 24 years later, Tom Dollery recalled how he took on the county captaincy 'with great trepidation' but nevertheless refused the Committee's request not to change with his fellow professionals. He also recalled that at the end of that season, after it was certain that Warwickshire had won the championship for only the second time in their history, he arranged a party for the players. The bill came to between £15 and £20, but the Club refused to pay – the Chairman said, 'Tell them to pay it themselves'!

In the increasingly liberal post-War years professional county captains were a more common sight. Doug Wright captained Kent from 1954 to 1956; Dennis Brookes, Northants from 1954 to 1957; Maurice Tremlett, Somerset from 1956 to 1959; Reg Perks, Worcestershire in 1955; and finally, in 1960, Yorkshire succumbed to reality and appointed Vic Wilson as captain.

Cyril Washbrook could rightly have expected the Lancashire captaincy several years before he was eventually granted it in 1954. Five years earlier the matter had come up for discussion on the Committee. Washbrook, who joined the staff in 1933, had been overlooked in favour of Nigel Howard, an amateur who made his county debut in 1946. But Nigel was the son of Rupert Howard, the Lancashire secretary. According to John Kay's *Lancashire,* the young Nigel used to receive advice by telegram from the county's Chairman and his secretary-father. On one occasion the telegram mistakenly advised 'Put Greenwood in first' instead of 'Put Greenwood on first', but Nigel Howard, true to the telegram, did the former.

THE SURREY YEARS

Surrey dominated the county championship in the 1950s. After sharing the title in 1950 they won it outright from 1952 to 1958 inclusive. In those seven seasons they lost only 28 championship matches.

Jack Parker and Laurie Fishlock retired, on a high note, in 1952. Both players had joined the staff in the early 1930s and in the post-War years graduated to share the role of senior professional. The Committee showed some fresh wisdom by informing the pair one year in advance that the Club would not require their services after the 1952 season. Parker died in 1983 and Jim Laker wrote in *Wisden Cricket Monthly*:

> If I ever needed advice in my early days at the Oval, the one person I turned to was Jack Parker. I picked up more about the game from him on train journeys, in hotel bars and in dressing rooms – where he was an avid watcher – than during the hours spent at net practice. He too had learned the game the hard way. No sponsored scholarships or winter cricket holidays, but instead two months working his passage on a cargo boat to Australia to further his own cricket education.

Jim Laker, a Yorkshireman, had made his debut in 1946 and was described by the amateur captain Errol Holmes in his report to the Committee the following year as 'a real "find" . . . outstandingly good as an off-spinner . . . excellent gully . . . full of guts'. Tony Lock also made his first Surrey appearance in 1946. Holmes said of Lock 'very young and very pleased with himself'.

Alec Bedser, who had joined the staff in 1938 on £2 per week in summer only, returned to the Oval after war service in the RAF to become England's principal seam bowler. Holmes remarked, 'slightly swollen-headed . . . firm handling is essential'. In 1947 the youthful Ken Barrington joined the Surrey staff on 50 shillings per week and a season ticket from Reading to the Oval. Andrew Sandham, appointed as county coach in 1945, noted that Barrington was 'quite a good bowler . . . shapes fairly well with the bat'. It was six years before the determined Barrington made his county debut.

Peter May, an amateur and the most gifted batsman of his generation, gained a place in the Surrey eleven during his first year at Cambridge University in 1950. The following summer he returned to play during the University vacation, with the professionals being dropped in rotation to ensure May's inclusion. Finally, in 1952, Stuart Surridge assumed the captaincy, a man who has been described as an amateur who led the eleven with the ruthlessness of a professional.

The sustained brilliance of the Surrey professionals was relatively well-rewarded by the Committee. In 1948 the basic weekly wage of a capped Surrey professional had been increased by £1 to £7 10 shillings and it stayed at that level until November 1951. The previous year the best-paid Surrey player received total earnings of £760, including match fees, talent money and win bonuses.

The Surrey professionals had two problems however. First, in general retail prices were rising sharply as a consequence of the Korean War. Prices rose by almost 10 per cent in 1951 and again in 1952. And second, they complained of a 'very fluctuating income' due to the relative importance of match fees in their total earnings. As a consequence the players experienced a 'very real anxiety in balancing their budgets'. The Committee's response was that large match fees 'engendered keenness, prevented scrim-sharking and gave disciplinary control'. The last-mentioned point was clearly important to the Committee, but they did also recognise that discipline could be maintained by 'witholding of talent money and win money' or suspension on half-pay.

The compromise reached in November 1951, and 'welcomed' by Fishlock and Parker, the players' representatives, recognised the principle of 'a much increased weekly wage with a corresponding decline in match money'. Capped first eleven players were to be paid £10 10 shillings per week; £8 for an away match, instead of £12; and £4 for a home match instead of £5. As an incentive the Committee raised the win bonus to £5. Two years later the win bonus reverted to £2 as part of a package which saw the away fee rise to £10 10 shillings and the home rate to £7. By then the senior staff at the Oval had achieved the important goal of making their income more dependent on a regular weekly wage and less determined by a payments-by-results system.

In 1953 and 1954 the Committee allocated £800 as talent money for the championship-winning sides which meant that a leading professional received an additional £60-100. From 1955 to 1959 the sum to be dispensed rose to £900 and star players, like Jim Laker, benefited by more than £100 at the end of the season. Towards the end of the 1955 season the Club secretary, B. K. Castor, met the professionals' representatives, Alec Bedser and Arthur McIntyre, to hear the players' case for a better pay deal. Bedser and McIntyre argued that not only was it three years since there had been a pay adjustment but also, in that time, the cost of an away trip had increased. They cited the case of a visit to Weston-super-Mare to play Somerset for which the fee was 10 guineas but the hotel bill £6. However the most novel proposal advanced by the two players was that talent money should be calculated on the number of appearances, not match performances.

In January 1956 the Committee rejected the Bedser-McIntyre talent money proposal on the grounds that it was vital to 'distinguish the great and successful player'. Further, they noted, Jim Laker opposed any idea of talent money being based solely on appearances. A 5 per cent pay increase was granted, while at the same time the Committee minuted that the professionals at the Oval earned £100 per annum more than at any other county. None the less the following July the players again raised the question of away expenses and stated that it had become 'extremely difficult to make ends meet'. Clearly the Committee agreed because the fee for a mid-week away fixture was increased to £13 10 shillings, with an additional £2 10 shillings for a weekend away match.

By the end of the 1950s a leading Surrey player – the best paid professional cricketer in England – could expect to earn between £900 and £1000 from the county. From that he would have to deduct his away expenses, maintain and renew his equipment and, of course, pay tax. The average male earnings in the manufacturing sector were about £750 gross. The professional's life may have included some fame but it did not produce much of a fortune. After his retirement Alec Bedser wrote an article for the 1961 edition of *Wisden* in which he commented that:

> Fewer people are taking up cricket professionally these days. The rewards are not very great and, with advanced education and higher wages, there are safer and definitely more attractive prospects for the average youngster outside the game.

ORDERED OUT OF THE GROUND

In the 1950s and early 1960s British employers, in line with their North American and European counterparts, began to consider and implement more sophsticated management techniques. Realising that there was more to working life than pay and a forty-hour week, the new breed of personnel managers introduced ideas like job satisfaction, motivation, employee participation, improved communications and fringe benefits. 'Man management' became the vogue.

Relations between cricket's employers and their employees remained virtually unchanged from the pre-War days. In 1954 Harold Gimblett, who had joined the Somerset staff in 1935, was ordered out of the Taunton ground by the county secretary. The incident occurred at the end of July during the match against Pakistan. Gimblett had been put on electro-convulsant therapy treatment during the winter of 1953-54, but reported for duty with Somerset the following April. In his second match of the season against Yorkshire at Taunton, after making a duck in the first innings, Harold Gimblett suffered a breakdown. In David Foot's biography he recalled:

> I came in and said I couldn't take any more. I was finished. It was my last game for Somerset. I knew I shouldn't have played. I packed my bags and went home. I moped about the house. Soon I was to return to hospital as a voluntary patient.

During his first-class career for Somerset and England, Harold Gimblett scored more than 23,000 runs and remains the greatest batsman the county ever produced. To order such a player from the ground seems incredible. As Gimblett remarked, 'I was speechless.'

Harold Gimblett's Somerset career overlapped very briefly in 1954 with that of expatriate South Australian John McMahon. After playing for the Australian Services side in England in 1945, McMahon, a slow left-arm bowler, joined the Surrey staff. He remained at the Oval until 1953 when he was 'dismissed' for 'insubordination on the field' and being 'exceedingly truculent' to the second eleven captain and county secretary. Despite Surrey verbally informing Somerset, McMahon still moved to the west country and represented Somerset until 1957, after which he played in the Lancashire League. Forty-three years earlier Surrey had sacked another Australian, Alan Marshal, for 'insubordination'.

The most famous cricket dismissal in the 1950s occurred in 1958 when Yorkshire dispensed with the services of Johnny Wardle, a slow left arm bowler, still at the height of his powers. Wardle had played in 28 Tests for England, capturing 102 wickets, and on 27 July 1958 received the expected invitation to tour Australia during the forthcoming northern winter. Three days later the Yorkshire secretary tersely announced that the county would not be calling on Wardle's services after the end of the season. Wardle asked to be stood down from the next match because of comments he intended to make in his column in the *Daily Mail*. The Club agreed, but after seeing the article terminated Wardle's engagement at once. Eight days later the MCC withdrew their invitation for Wardle to tour Australia on the grounds that he 'did a grave disservice to the game' and that 'the welfare of cricket as a whole in terms of loyalty and behaviour must override all other considerations'.

The first-class career of Johnny Wardle had come to an end, although he continued to play in the Lancashire League and for Cambridgeshire with considerable success.

In 1970 Yorkshire made him an honorary life member, as did the MCC.

Two years after the Wardle incident another England spin bowler, Jim Laker, also found himself in bother after putting pen to paper. After the publication of his memoirs *Over To Me*, Surrey and the MCC withdrew Laker's honorary memberships, although in later years these privileges were restored.

THE ABOLITION OF THE AMATEUR

The Advisory County Cricket Committee, meeting on 26 November 1962 at Lord's, 'decided by a clear majority to abolish amateur and professional status and call all players cricketers'. By a margin of eleven votes to seven the anachronism of gentlemen and players had finally been laid to rest.

In its 1963 edition *Wisden* exclaimed that the abolition of the amateur came as 'yet another big surprise', but the reality of first-class cricket was that the true amateur had virtually disappeared. In 1959 only 39 amateurs appeared in the county championship and less than half of that number played in 10 or more fixtures. Thirty years earlier the comparative figures were 205 amateurs of whom 46 played in 10 or more matches. Furthermore, several of the regular amateurs were employed as county secretaries, for example, Donald Carr (Derbyshire), Trevor Bailey (Essex) and Wilfred Wooller (Glamorgan), putting into doubt their amateur status.

During the winter of 1957-58 the MCC had established a special sub-committee to 'examine the problems of amateur status in the light of the present-day conditions'. Under the Chairmanship of the Duke of Norfolk, the President of the MCC, the sub-committee rejected any solution which involved abolishing the amateur-professional distinction on the grounds that 'the distinctive status of the amateur cricketer was not obsolete, was of great value to the game and should be preserved.' Such a proposition is dubious given the small numbers of genuine amateurs playing first-class cricket at the time. The sub-committee saw no reason to question the status of 'amateurs' who were employed as county secretaries or who made their living by broadcasting and writing about the game, or who received income from advertising.

However, even they could not ignore the 'pseudo assistant secretary . . . paid for playing cricket under the umbrella of his nominal secretarial duties', and 'were disturbed by the apparent over-liberal interpretation of the word "expenses" in certain cases'. Since the 1880s the authorities had turned a blind eye to both these issues and 70 years later they still felt unable to 'legislate for these cases under any general formula'. The 'machinery' of a 'standing committee' was proposed to examine cases individually with the proviso that any reports 'shall at all times remain confidential'. No similar protection was ever afforded to a professional whose qualification or conduct was brought into question.

The sub-committee concluded that at home amateurs were 'fully entitled' to continue to receive 'genuine out-of-pocket expenses' and that on major overseas tours there should be 'a graded system of broken-time payments'. This decision to allow amateurs compensation for loss of earnings was the major innovation in the sub-committee's report. In other sports, such as rugby union, athletics or rowing, broken-time payments would have contravened the status of an amateur.

The sub-committee's report is interesting for its lack of a definition of an amateur, although it does state that a professional is 'any cricketer directly or indirectly paid for playing cricket'. By making the definition of a professional so specific, that is, refering only to payments for playing cricket, the sub-committee implicitly made the status of the amateur much wider. It is worth comparing the MCC sub-committee's statement to the entry in the *Oxford English Dictionary* that a professional is a person:

> That follows an occupation as his (or her) profession, life-work, or means of livelihood; spec. applied to one who

follows, by way of profession, what is generally followed as a pastime.

It could surely be argued that a person who played cricket all summer and received expenses, who wrote about the game in the press or was employed as the county secretary, and who went on tour with England in the winter and received broken-time payments was pursuing cricket, not as a 'pastime', but as a 'profession, life-work or means of livelihood', and therefore was a professional.

Between 1958 and 1962 the discussion continued over the future place of the amateur in county cricket and even within establishment circles there were differences of opinion. For example, in September 1959 the Surrey Committee passed a resolution which 'strongly opposed' broken-time payments, while Gubby Allen, an influential member of the MCC Committee, would have prefered the retention of amateurs in the game, via broken-time payments, even after 1962.

Les Ames, the Kent secretary-manager and Committee member, voiced the opinion of many older players when he said in a recent interview that the abolition of the amateur was 'a sad day' for cricket, but as *The Times*' cricket correspondent wrote at the time it was 'a realistic decision'.

The abolition of the amateur-professional distinction obviously meant the end of the Gentlemen versus Players fixture, an institution since 1806. A total of 273 matches had been played, the Gentlemen won 67 and the Players 126, there was one tie and the rest were drawn.

Two months after the Advisory County Cricket Committee's historic decision Sir Pelham Warner died, aged 89. Warner, born in Trinidad in 1873 was the youngest of 18 children; his father was the island's Attorney-General. After completing his education at Rugby school and Oriel College, Oxford, Plum Warner sat for his bar finals before embarking on the first of numerous cricket tours. In 1903-04 Warner captained the first MCC tour to Australia and was always keen to stress the imperial and moral values of the game. Shortly after arriving in Australia in 1932, in his capacity as joint tour manager he said that the aim of the MCC 'of which I am a humble if devoted servant – in sending teams to all parts of the world is to spread the gospel of British fair play'.

Sir Pelham Warner, a contemporary of Lord Harris, Lord Hawke and Sir Stanley Jackson, was steeped in cricket's traditions and like them he always urged the amateur domination of the game. Warner's death and the ACCC meeting which abolished amateur status marked the end of an era.

At that same meeting in November 1962 it was also decided to organise a national one-day knock-out competition with commercial sponsorship. At last, nearly a century after the idea was first raised, there was to be a knock-out competition between the counties. The Gillette Razor Company paid a mere £6500 to be the initial sponsors and, in retrospect, the asking price was a bargain.

The Gillette Cup, first played for in 1963, opened a new epoch in the history of cricket. The commercialisation of the game had begun. In the next 25 years sponsorship deals and the sale of television rights would put millions of pounds and dollars into cricket, but would the players, or cricketers as they were all now to be called, receive a just reward?

CHAPTER 12

The Making of the Modern Professional

SINCE the abolition of the amateur in 1962 two developments have changed the working life of the professional cricketer. The first was the establishment of the Cricketers' Association in 1967. The second involves the greater commercialisation and overt politicisation of the game, exemplified by the creation of World Series Cricket in 1977 and the mis-named 'rebel' tours of South Africa.

THE CRICKETERS' ASSOCIATION

In an article in the *Cricketer* in 1974 John Arlott, currently President of the Cricketers' Association, stated that a decade ago:

> Cricketers were the only body of British wage-earners with no freedom of choice of employment, no representation, negotiation, arbitration, protection of independently-framed conditions of employment. Most administrators believed that state of affairs should continue; while many players were alarmed by the possible consequences of attempting to redress it.

Fred Rumsey, during his six years with Somerset, did not accept the 'alarmist' argument and during the 1966 and 1967 seasons made the rounds of the county dressing rooms lobbying for the creation of a cricketers' association. In

October 1967, at a meeting of 70 players in London, the Cricketers' Association was founded. Rumsey took on the responsibilities of being secretary, while Jack Bannister, whose career with Warwickshire had begun in 1950, became the treasurer. Subsequently, in 1970, Bannister assumed the secretary's job on a full-time basis (John Arlott described him as 'over-worked and underpaid') and he remains the organisation's only paid official.

At the Association's first Annual General Meeting, which took place in March 1968 at Edgbaston, membership had reached 130 or about one-third of first-class professionals. Apparently many of the county captains and senior professionals remained unconvinced of the need for such an organisation. They felt that the Cricketers' Association would mirror the 'militancy' of the Professional Footballers' Association, while many players opposed the idea of a union per se or feared victimisation if they joined. From the authorities' standpoint the paternalism which had governed Committee-player relations since the 1880s was under serious threat.

Within three years the Association had achieved virtually 100 per cent membership and today has more than 350 members (only current county cricketers can join) with the only exceptions being a few of the overseas players. The Association is funded by an annual donation from the Test and County Cricket Board (TCCB), usually around £20,000, which puts the organisation in the anomalous position of being financially supported by its members' employers.

Despite some players and Committee members' fears, the Association has always acted responsibly and with restraint, while at the same time achieving some important gains for its members. Jack Bannister considers the three most significant to be:

* The creation of a Group Retirement Scheme in 1975;
* The minimum wage for all county players won in 1979; and
* The Association's representation on the TCCB's registration and disciplinary committees.

FROM REGISTRATION TO THE TRANSFER MARKET

Since the establishment of the Cricketers' Association not a single player has been barred from playing for a full season because of their decision to move from one county to another. Between 1956 and 1961 three England cricketers – M. J. K. Smith, Peter Richardson and Tom Graveney – failed to convince the MCC's Registration committee that they should be specially registered and allowed to forego the necessity of the one-year residential qualification. Interestingly, at the time, two of this trio – Smith (moving from Leicestershire to Warwickshire) and Richardson (Worcestershire to Kent) – were amateurs. Under the rules of county cricket an amateur could not transfer to another county if he was 'still required by the county for which he is qualified' and 'whose reasons for changing his county are not considered adequate by the Registration committee'. In the case of a professional he could not move if he was 'required by the county for which he is qualified and whose terms of re-engagement are considered by the Registration committee to be reasonable'.

The inadequacy of these rules was highlighted by the case of Tom Graveney in 1961. Graveney had been the professional captain of Gloucestershire in 1959 and 1960. After finishing second in 1959 the county dropped to eighth the following season.

Wisden recognised that the side had been 'plagued by injuries', including to Graveney who missed seven matches but still headed the Gloucestershire batting averages with 1394 runs. The Committee's response to the decline was to deprive Graveney of the captaincy and appoint the amateur C. T. M. Pugh in his place. Understandably Tom Graveney was dismayed and resigned from the county, but given that Gloucestershire wanted to retain the services of its most accomplished batsman and had made him a 'reasonable' offer, the MCC Registrations committee insisted that he sit out the 1961 season. The following year he represented Worcestershire.

Eleven years later, in February 1972, the TCCB's Registration sub-committee had to consider the cases of Bob Willis and Bob Cottam who wanted to leave Surrey and Hampshire respectively. Through such a move Willis expected to gain a regular first-eleven place with Warwickshire. Despite being chosen for the 1970-71 England tour of Australia and New Zealand, Bob Willis made only 14 county championship appearances for Surrey during the 1971 season. Bob Cottam's reasons for moving were not made public, but given that he forfeited his benefit, having made his Hampshire debut in 1963, they must have been strongly felt. The Registration sub-committee decided that Willis could not play in competitive matches for his new county until 1 July 1972, while for an unexplained reason, Cottam was allowed to re-appear from 17 June.

Writing in *Playfair Cricket Monthly,* Rex Alston wondered how strong the influence of the Cricketers' Association had been within the sub-committee, particularly in light of a referendum, organised by the Association, which showed that the players 'were loyal to their counties and would not consider uprooting themselves and their families unless for a very strong reason'. During the 1970s and 1980s more and more players changed counties – in 1981 47 cricketers had represented more than one first-class county, while a further 30 had played second eleven cricket elsewhere. Frequently players changed counties because their first eleven opportunities were restricted or they were young players who the county coach considered would not make the grade or they were older members of the staff who the committee felt were no longer integral to the county's future.

Since 1873, when the MCC first imposed a restriction on a professional's mobility of labour, the spectre of a transfer market, akin to that of professional football, has been raised by the cricket establishment. In 1980 Barry Wood moved from Lancashire to Derbyshire, but the TCCB Registrations committee blocked the move claiming it was 'not in the best interests of cricket', undoubtedly because Wood left Old

Trafford shortly after receiving a testimonial cheque of £64,429. However, as Barry Wood explained, 'that was awarded for services rendered. I have given 14 years to Lancashire.' Significantly, the committee also stated that they wished to avoid 'the development of a transfer system'. Wood appealed to the Cricket Council and was given 30 July as the date for the resumption of his career. When faced with legal action, the TCCB further reduced the ban to 4 June and accepted the player's registration with Derbyshire. The TCCB would have had no defence in the courts in their obvious attempt to effect a restraint of trade.

During the winter of 1986-87 the transfer issue re-emerged following the decisions of Ian Botham and Graham Dilley to leave Somerset and Kent respectively and join Worcestershire. Both players' contracts had expired on 1 January and they were at liberty to approach, or be approached by, other counties. In March 1987 Christopher Martin-Jenkins editorialised in the *Cricketer* that 'County cricket is hovering on the brink of a transfer problem which has tarnished football and will certainly break down loyalties in cricket too.' Mike Selvey, a former player and county captain and subsequently a journalist, asked in the June issue of *Wisden Cricket Monthly*, 'What's so wrong with a "transfer" system?' He argued further 'that clubs over the years have become complacent about how they treat their players, expecting loyalty while doing little, particularly financially, to command it.' To strengthen his case Selvey quoted Phil Carling, the Glamorgan secretary, who said:

> Players are employees as in any other job and if they sign a three-year contract there is no commitment by club or player after that time. At the end, you should be a free agent to play for whomsoever you please.

Peter Roebuck, writing in the *Cricketer* in July 1987, expounded on the positive aspects of the free movement of players between counties. Among its virtues were 'to revive flagging careers, to give frustrated talent its chance, and to take unhappy employees into fresher, greener pastures.' The Somerset captain continued that players do not 'move willy-nilly, do not abandon their friends, their roots, or their children's education easily'. Like everybody else a cricketer changes employer to 'further their careers'. In fact, Roebuck felt that the transfer of players improved the game because new signings generated interest and members' subscriptions as well as strengthening the playing staffs of weaker counties. However, his basic point was that cricketers cannot be denied the same rights as any other employee to 'search for work that is satisfying and a working relationship that is cheerful'.

The reality of the lives of professional cricketers is that until the 1980s they were not accorded the same rights as employees in any other job. Until the abolition of the residential qualification their ability to sell their cricketing skills in the market place was severly restricted. After more than 100 years the professional cricketer is now able to sell his labour like any other worker, and the onus is on the county clubs to put together packages covering earnings, bonuses, benefits and pensions which offer reasonable rewards and security. In other words, the county clubs now have to behave like other employers.

Inevitably 'star' players are going to command more valuable contracts, as they always have done, but today the county clubs may have to seek additional commercial sponsorship if they wish to retain or sign particular players. At the turn of the century wealthy clubs like Surrey or Lancashire could meet the demands of Lohmann, Richardson and Hayward or the amateur MacLaren from their normal revenue or substantial reserves generated from gate receipts, but with the steady decline of spectators at county championship matches other sources of income have had to be found.

With players being able to move more freely between counties the matter of compensation for their previous employers has been raised. The arguments in favour of such a scheme are that the player's former county has invested time, money and coaching in him and it should be compensated by the cricketer's new county. Various scales have been proposed with the final amount to be paid being dependent on the professional's length of service and status. Compensation is also seen as a way of ensuring that there is a redistribution of income within the counties from the rich to the poor.

The Test and County Cricket Board discussed such compensation payments at its spring meeting in 1981 and rejected the idea because 'It was feared that a football-style transfer system might develop.' The spectre of soccer's spiralling transfer fees does seem misplaced given the smaller numbers involved of cricket clubs (17 as compared to more than 40 in the English first and second divisions alone) and players (the Professional Footballers' Association had 2629 members in 1985 as compared to just over 350 in the Cricketers' Association). Also, there is no cricketing counterpart to the wealthy European soccer clubs offering big money over the same season and adding to the transfer fee spiral.

The other argument against compensation payments or transfer fees is that it will create a situation where a few wealthy counties gather all the best talent and dominate the various competitions. Yet the presence of one or more overseas Test cricketers with 16 of the counties works against such a concentration of talent, while it is also worth noting that 'buying' players to win championships does not always pay. In Australia, Queensland have pursued such a policy in their attempt to secure the Sheffield Shield, but after 54 seasons they have yet to carry off the trophy, despite enticing Allan Border, Greg Chappell, Jeff Thomson and Kepler Wessels to Brisbane.

In the 1890s many counties opposed the introduction of winter pay for their professionals, but were forced to accept it. Similarly when the Cricketers' Association won its campaign in 1979 for the introduction of a minimum wage several counties claimed it was a financial impossibility, but were proved wrong. Today, as leading cricketers insist on better contracts or offer their proven talents to another county, the bogey of a soccer-style transfer system is being raised. The consequences of winter pay and the minimum wage were increased pay and greater security for the game's professionals and, no doubt, that will be the eventual outcome of increased player mobility between the counties. As Christopher Martin-Jenkins wrote in the *Cricketer* in March 1987:

> The county clubs may also need to revert to longer contracts in order to keep their players. In return, it is time for the clubs to take expert financial advice about the possibility of setting up a proper pension scheme. The maturity value of this would increase sharply each year that a cricketer plays for his club . . . it would give players an incentive to remain loyal.

In many respects professional cricketers have lagged behind their brethren in the Professional Footballers' Association who, apart from higher earnings, have negotiated a good retirement benefit scheme which pays a lump sum at the age of 35 based on salary; a private medical scheme; vocational education programmes; help in finding a career after soccer; and a standard contract. Perhaps similar developments will follow in English county cricket; after all, cricketers are now in the same position as soccer players who achieved the abolition of the maximum wage in 1961 and freedom of contract in 1979.

WORLD SERIES CRICKET

The establishment of World Series Cricket in 1977 by Kerry Packer shook the cricket authorities. The first-class game has never been the same since 9 May 1977 when a leaked press story revealed that 34 top international cricketers had signed to play for World Series Cricket (WSC).

The long-term significance of WSC was that it forced cricket's governing bodies to seek greater commercial sponsorship for the game, to demand more money for broadcasting rights and, particularly in Australia, to place greater emphasis on one-day international matches. Australia, less constrained by tradition and more accepting of aggressive marketing, quickly introduced the innovations of day-night matches under floodlights, coloured clothing, the white ball, fielding circles and strong media promotion.

Since World Series Cricket attendance at first-class and one-day matches in Australia has increased considerably from 400,000 in 1977 to around one million in the 1980s. Of course this growth has been at the one-day, particularly day-night, international games, not at the Sheffield Shield matches, but it cannot be denied that a new audience has been attracted to the game. Children, women and the working class have been enticed back to cricket. As Andrew Caro, the Managing Director of WSC commented in 1978, 'A pure game that nobody watches is a dead game.'

Australian television has provided excellent and extensive coverage – usually 600 hours each season – and, as a consequence, Packer's Channel 9 generated huge advertising revenues. According to the station's promotional material a television cricket sponsor's commercial will be seen 94.4 million times in Sydney and Melbourne in the course of the season! During the 1984-85 World Series Cup and the World Championship of Cricket it was claimed that 60 per cent of all women, 74 per cent of all teenagers and 57 per cent of all five to 12-year-olds tuned in to Channel 9's coverage. In a newspaper interview the executive producer of sport at Channel 9 explained his approach, 'I aim our coverage at my mother. She had three kids who played cricket but she never really understood it.'

The decisive battles over the future of WSC and cricket itself were fought through the turnstiles and in the English High Court. Pressure mounted on the various national governing bodies and the International Cricket Conference to resolve the dispute with WSC. The Australian Cricket Board, in particular, incurred heavy losses due to the competition from the all-star World Series matches. It is estimated that the Australian Board lost £445,000 during the two-year dispute.

However, the most significant defeat for the cricket establishment came in the High Court in the cases of *Greig and others* v *Insole and others* and *World Series Cricket Pty Ltd* v

Insole and others heard before Justice Slade over 31 days between 26 September and 25 November 1977. The Test and County Cricket Board meeting on 15 July 1977 decided in principle to ban from county cricket those players contracted to WSC, subject to the International Cricket Conference introducing a similar ban at Test level. Eleven days later the ICC effectively endorsed such a ban. The TCCB proposed to hold a meeting on 5 August where it was expected that a resolution would be carried which would have disqualified from county cricket for two years any player who contravened the ICC's ruling. On 3 August Tony Greig, John Snow and Mike Procter struck back issuing a writ against the Chairmen and secretaries of the TCCB and ICC seeking a declaration that the various rule changes were '*ultra viries* and in unlawful restraint of trade'.

Justice Slade found for the plaintiffs, that is, the players, and WSC, in both actions. *Wisden* estimated that the case cost the TCCB and ICC £200,000, but, even more significantly, it fundamentally altered employer-employee relations in the world of professional cricket. In his judgement Justice Slade stated that the new ICC and TCCB rules:

> if implemented, substantially restrict the area in which it will be open to professional cricketers to earn their livings. It is common ground that the rules of an association which seek substantially to restrict the area in which a person may earn his living in the capacity in which he is qualified to do so, are in restraint of trade.

Justice Slade agreed with Greig, Snow and Procter that they were being unjustly denied 'the right to work' and 'for two of the plaintiffs it would have had the effect of driving them permanently out of first-class cricket'. Justice Slade also did not accept criticism of the players 'on moral grounds . . . for entering into contracts with World Series Cricket'. His Honour continued:

> A professional cricketer needs to make his living as much as any other professional man. I think it is straining the concept of loyalty too far for authorities such as the

> defendants to expect him to enter into a self-denying ordinance not to play cricket for a private promoter during the winter months, merely because the matches promoted could detract from the future profits made by the authorities, who are not themselves willing or in a position to offer him employment over the winter or to guarantee him employment for the future.

Earlier in his judgement Justice Slade had touched on this lack of security for the players when he commented that:

> In a world situation, however, where no country save the United Kingdom offers any real career structure for an aspiring professional cricketer, and the United Kingdom itself only offers rewards which many professional cricketers have considered inadequate, the path open to an aspiring commercial promoter of cricket is a much easier one.

Ten years later Tony Greig justified his part in WSC in a newspaper interview with the remark that 'Fundamentally, the initial thing was "what's best for me?" ' . . . I look after number one and my family first.' For leading players, who lacked security and justifiably considered themselves undervalued and underpaid, the attraction of WSC was irresistible. After signing up with WSC Derek Underwood commented:

> For me the security offered by the Packer contract is vital. In this one season I can double the income I collected in the tax year April 1976 to April 1977, when I played a series against the West Indies, had a full season for Kent and went on a four-month tour of India . . . One of my greatest worries has always been – what would I do when my playing career is over? I have no qualifications. Up until now I have been unable to save much from my income. It's nice to feel that at last I am earning the sort of money that other international sportsmen have enjoyed for years.

Underwood's complaint that he had 'been unable to save much' was not surprising given the increase in the cost of living between 1973 and 1977 of 96 per cent. Over that same period the fee for an England appearance had risen by only 40 per cent (from £150 to £210). Overall, payments to England's leading cricketers had not kept pace either with the rate of inflation or the general increases in earnings achieved by the trade union movement. The players were justified in considering themselves undervalued and underpaid.

The financial rewards for World Series cricketers were substantial. According to evidence given in the High Court WSC contracts varied from one to three years and paid between A$20,000 and A$35,000 for each annual 'tour' of 55 days. Tony Greig, who prior to his 'defection' was England captain, received A$30,000, paid in three installments, plus a A$30 daily accommodation and meals allowance. WSC also established a Players Provident Fund and ensured that the players' wives and children could travel and live with the teams.

In 1977 the fee for an overseas tour with England was £3000 or the equivalent of A$5000, that is, 4-7 times less than the 'tour' payments offered by Kerry Packer's World Series Cricket. In the face of the WSC challenge to its authority over the game, and the danger of more England players 'defecting', the TCCB decided at its meeting on 5 August 1977 to implement a five-fold increase in the rate for a home Test. Instead of £210 per Test an England player received £1000 and further, a consortium of three businessmen agreed to pay a £1000 bonus to each of the nine England players who had declined to join Kerry Packer.

The TCCB also found a major new sponsor for Test cricket in the form of Cornhill Insurance who injected one million pounds over five years into English cricket. As a consequence the fee for an overseas England tour was raised by £2000 to £5000. Clearly, when forced to do so, the TCCB could find corporate support and ensure the financial security of some of its leading players. The obvious question is why hadn't these decisions been taken a decade earlier?

It is clear that the Test players who joined WSC gained financially, but there has been some contention as to whether there were any benefits from World Series Cricket for the county professionals. Three important points need to be made. First, the resolution of the crisis required the involvement of the Cricketers' Association and, as *Wisden* noted in its 1979 edition, 'the Cricketers' Association was able to play a substantial part in striving for peace'. Again, the Association was seen to be acting responsibly and in general could justly expect to play a more active role in the discussions of cricket's future. This newly-acquired status helped in the negotiations around the introduction of the minimum wage in 1979.

Second, the involvement of companies like Cornhill Insurance and Packer's Channel 9 indicated that substantial corporate sponsorship could be found for the game and, in turn, some of that income has been passed on to the players in the form of better wages, conditions and prize money. The introduction of the minimum wage substantially increased the counties' wages bill (£700,000 in 1978 as compared to over two million pounds today), and that has been met through the greater commercialisation of first-class cricket.

And finally, but very significantly, the *Greig* v *Insole* case represented the first-ever legal challenge by a group of players to the authorities. Furthermore, Greig, Snow and Procter won the case and set a precedent which showed that the TCCB and ICC could not impose bans and rules which restricted a professional's right to work and were a restraint of trade. The legal status of registration periods and enforced residential qualifications for county professionals were brought into question. According to *Wisden*, at the TCCB meeting in Spring 1980 it was agreed that 'English players not required by their county could move to another with greater ease.'

Professional footballers had already fought and won a similar legal battle in 1963 in the case of *Eastham* v *Newcastle United Football Club Ltd*. George Eastham had asked to be transferred, but Newcastle United gave notice of retention and refused to release him. The player declined to re-sign and took the matter before the courts. In the High Court Justice Wilberforce held that the retention provisions, which operated after the end of the employee's employment, substantially interfered with Eastham's right to seek employment and therefore operated in restraint of trade. Similar retention provisions existed in the rules which governed county cricket but were never legally challenged.

After the *Greig* v *Insole* case professional cricketers had a precedent which showed that they had rights, like other workers. It is interesting to note that the TCCB quickly reduced the length of Barry Wood's suspension in 1980 when he threatened a restraint of trade action in the courts.

While the brief existence of World Series Cricket played a part in the consolidation of the Cricketers' Association in England, the same cannot be said for the Players' Association in Australia. Ian Chappell, who captained the WSC Australian team, recently reflected on the state of Australian cricket since the WSC-Australian Cricket Board compromise and remarked:

> Apart from the fact that they are getting paid better I'd go so far as to say that they (the players) are back to 1977. That really disappoints me. I think it is a pity the players didn't grab hold of the game more than they have . . . the Players' Association (now the cricket committee) has been a paper tiger really. I think 1979-80 provided a great opportunity; an opportunity to start afresh. I think, somehow, it didn't happen.

In retrospect the cricketers who joined World Series Cricket appear to have no regrets about that decision. Alan Knott, in his autobiography, *It's Knott Cricket*, remarked that WSC had benefited cricket by 'improving the standing of the player and his position in the game'. He continued, 'I can only repeat that it was a direct consequence of having two employers where before there had been only one.'

In an article in the *Cricketer* in March 1983 Asif Iqbal, the former Kent and Pakistan captain, makes a similar point.

He argues that the reason the authorities were so concerned about the appearance of WSC was because:

> It was a first step to creating an independent market for professional cricketers and thus was an alternative to the take-it-or-leave-it position . . . Its expansion could well have spelt the total erosion of the cricketing power structure that existed not only at Lord's but in all the cricket headquarters of the world.

Seen in that light World Series Cricket was not new. In the late 1860s and early 1870s the MCC had decided to curtail the influence of the professional touring elevens, and particularly the All-England Eleven, while 40 years later the fledgling Australian Board of Control confronted the players in an attempt to gain control over the tours to England. On both those occasions the authorities achieved their aims and the influence of the players was broken. In 1977-79, under very different economic and social circumstances, the cricket establishment was less successful.

THE NEW PATRONS

Patronage is not new to cricket. Individual benefactors, from the Earl of Stamford in the 1850s to Sir Julien Cahn in the 1930s, while not always popular with Lord's, have helped to financially ensure the survival of the game. Today the new patrons are cigarette manufacturers, insurance companies and television stations.

Since the compromise was reached with World Series Cricket in 1979 corporate sponsorship has expanded dramatically. In 1977 the TCCB had sponsorship deals worth £476,000 but by 1986 they exceeded two million pounds. In 1987 Cornhill Insurance announced a new sponsorship for Test cricket which will inject £4.5 million into English cricket over five years. In turn this has meant the substantial sum of £330,575 was available as prize money during the 1987 season.

Benson and Hedges has been the major sponsor of cricket in Australia since 1973. Their most recent three-year contract with the Australian Cricket Board was apparently worth A$5 million to the Board. Benson and Hedges is also one of the six most significant sponsors of English cricket. The ethics of allowing a cigarette manufacturer to sponsor cricket is rarely questioned. In an article in 1982 about 'cricket's sticky wicket' the *Economist* put the matter simply, 'Cigarette makers have been eager to use cricket's clean, healthy image to counteract the popular image of smoking as a dirty, unhealthy addiction.' For Benson and Hedges, as an Australian spokesman said, cricket sponsorship is 'desirable in terms of public relations and public image'.

For Cornhill Insurance, cricket sponsorship was a means to raise their market profile. According to the *Economist* 'Its "awareness level" – ie, the number of people who included Cornhill when asked to name all the insurance companies they could – jumped from 2 per cent in 1977 to 17 per cent' at the end of the 1981 season.

Nevertheless, the *Economist* concluded that the influx of this commercial money has only provided cricket 'with a lifestyle of shabby gentility', especially in regard to the lack of 'well-appointed facilities' and has left 'cricketers . . . among the lowest-paid sporting professionals anywhere'.

EARNINGS

In 1985 a handful of star England cricketers earned in excess of £40,000. The unique talents of Ian Botham were even more handsomely rewarded. According to the *Australian*, in February 1987, 'his worldwide income from playing cricket, sponsorship, media work, endorsements and personal appearances' should exceed 'A$500,000 this year'. The goal of Ian Botham's English and Australian agents is simply to make him the first cricketing (sterling) millionaire.

Ian Botham's high public profile guarantees him a lucrative income from product endorsements and advertising. Despite the hectic tour schedule in Australia in 1986-87 Botham made television advertisements for a floating hotel, an electronics company and Overseas Telecommunications as well as a number of personal appearances. Like all successful contemporary sports stars, Ian Botham endorses equipment, in his case this is particular brands of boots and bats. A glance through any cricket magazine demonstrates the extent of player endorsements with everything from sun hats to wicket covers bearing the names of leading professionals.

In Australia, according to a survey in June 1987 by *Sportsweek*, only Allan Border and Kim Hughes earned more than A$200,000 from cricket and associated work. While that sum is almost 10 times higher than average annual earnings in Australia it leaves the pair well down the list of Australian sports earnings, way behind golfers Greg Norman (A$2 million), Bruce Crampton (A$1 million), Rodger Davis (A$600,000), David Graham (A$500,000) and Graham Marsh (A$450,000); tennis player Wendy Turnbull, marathon runner Robert de Castella, soccer stars Craig Johnson and David Mitchell, and cyclists Phil Anderson and Danny Clark (all A$250,000 plus). Languishing at the bottom of the 'star' earnings list were Australian Test players such as David Boon, Dean Jones and Craig McDermott with A$60-70,000 which put them on a par with boxer 'Aussie' Joe Bugner.

Nevertheless, the earnings of Australian Test players are in excess of £25,000 and are substantially more than an English county professional would expect to receive from all sources annually. Jack Bannister, writing in the 1986 edition of *Wisden*, claims the earnings of a county player had risen to £12,000 in 1985. Eight years earlier the figure was £3500.

In 1986 a capped player was paid a minimum salary of £8000 for five and a half months work. If he was playing for an average county side a first-eleven professional might expect another £600 in bonuses to accrue during the season. Several counties pay loyalty bonuses, for example, an additional £50 per annum for each season the player remains with the Club, while prize money and win bonuses are pooled and divided out according to match appearances. Most Clubs provide their players with a county-championship incentive of a bonus for each win over five. A side achieving more than five wins would almost certainly be challenging for the title. For example, Middlesex topped the table in 1985 with eight victories.

Of course the modern professional also receives a number of non-wage benefits or perks. In *It Never Rains*, published in 1984, Somerset's Peter Roebuck wrote that he had not bought a car for five years thanks to one of the county's sponsors, that during the season most of his meals were free, that he received 'generous expenses', never paid for his kit and even obtained free haircuts in Taunton.

The introduction in 1979 of a minimum salary of £4500 for a capped player definitively shifted the emphasis of a professional's earnings away from payments-by-results which had for so long been dominant in cricket. As late as the early 1970s the leading Notts professionals received a salary (£850) and then match appearance fees of £7 in the championship and £15 for Sunday League fixtures. Other counties had moved away from this traditional pattern. In 1969 Lancashire, for example, paid their capped professionals £1600 per year with the possibility of an additional £200 bonus. The introduction of the Sunday League in 1969 prompted the Old Trafford Committee to increase salaries by £500, rather than pay a match appearance fee.

Another important development which has added to the players' security has been the implementation by the Test and County Cricket Board of a 'Group Retirement Scheme' under which the TCCB pays the equivalent of 5.25 per cent of a player's earnings into a pension fund. Because of the nature of such schemes this contribution of about £400 is tax free.

The Cricketers' Association has also ensured that a salary scale exists for young and uncapped members on the county staffs. In 1986 an uncapped player over the age of 23 received a minimum salary of £4250 plus rewards for length of service and a mandatory minimum of £10 for each day played in the first eleven including one-day fixtures.

The existence of agreed and enforced minimum salary rates and the Group Retirement Scheme not only provides greater security for the county professionals but it has also eliminated the obvious division that previously existed, at least in terms of financial rewards to the players, between a few wealthy clubs, such as Surrey and Lancashire, and their poorer counterparts. While the salary structure agreed with the Cricketers' Association establishes minimum rates, according to Jack Bannister at least five counties pay more and one considerably more than the minimum.

The Cricketers' Association has also acted to ensure that there is some recourse for retired cricketers who find themselves in need of financial support. In January 1982 the TCCB agreed to the Association's proposal that the over-rate fines paid by the players would be used to establish a charitable trust for destitute cricketers. By that means the Cricketers' Association Charity was created with assets in excess of £60,000 and it has already provided assistance to three former professionals.

THE 'ENDURANCE TEST'

In 1966 the first experiments were made with first-class cricket on Sundays. *The Times* commented, 'Not many years ago people were saying that Sunday cricket would "never come in our lifetime". Now it is here to stay.' The cricket establishment had rejected the idea on several occasions but relented in the face of public and commercial pressure. The existence of three one-day competitions, along with Sunday play, means that the modern county professional is likely to take the field, weather permitting, on more than 100 days during the summer.

Peter Roebuck has written that between 27 April and 15 September 1983 he was required by Somerset on 121 days while on 10 of the remaining 26 days he expected to be appearing in local fixtures for the county's beneficiary. In other words, Roebuck would be playing on nine out of every 10 days. Since the so-called golden age the number of days a professional appeared has increased significantly. In 1905 each county organised their own championship fixture list which, apart from Northants who arranged only 12 matches, varied between 18 and 28 games or 54 and 84 playing days. Thirty years later the number of fixtures still remained at the discretion of each county, but the programme had increased to between 24 and 32 games or 72 and 96 playing days. In 1955 the championship had been stabilised at 28 matches or 84 playing days.

In all those seasons cited, a small number of star performers did play more frequently due to representative and festival games. For example, George Hirst in 1905, Walter Hammond in 1935 and Fred Titmus in 1955 all made 35 first-class appearances in those respective seasons. Since the turn of the century, however, there has been a clear trend for the county professional to be working more first-class days per season.

In *It Never Rains* Peter Roebuck depicts the summer as an 'endurance test'. He continues by describing the Somerset dressing room on a Saturday in August in Derby:

> Seven of our party are lying around sound asleep, heads on pads or towels. I've never seen a team so white and drawn . . . the barrage of travelling and concentration has taken its toll . . . County cricket is rather like trench warfare at times; the qualities you most need to survive are graft and endurance.

Similarly, the contemporary Test cricketers have to undertake more arduous playing and travelling schedules than their predecessors. Not only are there more Tests played, but air travel has eliminated the restful sea and rail journeys. A touring party visiting Australia, especially given the large number of one-day internationals now included in the itinerary, has to crisscross the continent. During their 1986-87 Australian tour the England party flew in and out of Perth in Western Australia from the East coast (a distance of 3500 kilometres) on three occasions. A similar number of trips was made to Adelaide and Brisbane and even more to and from Sydney and Melbourne. In total the tourists made over 30 internal flights in the space of four months. Not surprisingly Mike Gatting publicly complained about the tour schedule.

The modern player also needs stamina to endure the pressure of media interest and public attention. The private lives of a nation's sporting heroes are no longer sacrosanct. An issue of *Wisden Cricket Monthly* reported in 1985 that one well-known player was involved in divorce proceedings and that the judge had lifted a non-molestation order; that another had divorced and remarried; while a third's business had collapsed leaving him with debts of £700,000. All these players were named yet these disclosures are minor in comparison to the gross intrusions into Ian Botham's private life. With the omnipresent media at his heels is it surprising that on tour Ian Botham often prefers the seclusion of a hotel suite or a cinema? In *It Sort of Clicks* Ian Botham compared the 1977 and 1984 tours of New Zealand. 'Now I was a marked man. Everywhere I went people would be pointing at me . . . I went to cinemas a lot. I go even more nowadays. I can sit down and once it gets dark I know I'm safe.' In *It Never Rains* Peter Roebuck describes the county professionals search for privacy:

> The dressing room, the car and the field are private places . . . It's the bits in between – the autograph hunters or the newspapermen, the cameras and the outsiders – that are difficult to endure . . . our craft is performed on a public stage.

In an article in the *Cricketer* in October 1982 Frank Hayes, the Lancashire and England batsman, argued that 'temperament' was an ability to accept and cope with the 'extra pressures sometimes not easily understood by those not under the spotlight'. In the same magazine James Graham-Brown was brutally frank when he admitted that his professional career had been a 'total misery' due to his inability to 'relax or be natural' and it was only away from the public gaze 'in the security of the second eleven' that he could perform.

WINTER WORK – STILL A PROBLEM

During the English winter more than 300 first-class cricketers begin to look for work and with unemployment exceeding three million that can be hard to find. In *Yorkshire and Back*, published in 1980, Ray Illingworth, a former England captain, remarked that 'One of the eternal problems of the average first-class cricketer is to find a suitable job between seasons.' Illingworth remembers spending 17 winters selling Christmas cards and fireworks on a commission basis in Scotland.

Since the first ground staffs were created more than a century ago the problem of finding winter work for cricket's seasonal employees still remains to be satisfactorily resolved. Among the comments made by players in *The 1986 Cricketers' Who's Who* are, 'Counties should try harder to find winter employment for players' and 'I wish employment could be found for more cricketers when the season ends'. Writing in the *Cricketer* in October 1986 Simon Hughes, the Middlesex fast-medium bowler, educated at Durham University, remarked:

> Without doubt at least 50 per cent of county players dread 30 September. This is D Day. No more handy expenses to collect; no more away trips; hand the sponsored car back; salary cheques dry up – that's worst of all . . . (counties) virtually disown their players come October.

The 1986 Cricketers' Who's Who asked the 352 players listed what they would be doing, or expected to be doing, during the 1985-86 northern winter. Apart from the 40 overseas professionals, more than 30 had been selected for the England and England B tours; 84 intended to coach overseas with the most popular destinations being Australia (36), South Africa (23 – although the numbers have been declining during the 1980s) and New Zealand (16); seven were studying; two organising their benefits; two employed at indoor cricket schools; one playing soccer and 42 'hopefully' working. That list fails to account for the remaining 140. According to Simon Hughes, who made his county debut in 1980, finding winter work is 'becoming more tricky', and 30 players were on the dole during the 1985-86 winter.

An overseas coaching job, a popular winter occupation, would be expected to net the professional £4000, given that his employers usually provide nominal or rent-free accomodation, a car and other perks. Simon Hughes is less complimentary, describing the financial rewards as 'just enough to live on' and comparing his enthusiasm for a winter overseas in club cricket with 'an evening in the laundrette'.

A BETTER EDUCATION AND HIGHER QUALIFICATIONS

Again based on information provided in *The Cricketers' Who's Who,* it is apparent that the modern professional is more aware of his future beyond the game than his predecessors. The professional cricketer has never been better educated. Of the 312 English professionals 97 had tertiary-level academic qualifications, while a further 28 had remained at school to take and pass their A levels. Among the university-educated cricketers Oxford and Cambridge accounted for only 19 professionals while the other universities, particularly Durham (with 10), provided 33. This latter figure emphasises the need for a rethinking of the role of Oxford and Cambridge University cricket and the justification for a combined University eleven being established to play against the counties.

While many players are able to employ their academic skills either in winter, or after they retire from first-class cricket, as teachers, accountants or running their own businesses, many others have chosen to obtain a National Cricket Association or MCC coaching qualification. No doubt Sydney Barnes would be delighted to find that today most of his successors are not 'trading as best they could upon their faded glories' in 'a fourth-rate beerhouse'. Nor are they returning to the factory or mine, once fêted but now forgotten, for the simple and disappointing reason that fewer young working-class men either have the ability to become professional cricketers or see it as a viable future. The same cannot be said of soccer which continues to attract talented working-class youngsters.

The mines once provided England with a seam of fine fast bowlers. In the 1930s half the Nottinghamshire side came from the collieries. But the dramatic pit closures of the past two decades have meant that the Test selectors have had to turn to teachers, clerks and diamond setters. In 1986 there was only one former miner playing county cricket.

The working-class communities which provided the socio-economic base for the fine Derbyshire, Lancashire, Nottinghamshire and Yorkshire sides prior to the Second World War have disappeared and with their decline the century of dominance of the northern working-class professionals has drawn to a close. Between 1965 and 1984 Lancashire and Notts lost more championship matches than they won, whereas in the 1970s Kent achieved remarkable success. And today the question is whether Essex or Middlesex will be the team of this decade. Despite the 1987 season, it appears that in contemporary Britain it is not just prosperity and employment but also cricket success that is to be found in the South of England.

THE BENEFIT – AN OUTDATED IDEA

As long as there has been professional cricket there have been players' benefits, but in the 1980s the benefit, as a reward for loyalty or long-service, has been questioned. In *The 1986 Cricketers' Who's Who* players commented that the benefit system was 'haphazard' and should be replaced with either 'a sum at the end of their careers dependent upon their length of service' or by an 'endowment scheme when the player is capped'.

The two basic principles of a benefit have remained unchanged since the last century. First, it is not a right but 'awarded' by the county after an application by the player and, second, a benefit is usually granted only if the cricketer has been capped for 10 years. The problems which have dogged the benefit system over the years remain. Writing in *Wisden* in 1975 Bob White, the former Middlesex and Notts player, explained that it took him 'twenty-one years from the time I started, but I'm lucky in as much as at least I did get a benefit. Some players and good ones never do.' Bob White had joined the Lord's staff in 1953 but did not receive his Middlesex cap until 1963; three years later he joined Nottinghamshire. Similarly, Eddie Hemmings, another Notts player, did not receive a benefit until 21 years after he made his county debut for Warwickshire in 1966. Hemmings was not awarded his cap at Edgbaston until 1974. Five years later he moved to Trent Bridge, was capped there in 1980, and awarded a benefit in 1987 at the age of 38.

The nature of the benefit system ensures that the returns are not uniform between players and counties. For example, in 1980 Lancashire's Jack Simmons received £128,000 (an all-time record until Graham Gooch's £153,906 in 1985), whereas Worcestershire's Ted Hemsley achieved only £10,000 while Alan Hodgson, the Northants fast-medium bowler forced into retirement due to a back injury, had a £3466 testimonial. Obviously a cricketer with one of the larger county Clubs, in a more populated part of the country or with a strong local following, is still likely to receive a more substantial reward than one of his colleagues, no matter how loyal, who represents a smaller and poorer county. It is not surprising that the highest benefits in the 1960s (Brian Statham £13,047), the 1970s (Barry Wood £62,429) and in the early 1980s (Jack Simmons) were achieved in Lancashire.

In 1981 Jack Simmons wrote an article in the *Cricketer* advocating the maintenance of the present system as a 'reward for loyalty'. He explained that his £128,000 was raised via a committee blessed with 'endless energy' and his willingness to visit every part of Lancashire and more than 100 local cricket clubs. Eleven matches were organised within the county, including one against a West Indies eleven; there were evenings in working men's clubs, cabarets, bingo and sporting dinners. These details highlight the difference between a modern benefit and one arranged prior to the Second World War. In the pre-War era most of the money was generated from gate receipts (less expenses) during the benefit match, a subscription list and ground collections, whereas today a successful benefit requires the organisation of a series of social occasions, raffles and pontoon tickets. Mike Hendrick, the Derbyshire and England bowler, having been obliged to return home early from the 1979-80 tour of Australia due to injury, began to organise his benefit. He commented in the *Cricketer*:

> My main venture is a darts competition . . . We are aiming to get 25,000 people competing . . . The only way to spread the word is to visit the places . . . I might visit up to ten pubs in a lunchtime session . . . five hours (a day) on these delivery missions.

With so much off-the-field benefit activity to arrange, it is hardly surprising that a player's form can suffer. Alan Knott wrote in *It's Knott Cricket* that a benefit year is a 'very hard one to get through . . . it is difficult to get your mental approach to the game right and your energy is drained'. Instead of the benefit system Alan Knott proposed that the counties should be engaged in general fund-raising activities for the purpose of paying higher wages. In 1981 Phil Carling, then the Notts Chief Executive, made the remark that 'What I want to see is players getting a really good salary instead of their financial future being dependent on one hectic benefit year.' Eighty-seven years earlier in *Cricket* the Rev. Holmes had made exactly the same point!

Jack Bannister, the Secretary of the Cricketers' Association, would prefer a situation where benefits were less significant as a source of income and instead the counties established good portable endowment schemes. Portability is very important to avoid a player's ability to change county being restricted. In 1968 Ray Illingworth, then aged 36 with 17 years of professional experience, asked Yorkshire for the security of a three-year contract as opposed to their usual annual agreements. The Club refused. Ray Illingworth resigned, but Yorkshire did not pay over his endowment policy.

The Australian Cricket Board has established a lump-sum pension scheme for its Test players which accumulates according to the number of international appearances and falls due when the cricketer retires. Rodney Marsh, for example, received in excess of A$50,000.

The obvious problem, however, is that benefits, unlike endowment schemes, are tax free. Despite that, it seems invidious that a professional cricketer's financial future should be dependent on a system which is sophsticated 'begging', and a lottery. It would seem to be time to remove the uncertainty and insecurity and in one more regard put cricketers on an equal footing with other employees.

1900 TO 1986: COMPARISONS

Are professional cricketers better off today than they were in the so-called golden age, or after the Second World War? As far as earnings and benefits are concerned, Table 10 indicates that in real terms, measured by the purchasing power of the pound, the contemporary player is more prosperous than his predecessors.

Table 10 provides a comparison across decades by standardising the information into 1986 prices. Graham Gooch's 'huge' benefit in 1985 is not significantly higher than George Hirst's in 1904, while it is only since the Second World War that an average professional's benefit has shown any real improvement on the figures being returned in the so-called golden age.

Similarly, it is only in the last 30 years that the earnings of an uncapped member of the ground staff have bettered those achieved in 1900. In fact between the First and Second World Wars, in real terms, the earnings of uncapped players declined dramatically.

From 1900 until the 1950s capped county professionals and the few 'star' players managed to maintain the earnings differential between themselves and skilled workers. For more than half a century a capped professional's earnings were twice those of a skilled worker, while 'star' players were five times better off. By 1950 in real terms they had between 7 and 14 per cent more purchasing power than their brethren in 1900.

Table 10: A comparison of earnings and benefits, 1900–85 (£)

	Earnings Uncapped	Earnings Capped	Earnings 'Star'	Average Benefit	Highest Benefit	Earnings Skilled
1900	90	200	450	1000	3703	100
1986 Prices	3150	7000	15750	35000	129605	3500
	100	**100**	**100**	**100**	**100**	**100**
1930	100	400	1200	1500	4016	220
1986 Prices	2100	8400	25200	31500	84336	4620
(1900 = 100)	**67**	**120**	**160**	**90**	**65**	**132**
1950	300	750	1800	3000	14200	400
1986 Prices	3000	7500	18000	30000	142000	4000
(1900 = 100)	**95**	**107**	**114**	**86**	**110**	**114**
1977	1500	3500	8000	23000	62429	4000
1986 Prices	3000	7000	16000	46000	124858	8000
(1900 = 100)	**95**	**100**	**102**	**131**	**96**	**229**
1986	4250	12000	40000	50000	153906	10000
(1900 = 100)	**135**	**171**	**254**	**143**	**119**	**286**

By 1977 the situation had changed markedly. Shortly before the establishment of World Series Cricket the earnings of English cricketers had declined to such an extent that capped players found themselves receiving less per year than a skilled worker, while a 'star' player was now only two times better off. During the 27 years from 1950 skilled workers had doubled their income in real terms, while professional cricketers' earnings had declined and they were barely better off than their predecessors at the turn of the century!

Cricketers were paying dearly for their lack of union organisation. From 1970 to 1974, under Edward Heath's Conservative Government, the trade union movement achieved significant wage increases. Real take-home pay rose by 3.5 per cent per annum from 1970 to 1973. In 1974, in the wake of the successful miners' strike, the Labour Party was swept into government. For the next three years earnings exceeded the cost of living, despite the latter running at unprecedented post-War levels. In July 1975, for example, the cost of living was 26.3 per cent higher than the previous year.

Unfortunately county cricket was in a state of financial crisis and several clubs came close to bankruptcy. The downward trend of attendances at first-class matches continued while in general inflation soared. A glance through the relevant volumes of *Wisden* highlights the problems. In 1970, with the cancellation of the South African tour of England, every county made a loss, indicating how dependent the counties had become on Test match revenue. Four seasons later more heavy losses were recorded. Gloucestershire launched a fund to raise £25,000 to overcome the worst financial crisis in the Club's history, while Middlesex warned their members that unless £20,000 was found the Club faced bankruptcy by the end of the year.

These crisis years reached their zenith at Worcestershire in 1975. In September the players dispatched a letter expressing their 'complete lack of confidence' in some leading members of the Club's administration. Four days later the Committee sacked six players including Brian Brain, Rodney Cass and Jim Yardley. An extraordinary general meeting was called but abandoned when 1000 members were unable to gain admission to Worcester's Guildhall. During 1975 Worcestershire made a loss of £6915 despite improved income from membership subscriptions, gate receipts and other income, but over a two-year period expenditure had risen by £30,000. *Wisden* expressed the hope 'that peace would be restored in time for the new season'. In the event during 1976 the Cricketers' Association was obliged to intervene to solve a situation which by August still found nine players without contracts.

In the late 1970s and post-WSC 1980s, capped professionals, and particularly the 'star' players, have improved their financial position. The earnings differential with a skilled worker has widened again, albeit not to the pre-War levels, but assuming the continued availability of commerical sponsorship and prize money there is every reason to expect improved earnings and a better deal for the players.

IS THERE A FUTURE FOR THE PROFESSIONAL CRICKETER?

From time to time a voice within the cricket world has raised the contentious point that perhaps there is no future for the professional cricketer. In 1963 in *Beyond a Boundary* C. L. R. James argued that he saw

> . . . the rejuvenation of the game not in legislation but in a changing relation of the cricketer to the life around him. He must become an ordinary member of the community who will play cricket for the fun of it, which does not mean that he will not play it seriously.

For C. L. R. James the intention is to retrieve cricket as 'an artistic expression of life' and by abolishing the specialist professional create a cricketer whose play represents 'an artistic expression of his own individual life'. James is searching for the lost halcyon days of the so-called golden age prior to the First World War.

A recent and perhaps surprising convert to the cause of part-time professionals is Tony Greig. Interviewed in May 1987 in the *Australian* he reflected on the career of South Africa's Graeme Pollock:

> Graeme has never been a fully-fledged professional; in other words, he has never had to rely on cricket for a living. That means he has retained some flair, it's not the end of the world if he has a bad trot. Security is provided by his job and he doesn't get absolutely sick of the game by virtue of having to play it every day of the week.

Tony Greig argues that because Pollock was a part-timer he has been able to remain in the game until he was 40 and entertain people, in comparison to other leading players who have become sick of playing cricket day-in, day-out and have either retired or demanded a break from touring overseas.

The problem is that today there is too much cricket and such a programme is sustainable only through extensive corporate sponsorship. Writing in the *Cricketer* in 1983, Paul Parker, the Sussex and England batsman, advocated the 'radical idea' of two geographical divisions of nine teams each, playing eight four-day matches from Friday to Monday. The other 10 weekends would be used for one-day matches. In such a proposal there would be no place for full-time professionals. Parker envisaged that local league cricket would be strengthened by the influx of former county professionals; that young players could graduate quickly from club to representative cricket; that the quality of pitches would improve and cricketers chosen for the four-day county matches would be 'fitter and fresher'.

None of these proposals would eliminate professional cricketers. League clubs would be keen to sign the best available talent, while others would find county sinecures paid for by corporate sponsors. In theory Australia has a system of non-professional cricketers but the demands of one-day internationals, Test matches and the increasing number of overseas tours means that it is very difficult for a leading Australian player to develop a career parallel to cricket. Instead many Test players are effectively full-time professionals or have left the game relatively young in order to secure their business future. Nor is it the case that Australia's Test and state players are to be seen playing grade cricket at the week-ends; again, the demands of the international and representative circuit make this an impossibility on a regular basis.

The trend internationally is for cricket to be more rather than less professional, especially as the influence of commercial sponsorship continues to grow and prize money increases. In the 1980s several English counties have been recording profits annually, most notably Essex which posted a £100,000 profit in 1986 for the third successive year. Leicestershire, which justifiably has a reputation for being a pioneering county Club, has made a profit for the last 18 seasons.

While cricket has become more professional so has the marketing and the administration of the game. Many county secretaries now have a background in business or accounting and with their staff have gone out to seek local business sponsorship. Such a move has been essential given that the total membership of the county clubs has hovered around 92,000 since 1983. While Essex are one of the few counties to have increased their membership (from 6500 in 1983 to 8954 in 1987) they also generate nearly £100,000 per season from advertising and local sponsors, the most significant being the Suffolk brewery, Tolly Cobbold (£60,000). Every county has followed this course and among the deals announced in 1987 were Carphone (£100,000) and the Midlands Electricity Board (described as 'lucrative') with Worcestershire; James Capel, the stock-brokers, with Kent (£100,000 over two years); TNT with Leicestershire (£30,000) and Hampshire; and Bassett Foods (£250,000 over three years) with Yorkshire.

Sponsors want to be associated with a successful side and in that regard the Essex players have delivered the goods. In a recent interview in the *Cricketer* Peter Edwards, the Essex secretary, commented that 'The playing side of the Club is very much in the hands of the players. At some Clubs, I think, the Committee members get too involved on the playing side.' Undoubtedly the contemporary professionals have a stronger and more accepted voice within their county clubs. An example of this was the lobbying by Sussex players for the removal of Stewart Storey as Club manager. But players also know that the failure to produce success can lead to swift retribution, such as the sackings in 1986 of Joel Garner and Viv Richards at Somerset and Peter Lever and Jack Bond at Lancashire.

In 1851 Felix, the President of the All-England Eleven, made a retirement speech which more than 130 years later contains many pertinent reflections on the life of a professional cricketer:

> Be grateful to God that He has given you health and strength to go through the great fatigue and dangers of

> your professional career, and that it hath pleased Him to suffer you to return to the bosom of your families after six months' laborious avocation, and that you carry back to your homes the good name which the foul slander of your enemies would take from you. They may well envy you your reception as you journey through 'the land', where you have had the opportunity of visiting some of the noblest cities in the world. They may well envy you the character which you deservedly enjoy for prosecuting the interests of your profession with such a determination to do what is right; and be assured, though strange it may appear, that the more you succeed by a principle of action unimpeachable and true, just so you will provoke the envy and slander of your fellow creatures.

The professional cricketer has been, and will remain, indispensable to the success of first-class cricket. It seems remarkable that the issues which concerned the players prior to the First World War, such as winter work, future security, the benefit system, lack of consultation and relatively poor earnings, are either only just being addressed or remain unresolved. Recent improvements have happened, in part because the players themselves, like William Clarke and his All-England colleagues in the 19th century, have taken intiatives. The creation of the Cricketers' Association in 1967 was an important landmark – although it is to be regretted that this could not have happened 80 years earlier. Nevertheless, as Vic Marks, the Oxford University educated, Somerset and England all-rounder, wrote in 1986, 'Professional cricket is a precarious, cut-throat means of earning a living.'

Cricket Bibliography

Place of publication is London unless otherwise stated

ANNUALS AND PERIODICALS

Australian Cricket Journal, 1985 to date
Cricket, 1882-1913 and in 1914 as *The World of Cricket*
The Cricket Field, 1892-95
Cricket Quarterly, 1963-70
Cricket Scores and Biographies, Volumes I-15
Cricket Society Journal, 1961 to date
The Cricket Statistician, 1973 to date
The Cricketer, 1921-1974, subsequently *The Cricketer International*, 1974 to date
The Cricketers' Who's Who, 1979 to date
Denison's Cricketer's Companion, 1843-46
Frederick Lillywhite's Guide to Cricketers, 1849-66
James Lillywhite's Cricketers' Annual, 1872-1900
John Lillywhite's Cricketer's Companion, 1865-85
Playfair Cricket Monthly, 1960-73
Wisden Cricket Monthly, 1979 to date
Wisden Cricketers' Almanack, 1864 to date

BIOGRAPHIES AND AUTOBIOGRAPHIES

Alcock, C. W. *Famous Cricketers and Cricket Grounds*, Hudson & Kearns, 1895

Ames, L. E. G. *Close of Play*, Stanley Paul, 1953
Arlott, J. *Fred*, Eyre & Spottiswoode, 1971
Arlott, J. *Jack Hobbs*, John Murray, 1981
Andrews, B. *The Hand that Bowled Bradman*, Macdonald, 1973
Bailey, P., Thorn, P. and Wynne-Thomas, P. *Who's Who of Cricketers*, Newnes Books, 1984
Barlow, R. G. *Forty Seasons of First-Class Cricket*, Manchester: Heywood, 1908
Bedser, A. E. and Bedser, E. A. *Our Cricket Story*, Evans Bros., 1950
Bowes, W. E. *Express Deliveries*, Stanley Paul, 1949
Brodribb, G. *The Croucher*, London Magazine Editions, 1974
Brodribb, G. *Maurice Tate*, London Magazine Editions, 1976
Brooke, R. *John Edward Shilton's Book*, Haughton Mill: Association of Cricket Statisticians, 1984
Caffyn, W. *Seventy-One Not Out*, Blackwood, 1899
Coldham, J. D. *Lord Harris*, George Allen & Unwin, 1983
Coldham, J. D. *William Brockwell*, Privately Printed, 1970
Daft, R. *Kings of Cricket*, Bristol: Arrowsmith, 1893
Daft, R. *A Cricketer's Yarns*, Chapman & Hall, 1926
Davies, D. *Dai Davies Not Out . . . 78*, Llanelli: Dyfed Publications, 1975
Denison, W. *Sketches of the Players*, Simpkin Marshall, 1846
Dollery, H. E. *Professional Captain*, Stanley Paul, 1952
Down, M. *Archie*, George Allen & Unwin, 1981
Duckworth, L. *S. F. Barnes – Master Bowler*, Hutchinson, 1967
Duckworth, L. *Holmes and Sutcliffe*, Hutchinson, 1970
Ellis, C. *C. B. The Life of Charles Burgess Fry*, Dent, 1984
Foot, D. *Cricket's Unholy Trinity*, Stanley Paul, 1985
Foot, D. *Harold Gimblett*, Heinemann, 1982
Ford, W. J. *A Cricketer on Cricket*, Sands & Co, 1900
Harris, G. R. C. 4th Baron *A Few Short Runs*, Murray, 1921
Hawke, M. B. 7th Baron *Recollections and Reminiscences*, Williams & Norgate, 1924
Haynes, B. and Lucas, J. *The Trent Bridge Battery*, Collins Willow, 1985

Hitchin, S. W. *A Biographical Sketch of Arthur Shrewsbury*, Nottingham: Hitchin, 1890
Hobbs, J. B. Sir *My Cricket Memories*, Heinemann, 1924
Hobbs, J. B. Sir *My Life Story*, Star Publications, 1935
Holmes, E. R. T. *Flannelled Foolishness*, Hollis & Carter, 1957
Howard, R. E. *Fifty Years of Cricket Reminiscences of a Non-Player*, Manchester: the Author, 1928
Howat, G. *Walter Hammond*, George Allen & Unwin, 1984
Hutton, L. Sir *Just My Story*, Hutchinson, 1956
Illingworth, R. *Yorkshire and Back*, Queen Anne Press, 1980
Jessop, G. *A Cricketer's Log*, Hodder & Stoughton, 1922
Knott, A. *It's Knott Cricket*, Macmillan, 1985
Kynaston, D. *Bobby Abel*, Secker & Warburg, 1982
Laker, J. *Over to Me*, Muller, 1960
Larwood, H. *The Larwood Story*, W. H. Allen, 1965
Lee, F. S. *Cricket, Lovely Cricket*, Stanley Paul, 1960
Lee, H. W. *Forty Years of English Cricket*, Clerke & Cockeran, 1948
Lilley, A. A. *Twenty-Four Years of Cricket*, Mills & Boon, 1912
Mason, R. *Jack Hobbs*, Hollis & Carter, 1960
Mason, R. *Walter Hammond*, Hollis & Carter, 1962
Midwinter, E. *W. G. Grace*, George Allen & Unwin, 1981
Oldfield, W. A. S. *Behind the Wicket*, Hutchinson, 1938
Parkin, C. H. *Cricket Triumphs and Troubles*, Manchester: C. Nicholls, 1936
Peebles, I. *Denis Compton*, Macmillan, 1971
Peebles, I. *'Patsy' Hendren*, Macmillan, 1969
Peebles, I. *Woolley – The Pride of Kent*, Hutchinson, 1969
Pullin, A. W. *Alfred Shaw, Cricketer*, Cassell, 1902
Pullin, A. W. *Talks with Old English Cricketers*, Blackwood, 1900
Pullin, A. W. *Talks with Old Yorkshire Cricketers*, Leeds: Yorkshire Post, 1898
Read, W. W. *Annals of Cricket*, S. Low, 1896
Robertson-Glasgow, R. C. *46 Not Out*, Hollis & Carter, 1948
Robertson-Glasgow, R. C. *Cricket Prints*, Laurie, 1943
Robertson-Glasgow, R. C. *More Cricket Prints*, Laurie, 1948
Roebuck, P. *It Never Rains*, George Allen & Unwin, 1984

Roebuck, P. *It Sort of Clicks*, Collins Willow, 1986
Rogerson, S. *Wilfred Rhodes, Professional and Gentleman*, Hollis & Carter, 1960
Root, F. *A Cricket Pro's Lot*, Arnold, 1937
Streeton, R. *P. G. H. Fender*, Faber & Faber, 1981
Strudwick, H. *Twenty Five Years Behind the Stumps*, Hutchinson, 1926
Sutcliffe, H. *For Yorkshire and England*, Arnold, 1935
Swanton, E. W. *Gubby Allen*, Hutchinson, 1985
Tate, M. *My Cricket Reminiscences*, Stanley Paul, 1934
Tennyson, L. H. 3rd Baron *Sticky Wickets*, C. Johnson, 1950
Thomas, P. *Yorkshire Cricketers, 1839-1939*, Manchester: Derek Hodgson, 1973
Thomson, A. A. *Hirst and Rhodes*, Epworth Press, 1959
Thomson, A. A. *Hutton and Washbrook*, Epworth Press, 1963
Titmus, F. J. *Talk of the Double*, Stanley Paul, 1964
Wardle, J. H. *Happy Go Johnny*, Hale, 1957
Washbrook, C. *Cricket – The Silver Lining*, Sportsguide Publications, 1950
Watson, W. *Double International*, Stanley Paul, 1956
White, W. S. *Sydney Barnes*, Birmingham: Hudson, 1937
Woolley, F. *The King of Games*, Stanley Paul, 1936
Woolley, F. *Early Memories*, Tunbridge Wells: *The Cricketer*, 1976
Wright, L. G. *Scraps from a Cricketer's Memory*, Derby: Derbyshire CC Supporters' Club, 1980
Wyatt, R. E. S. *Three Straight Sticks*, Stanley Paul, 1951
Wynne-Thomas, P. *'Give Me Arthur'*, Arthur Barker, 1985
Wynne-Thomas, P. *Nottinghamshire Cricketers 1821-1914*, Nottingham: Notts CCC, 1971
Wynne-Thomas, P. *Nottinghamshire Cricketers 1919-1939*, Nottingham: Notts CCC, 1980

HISTORY OF THE GAME

Altham, H. S. et al, *Hampshire County Cricket*, Phoenix House, 1957
Altham, H. S. and Swanton, E. W. *A History of Cricket*, George Allen & Unwin, 1948

Alverstone, R. E. W. Viscount and Alcock, C. W. *Surrey Cricket*, Longmans, Green, 1902

Arlott, J. *Vintage Summer: 1947*, Eyre & Spottiswoode, 1967

Ashley-Cooper, F. S. *Nottinghamshire Cricket and Cricketers*, Nottingham: H. B. Saxton, 1923

Association of Cricket Statisticians, *A Guide to Important Cricket Matches Played in the British Isles 1709-1863*, Haughton Mill: ACS, 1981

Association of Cricket Statisticians, *Cricket Matches 1860-1863*, Haughton Mill: ACS, no date

Birley, D. *The Willow Wand*, Queen Anne Press, 1979

Bowen, R. *Cricket: A History of its Growth and Development throughout the World*, Eyre & Spottiswoode, 1970

Brookes, C. *English Cricket*, Weidenfeld & Nicolson, 1978

Browne, E. *A Short History of Nottinghamshire Cricket*, Nottingham: Richards, 1887

The Cabinet, Melbourne: J. Reid, 1862

Caple, S. C. *A History of Gloucestershire County Cricket Club, 1870-1948*, Worcester: Littlebury, 1949

Cardus, N. *The Roses Matches 1919-1939*, Souvenir Press, 1982

Darling, D. K. *Test Tussles on and off the Field*, Hobart: the Author, 1970

Derriman, P. *True to the Blue*, Sydney: Richard Smart, 1985

Forsyth, C. *The Great Cricket Hijack*, Camberwell (Victoria): Widescope, 1978

Frith, D. *The Fast Men*, Reinhold, 1975

Frith, D. *The Slow Men*, Sydney: Horwitz Grahame, 1984

Gale, F. *Echoes from Old Cricket Fields*, Simpkin Marshall, 1871

Gale, N. *Cricket Songs*, Methuen, 1894

Genders, R. *League Cricket in England*, Laurie, 1952

Gordon, H. Sir *Background of Cricket*, Barker, 1939

Grace, W. G. *Cricket*, Bristol: Arrowsmith, 1891

Harris, G. R. C. 4th Baron and Ashley-Cooper, F. S. *Lord's and the MCC*, London & Counties Press Association, 1914

Holmes, R. S. *The History of Yorkshire County Cricket 1833-1903*, Constable, 1904

James, C. L. R. *Beyond a Boundary*, Hutchinson, 1963

Kay, J. *Lancashire*, Arthur Barker, 1972

Kilburn, J. M. *A History of Yorkshire Cricket*, Stanley Paul, 1970

Kingwell, P. (ed) *A Clarion Cricket Mixture*, the Editor, 1983

Laver, F. *An Australian Cricketer on Tour*, George Bell, 1905

Lillywhite, F. *The English Cricketers' Trip to Canada and the United States in 1859*, Fred Lillywhite, 1860

Mandle, W. F. 'The professional cricketer in England in the nineteenth century' in *Labour History*, Canberra, November 1972

Marshall, J. *Headingley*, Pelham Books, 1970

Marshall, J. *Old Trafford*, Pelham Books, 1971

Martin-Jenkins, C. *The Wisden Book of County Cricket*, Queen Anne Press, 1981

Page, R. *A History of Tasmanian Cricket*, Tasmania: Shea, 1958

Pollard, J. *Australian Cricket The Game and The Players*, Sydney: Hodder & Stoughton, 1982

Pollard, J. *The Formative Years of Australian Cricket, 1803-1893*, Sydney: Angus & Robertson, 1987

Pollard, J. *The Turbulent Years of Australian Cricket, 1893-1917*, Sydney: Angus & Robertson, 1987.

Pullin, A. W. *History of Yorkshire County Cricket, 1903-1923*, Leeds: Chorley & Pickersgill, 1924

Pycroft, J. *The Cricket Field*, St James's Press, 1922

Pycroft, J. *Cricketana*, Longmans, 1865

Richards, C. H. *Nottinghamshire Cricket Scores and Biographies 1838 to 1890*, Nottingham: C. H. Richards, 1891

Ross, G. *The Surrey Story*, Stanley Paul, 1957

Shaw, A. and Shrewsbury, A. *Shaw and Shrewsbury's Team in Australia 1884-5*, Nottingham: Shaw & Shrewsbury, 1885

Shawcroft, J. *A History of Derbyshire County Cricket Club*, Derby: Derbyshire CCC, 1970

Sissons, R. and Stoddart, B. *Cricket and Empire*, George Allen & Unwin, 1984

Snow, E. E. *A History of Leicestershire Cricket*, Leicester: Backus, 1949

Snow, E. E. *Leicestershire Cricket 1949 to 1977*, Stanley Paul, 1977

Swanton, E. W. (ed) *World of Cricket*, Collins, 1980

Trevor, P. C. W. *The Problems of Cricket*, Sampson Low, 1907

Vamplew, W. 'Not Playing the Game' in *The British Journal of Sports History*, December 1985

Vamplew, W. 'Playing for Pay' in Cashman, R. and McKernan, M. *Sport Money, Morality and the Media*, Sydney: New South Wales University Press, no date

Wanostrocht, N. *The Doings of the Eleven*, two volume manuscript available in the MCC library at Lord's

Warner, P. F. *Lord's, 1787-1945*, Harrap, 1946

Williams, M. (ed) *Double Century*, Collins Willow, 1985

Wynne-Thomas, P. *Cricket Records*, Hamlyn, 1985

Index of cricketers and officials

Index by subject